Words Never Spoken

Words Never Spoken

A

Memoir

by

Craig Stewart

Words Never Spoken
Copyright © 2012 Craig Stewart
All Rights Reserved

ISBN-13:978-0615645391
ISBN-10:0615645399

Published by Craig Stewart
Impeccable Works, LLC
www.impeccableworks.com

Cover Art and Photo Courtesy of Byron Holly

Legal Disclaimer

Dedication

To the love that lasted only a season, but helped me grow as an artist. *This* happened because you motivated me again. You're my real life *Love Jones*—the one who helped me reach a new level as a writer. Your discipline sparked the fire that began some of these stories in a blog, which ultimately became this memoir. In the words of Anita Baker, *'you're my angel.'*

Acknowledgements

I'm grateful to God for the gift to tell stories through song, plays, greeting cards and now in a book. Thank You for enough perseverance to never let go of the dream.

To my mother for her undying support and complete understanding through all of my flaws.

To my father for allowing me to be a little boy who could show his feelings, and pushing me to speak up.

To my sister who consistently reminded me there was enough time left to do everything I dreamed of and I had already done so much in my life—I was being way too hard on myself.

To my brother for becoming a better person after 23 years served.

To my cousin Tiffany for challenging me to continue on when the course got too rough, and for sending a few dollars here and there to help me get by.

To my cousin Byron for always coming through with my graphic design & photography needs.

God knows the needs of people and He knows the hearts of those who shall satisfy those needs. For me, He sent Angela Bolin, Adrian Yokley, Chet Brewster, Danielle Brown, Daren Favarote, Delores & Albert Stuart, Dwight Eubanks, Enrique Toliver, Felecia Townser, Freddie Hendricks, Georgiana Threats, Greg Tolbert, Jeff Welch, Jessica Jordan, Jodine Dorce, Juanita Jones, Kelci Stringer, Kelli Stuart, Kelli Wright, Kesha Kline,

Kim Davis, Larry Johnson, Dr. Marvin Ghourm, Oscar James, Patrick T. Cooper, Rashard Smith, Ron Neal, Scott Bogan, Sherri Brown, Tara Williams, Tanika Humphrey-Cabral, Tonye Hannah and Will Brown. Thanks for helping me in one way or another to push my dreams forward and teaching me one of life's greatest lessons—compassion.

Contents

FOREWORD.. i

PROLOGUE... iii

UNGLUED..1

BEAUTIFUL MINDS...23

FLIRTING WITH THE LAW...................................36

DREAM CHASING 59

THE OTHERSIDE 85

LIFE OUTSIDE THE CLOSET..............................111

JUST CALL IT LOVE..122

THERE'S NO GLUE...142

A WHOLE NEW WORLD.....................................156

THE HETTABRINKS 164

SETTING THE STAGE 170

LOVE IS IN THE AIR...192

RUNNING ON EMPTY 207

JUST A KEY...229

TESTING THE WATERS 238

DREAMING WHILE AWAKE.............................252

SURRENDERING ALL 270

THE WRITING ON THE WALL 285

YOU'RE GONNA LOVE ME.............................304

PATTERNS..316

LEAVING ATLANTA 327

EPILOGUE 335

FOREWORD

A "word" is defined as a unit of language, consisting of one or more spoken sounds or their written representation, that functions as a principal carrier of meaning.

When words are effectively assembled and arranged, they tell a story, teach and touch...

In *Words Never Spoken*, Craig Stewart uses words, personally, powerfully and prolifically, to help and heal. Sharing candid recollections of learning and loving in a lifestyle that comes with no rules or road map, this memoir will undoubtedly help men living a non-traditional lifestyle move beyond blame, abandonment, misinformation and isolation in an effort to use their own adversities to foster powerful pride, rather than weary defeat.

Speaking to and for those who may not have had a strong shoulder to lean on, a listening ear, a voice of reason, a confidant, or the mere courage to speak up, this prophetic testament of both growing pains and great victory admonishes the silence that handicaps and hinders the evolution of a complicated type of man.

As you turn each page, enjoy this journey through the life of a courageous man who has turned his life into exactly what he wants it to be. From enticing exploits and illicit interests, to quiet tears in the night, Stewart bares his soul in the coming pages. A long time advocate for the advanced evolution of the gay, African-American male, he climbs the mountain and speaks confidently to the power of purpose, prayer and promise. In the end, I promise, you will discover victory over hardship, joy from suffering, and learn how to turn tears to triumph.

Arthur Ashe once said, "Start where you are. Use what you have. Do what you can." Craig Stewart has done just that. From his stellar stage play *A Day in the Life*, to the prose that follows, he is speaking words that must be spoken.

I would be remised if I did not testify to the strength and sound knowledge that comes from Stewart's heart. He's lived, learned, loved and lost, unabashedly, with no dress rehearsal, knowing that the next act of his life will be stellar, with his legacy being a never-ending encore.

I invite you to revel in this collection of words. I urge you to always be heard, to speak boldly and meaningfully.

Satchel B. Jester, Jr.

Writer

Speaker

Human

PROLOGUE

The first man I developed real feelings for contracted HIV from the relationship he had prior to us meeting, but he found out two months after we met. It was October 1, 1999 to be exact. I'll never forget that date because that day also marks my youngest nephew's birthday. In truth, Saleem didn't know if he contracted the virus from his ex or a stranger because he and his boyfriend did whatever with whomever while in that arrangement. It was dysfunction from the onset. That relationship was indicative of all the fears I harbored about being with another man intimately—consistent heartache, one after another, fueled by a series of love triangles, cheating, and of course HIV. After all, haven't we all been programmed to believe the gay community is the breeding ground for this disease? I imagined to be gay would mean being lonely because it meant isolation from family, a life fraught with short-lived relationships ending prematurely because men are believed to be incapable of monogamy in heterosexual relationships. So the idea of two men living happily ever after was inconceivable for me. Thus, I didn't want anything to do with being gay and I prayed for years that I wouldn't grow up to be.

Saleem and Wayne never determined who was responsible for bringing the disease into their lives. All he knew was that during an argument that lasted until 4 a.m., his ex told him he needed to be tested. I had just begun exploring my sexuality the year before, so for me dating someone HIV positive was the equivalent of a girl getting pregnant during her first sexual encounter—a nightmare realized.

I had an idea of what being gay and *the life* entailed long before acting on the feelings that followed me through childhood because family members teased me—calling me sissy, fag or punk when upset with me—and seeing *Paris is Burning* for the first time cringing, yet, identifying with the people in the documentary.

The sneers and taunts from family were packed with enough power to shatter the best self-esteem, and confirmation that gay was wrong. It's the reason many of us grow up despising other gay men, refusing to date those with feminine qualities.

I know a great deal of men who struggle with their sexuality because they were molested as children. And a percentage of those men are confused with whether or not they are gay because they were victims of molestation. The answer to that question is deeply personal and specific to each individual. I wasn't molested and I know I was born gay. It wasn't a choice. It wasn't a decision nor was it learned. I knew at an early age, but chose to avoid it.

Prologue

From what I *knew* about gay people, all were interested in becoming women, wearing women's clothes, flamboyant or destined for hell. I wasn't. I concealed my feelings and innermost thoughts from puberty through my college years. I actually believed if I never acted on that which I was avoiding then I wasn't really gay, and I would somehow escape being gay. It was denial at best, and quite possibly how some men slip into double lives. I thought suppressing the feelings was the remedy for not being gay as an adult, and the route around all the labels that came with it. As a teenager, I was never attracted to any male in particular. I was simply intrigued by the male physique in gym classes and porn if my friends and I happened to watch.

My first sexual experience was with one of my childhood friends. His family had a motor home parked in their backyard, and from time to time his mother used it to watch the soaps or to nap. We climbed in one day when it was unoccupied, and took turns humping each other on the bed with our pants around our ankles and our penises pressed against each other. For years, I chalked it up as kids experimenting. I pushed the experience so far to the edge of my memory that I almost forgot it happened.

It was difficult denying to myself that I was gay when my wet dreams were no longer about girls, but boys. Dreams aren't planned. I couldn't control them. Then there were trips to Owings Mills in Maryland to sneak peeks at *Black Inches* magazine. This magazine wasn't as tasteful or artistic as *Playgirl* in the way they photographed their models. These men were Black, completely naked, erect and posed in a sleazy, leave nothing to the imagination kind of way. My heart raced, and my palms sweat as I carefully removed the magazine from the plastic cover while keeping an eye on the unassuming store clerk. I would stuff the plastic somewhere on the bookshelf, grab a copy of *Fishing and Hunting* magazine to conceal the smut then find a corner in the store to enjoy. It would have been easier to buy the magazine, but I could only imagine the puzzled look on the store clerk's face when I appeared at the counter to purchase a magazine full of naked men. Not to mention, all I needed was for my mother to find it stashed someplace in my room because she happened to find it. She's the mother that believes it's your room, but that room is in her house.

After years of concealing feelings and thoughts, I finally drummed up the courage to go to a gay bar back home in Baltimore after I moved away for school at Hampton University in Virginia. I don't think I could have gone to a gay bar in Baltimore had I not moved away because I never considered venturing to one in Virginia for fear of running into someone from campus. I was home visiting one weekend and decided to go to Club Bunns. Paranoia convinced me that someone would recognize my car or had even memorized my license plate number, so I parked a street or two away from the club. The mind has a wonderful way of convincing us our fears are fact and what isn't, is.

Prologue

I wore a wool newsboy hat pulled down over my eyes to avoid eye contact, and a teak colored pea coat with the collar popped to make it difficult to see my face. What I failed to realize, my attire created mystery that drew attention to me in the tiny, dark, sparsely furnished bar. I sat in a corner looking and observing. I didn't have enough sense to order a drink to appear normal. Instead, I gave a good impression of a recluse. One of the other patrons came over and asked if he could buy me a drink. I declined and he retreated to his place at the bar.

The club was dead with the exception of the bartender, dj and 2-3 patrons who appeared to be regulars, so I left. I returned months later on a night the club hosted strippers because I liked the idea of men being comfortable naked with other men looking and touching them. I got in the habit of taking the forty-five minute drive to DC during my visits home for the sake of seeing the strippers at The Edge and Club Wet. For the first time, I got the chance to actually touch another naked man. I got a rush from fingering the dancers' asses, and holding, feeling and caressing another man's dick. I rarely tipped. I just touched for the experience and the satisfaction of knowing what it felt like without being judged—for wanting to look and touch without shame.

Moving to Atlanta after college cemented my ambition to become a writer, but encouraged apprehension about having sex with men. Although my first boyfriend was HIV positive, I wasn't concerned about my health because I wasn't in the practice of having random, wanton sex. I prided myself on having self-restraint. Saleem and I hadn't done anything more than kiss. In fact, there was no sexual contact of any sort with anyone if I didn't think we'd graduate to a relationship. Jerking off was even excluded. My friends teased me, calling me "Mother Theresa," but I didn't care because they were all recovering drug addicts who were ten years my senior and all HIV positive. They grew up in a generation that had sex first and got to know the person later, so I wasn't concerned with what they thought. It seemed to me they should have encouraged me to continue being selective to avoid following in their footsteps. They were in the practice of sleeping with whomever they were attracted to, including strangers. Personal safety didn't seem to be of any concern to them.

One of the things I said I would never do was date someone HIV positive, until I was faced with that reality with Saleem. I consistently spoke in absolutes, saying what I would never do and what I always did. I learned as a result of that relationship not to speak in absolutes because we often find ourselves doing the very things we say we'll never do only to wonder how and why it happened to us. That relationship changed the trajectory of my life and it set the tone for my work, and a few of my relationships that stared HIV in the face.

UNGLUED

This story, my story, begins May 4, 1976 in Baltimore, MD. I'm the youngest of three children. I have an older brother and sister, and there's a 13-year gap between my brother and me. My mom, Gladys, was married to my sister and brother's father prior to marrying my father, Milton hence the large gap in age.

My nickname as a child was '*Dirt*' because, according to family, I liked to play in dirt. Personally, I remember having an affinity for dolls with long hair, and it was no coincidence that most of my girlfriends also had long hair.

My mother is the fourth oldest of thirteen children. All but one of her siblings had children, so it would be an understatement to say we have a large family. I spent every weekend and summer at my grandmother's house to be around cousins who were close in age. My mother's sister, Arlene, who knew my dad from high school, introduced my parents.

My father, Milton, is a simple man. Born in south Baltimore and raised by both parents, he worked as a baker for many years at a distributor that supplied a grocery store chain with a variety of breads for their bakery departments. My dad was earning a good living when he met my mother, and taught her some of the fundamentals of saving. He knew the value of money, since my grandfather worked in a bank for many years.

My mother was the first woman my father truly loved, so he accepted the responsibility of providing for my siblings because their father was on and off drugs and in and out of jail. My mom was a single mother living at home until she and my dad moved to a place together to start a life of their own.

My mother's mother adored my father, but my mom always believed my paternal grandmother disliked her because she was a single mother with two children from a previous marriage when my father stepped in to help raise my siblings, Jadonna and James. As my mother saw it, his mother didn't have much room to judge her considering my dad's sister was also a single mother with two boys from two *different* men when she married a man who wasn't father to either of them.

Frankly, I never felt especially close to anyone on my father's side of the family either. He, like me, has a sister and brother, but they both have children. My father has a host of uncles, cousins and aunts whom I barely know, if at all.

According to my mother, my paternal grandmother babysat the other grandchildren as well as the children of family friends, but rarely agreed to keep me because of her ill feelings towards my mother. The only memory I have of my mother and grandparents together is standing at a bus stop across from Bon Secours hospital and coincidentally running into my father's father. I was about 5 years old at the time. My grandfather asked my mom if I could have a peppermint. In my excitement, I began choking on the candy. My mother was frantic, as I turned red gasping for air and my eyes welled up with tears. I saw fear in her eyes that I had never seen before. My grandfather stood frozen with his mouth open as my mother pounded my back, yelling for me to hold my arms up in the air to open the passageway. I felt the peppermint slip down my throat whole, allowing me to breathe again. My mother's face was a mixture of relief and anger because my grandfather helplessly stood by.

I spent every weekend and summer at my maternal grandmother's house, 1819 W. Baltimore Street. Every Sunday after church, my cousins Danielle, Chanel, and I went roller-skating at *Shake and Bake* with friends from the neighborhood on Pennsylvania Avenue, also known simply as *The Avenue*. We walked to and from the skating rink to save our money for snacks once we got there, and to purchase loose cigarettes to smoke on our walk home.

The three of us also attended summer camp at the Salvation Army, and honestly speaking we *were* the camp because there were so many of us from our neighborhood enrolled at the day camp. Everyone wanted to be in our click for the privilege of sitting with us at lunch, on field trips and of course for the chance to perform with us at the closing ceremony at the end of the summer.

I've always been a talker and it didn't just pose a problem in school, but in Bible study at camp too. An evangelist came in on

Wednesday afternoons to teach Bible stories and songs. One afternoon in particular, I was sitting Indian-style on the first row of the sanctuary with my flip-flops resting on the floor in front of me. Both of my arms were tucked inside my tank top because the air conditioning was on full blast. Ms. Brown, one of the camp counselors, saw me talking and rushed over to shush me. When she approached she noticed I didn't have my sandals on.

"Close your mouth and put your shoes on! Where do you think you are?" she said with her teeth clenched.

She favored *Scarecrow* from *The Wizard of Oz*. Ms. Brown wore a short, curly, dusty brown wig and she had little age lines that marred her top lip. When I reached down for my shoes she stepped on my fingers with her leather hard-bottomed shoes. The pain summoned tears. I sat crying as she walked to the middle aisle in the sanctuary to continue observing.

Chanel made sure I told her mother once we got to my grandmother's. My Aunt Arlene accompanied me to camp the next morning to confront Ms. Brown. Naturally, Ms. Brown lied and recounted the story completely different from what actually happened.

"I never put my hands on Craig. I don't know why he would say such a thing," she said.

"He sure wouldn't make it up," my aunt argued.

"Craig is one of my favorites. I would never do a thing like that to him or any of these children."

My aunt turned to me, "Did she step on your hands?"

I could barely utter the words because I was crying, "Yes."

"All I know is you better not put your damn hands on him again. He has a mother. If he does something wrong you call her, but don't you put your hands on him again!"

Arlene either forgot we were in a church when she cursed or didn't care, but my superstition of cursing in church had me fearful for her. She was still fuming when we got outside to take the three-block walk home.

She mumbled the entire way, "I know her ass was lying. If she puts her hands on you again, you let me know 'cause I'm gonna go right upside her damn head with her ugly ass."

From that day and every summer that I returned to camp, I was Ms. Brown's favorite and the other campers knew it, but they never understood why and I didn't bother explaining.

I loved being at my grandmother's so much that I asked my mother if I could transfer to the school my cousins were attending, but she wouldn't budge. My cousins never understood why I wanted to spend so much time at their house since it was old and rickety. The three-story dilapidated house had only one bathroom for the ten plus people who lived there. On any given day the house was without heat or hot water to bathe. We were left with no choice but to boil water in the kitchen and make several trips upstairs with pots until there was just enough water in the tub to take a bath. There were also plenty of times the phone was disconnected. The front door didn't lock, and it required a piece of newspaper or cardboard to stay shut. You could always hear someone yelling, *"who forgot to put the paper in the door?"* as the winter draft barreled through the downstairs hallway on to the dining room then off to the kitchen.

There was always something going on at my grandmother's, and so much to do. It was the place where a single pearl slipped down into my ear canal, leaving my Aunt Gloria to rush me to University Hospital where my mother worked as a unit clerk. My grandmother's house was the place my cousin Danielle and I ran through the hallways, ducking from pillows my cousin Byron swung at us from my Aunt Gloria's bedroom.

Someone was always in trouble for back talking an adult, arguing, cussing, fighting or staying out too late. It was where I wanted to be because Mama's house was a catchall for family members who found themselves displaced or separated from their spouse or partner.

My parents' home was the complete antithesis. Our house was purchased in the Pimlico community from a Jewish man, just before I was born. He advised my parents to patiently furnish the house as opposed to going broke trying to impress people by filling the house with furniture before they could afford to. My parents took heed of the man's advice. Years later, they were involved in a car accident that left them severely injured and with a lump sum of money. My father was taking my mom to work when another driver ran the light and struck them. My father had to have shards of glass surgically removed from his eyes.

With the settlement, my parents decided to pay off our house and remodel. At the time of the accident my mother didn't drive, so they bought a new car for her and one for my dad as well. It took several attempts before my mother passed the driving test, but there would be no more days standing at a bus stop choking on peppermints. If I were to ever choke again she could drive me to a hospital.

I didn't care that we had a more comfortable living space than my grandmother. I loved being in a house full of people.

Because I slept on a cot at the foot of my grandmother's bed she taught me to pray. The first prayer I learned was the *Lord's Prayer* that she dictated to me every night before bed even after I knew it by heart.

"Now I lay,..." she said.

"Now I lay..." I repeated.

I'd pause and wait for the next line.

"Go ahead and say it. You know it by now," she said.

"I'm waiting on you," I replied.

She'd continue reciting the words to the end, and I'd climb on my cot.

"As long as you're able to get down on your knees to pray, you should," she said.

"But what if I'm really tired?" I quizzed.

"If the Lord gives you the strength to get down on your knees to pray, then you get down on your knees to pray. There ain't no such thing as too tired," she reinforced.

One night I said my prayers while she was in the bathroom, and when she returned I was already in bed.

"Get up and say your prayers."

"I did."

"I sure didn't see you say them, so get up and say them again."

I pushed the covers back and crawled down to the floor.

My grandmother said her prayers on her knees every night until they became arthritic. She lay on her back with her hands crossed at her chest.

"Mama, you look dead. Are you sleep?"

She was completely still. I couldn't tell whether or not she was breathing in the dark.

"Mama—"

"Boy, would you be quiet and let me say my prayers!"

Mama didn't curse, but I thought on a few instances she wanted to say damn when her patience was tested. The closest she ever came to cursing at me or anyone was to say, "you a dirty, nasty, filthy, stinking, liar."

One night I reminded her to say her prayers because I didn't *see* her say them.

"Mama, you didn't say your prayers."

"I did too."

"I didn't see you say them."

"You didn't have to see me, the Lord heard me. Now go to sleep."

Unglued

My father gave me an allowance every weekend to have at my grandmother's. She held it for safekeeping with other money she kept for my aunts and uncles. Mama kept a wad of money wrapped in a combination of napkins, plastic sandwich bags and safety pins. No one ever knew how she kept the bundle orga nized without confusing one person's with another. Whenever I needed some of my money, I'd ask her and she'd walk to her bedroom closet to pull it from her hiding spot. Carefully, she'd unwrap the money as I eagerly reached and grabbed for the first bills I saw.

"Would you wait a minute? That's not yours!"

I offered to buy her lunch because she was on a fixed in-come. Later the same day, I threw it in her face when she re-fused to let me have my way.

"I thought you bought it out of the kindness of your heart. Had I known you were going to throw it in my face I would've never allowed you to do anything for me. When you give, you're supposed to give from your heart," she scolded.

My feelings were hurt because I hurt hers, and I knew she was right. That very well may have been the last time I remind-ed someone of something I did for them.

Her patience level was amazing considering the number of grandchildren she had pulling her in every direction, still we never heard her curse because she didn't believe in it. Our laughter, at her frustration, only angered her more. She threat-ened to tell my aunts on my cousins and she told me I wouldn't be able to visit the following weekend, but like clockwork I was on the phone calling for my weekly visit anyway.

*****

The first time my parents separated I was in elementary school. My father believed their relationship became fragile after they received the settlement money from the accident. He said my mom made financial decisions without the two of them discussing it first, and she frequently complained about things they didn't have in comparison to their friends. My father worked tirelessly, but my mom accused him of cheating. Infidelity was a symptom of my mom's first marriage and possibly part of the reason she had trouble trusting my father. Sometimes it's difficult to see the good in people when we're accustomed to getting the bad. If my mother was upset with my dad, my sister and brother took her side, leaving him as the outsider.

I was slightly relieved when they separated because my father was always the disciplinarian of the house, and with him gone I figured I could have a bit more freedom. There would be no more whippings with a belt, but that wasn't the case. He simply picked me up and took me to his place for a beating.

I was around twelve years old when my dad and I drove to a neighborhood near my grandmother's. As we drove down the residential street, my father pointed at my mother's car parked in front of a row house.

"You see that? That's your mother's car. She's in that house *right there*. You see it for yourself. She's been running around with another man. When you talk to her, ask her who she knows on Appleton Street," he said.

My dad was hurt. The betrayal in his eyes and the anger in his voice said it all. A mixture of emotions provoked him to involve me in whatever was going on between him and my mother. We passed the house one final time before taking the short drive back to my grandmother's.

I ran up the stairs to use the telephone in her bedroom because it offered some privacy as opposed to the one in the dining room. My grandmother was sitting in her rocking chair alongside the bed watching television. I took a seat at the foot of the bed in front of her. I reached over for the phone resting beside her.

"Don't pull it out too far because you know the cord will come out," she said.

With all the able-bodied adults living in my grandmother's house, one would think the living conditions would have been better, but they weren't. The phone had to be rigged, so the phone cord wouldn't slip out and disconnect the calls.

I carefully dialed my mother's work number with my heart beating violently. I was unsure if my rapid heartbeat was from the run upstairs or what I was about to ask my mother.

"Twelve west, this is Gladys."

"Ma."

"Yes?"

"What you doing?"

"Working, what do you think I'm doing?"

"Who lives on Appleton Street?"

"Appleton Street?"

"Yeah, my father told me to ask you who you know that lives on Appleton Street. We saw your car parked there."

I could see my grandmother twitching in her rocking chair. The chair rocked forward and back once, before she looked over at me with her piercing gray eyes.

"Don't question your mother. You don't ask where she's been. Stay in a child's place," my grandmother interjected gently.

My grandmother was no longer tuned in to *The Young and the Restless*. Normally, it took a major distraction to snap her out of the trance that only a few shows kept her in; *The Young and the Restless* was one, *The Golden Girls* was the other. This time she was listening to my phone call the entire time.

As my mom searched for an answer my grandmother gave me a look that meant get off the phone, and so I did. My father's decision to involve me sowed my own fears of one day being betrayed by love.

I'm the only one of my mother's children to graduate high school and college. Both my brother and sister dropped out of high school, but later earned GEDs. My siblings often said I was our mother's favorite, but I argued that we all were afforded the same opportunities. She did no more for me than she did for

12

them. I did occasionally tease that they inherited different genes from their father's side of the family, but I know there's a fine line between what a parent can provide and what a child decides to make of his or her life. My mother expected the same from all of us. We simply chose different paths.

In one sense, my mom was more settled by the time she had me at 32 years old, so she was able to pour more into me as a child. I was on a little league baseball team, and in swimming, ice-skating, music, karate, and art classes growing up. Her focus may have been more concentrated with me, considering my sister and brother both ended up on wayward paths running the streets with the wrong crowds.

My brother Jimmy spent most of his teenage years incarcerated, leaving me very few childhood memories of him. I could probably count on two hands how many times I've seen him in my lifetime because he left home to live with my mother's sister Loretta in south Baltimore. I do remember women doting over him.

Jimmy was tall, handsome, golden brown with a lean frame, full lips, goatee, teeth so perfectly white they resembled dentures, and plenty of timber in his voice to lure women my mother's age.

There were women calling our house at all hours of the night for him. The majority of the phone calls to our house were for Jimmy. It was so bad that my mother started mixing up the names of the different women calling. After a few mistakes,

Jimmy instructed her to *just take a message* without volunteering a name because she was quick to say the wrong one.

Jimmy had lots of street sense, and book sense. He attended some of the best schools and excelled in the gifted program, but Jimmy was a truant and rebellious when it came to structure at home under my father's rules. Part of the reason he moved to my Aunt Loretta's was to escape the many rules my mother and father had in place. He knew he could run wild at Loretta's.

One of my most vivid memories of Jimmy was a newspaper story about him that my mother was reading. She was in our dining room, and I was standing in the kitchen peering over her shoulder at *The Baltimore Sun* newspaper. The big, bold headline read, *Sentenced to 45 Years*. Jimmy was incarcerated for child abuse and the murder of a 10-month-old baby girl in 1989.

At the time, my brother was dating a woman with two children, and he was babysitting the youngest. I was told he was bathing the baby in the bathroom sink and left her unattended to answer the telephone when she fell into the porcelain bathtub adjacent to the sink. Subsequently, the baby died and authorities believed he and the child's mother were in collusion because there was a cigarette burn on the baby's leg that hadn't healed. Though the baby's mother didn't want to press charges against Jimmy, the state prosecuted him because they believed the mother was trying to protect him.

I was 13 years old when he went to prison, and our home was flashed on the evening news. For the first time ever, my mother gave me the option to stay home from school to avoid embarrassment. I decided to go to school the next day because no one knew Jimmy and I were related because we don't share the same last name.

Although family and close friends never believed the charges, Jimmy, whose street name was Dollar, was selling drugs at the time, and the law had caught up with him one way or another.

We made frequent visits to see him at various prisons throughout Hagerstown and Jessup, Maryland. I knew why he was locked up, but no one ever took the time to discuss the meaning of it all. The bits I knew were pieces I gathered from the news and conversations I overheard around the house.

Visiting those prisons had an impact on me. Our family dynamic had changed. Jimmy was our family, but the only way we could see him was to be put on a list, take an hour-long drive or so to an enclosed facility where we could barely embrace each other without a prison guard interfering. The psychology behind it all baffled me.

The sound of gravel crackling under car tires still remind me of the prison parking lots. There were hundreds of other cars and visitors passing by in the lot with their own stories and reasons why they were visiting family or loved ones.

The entire prison structure was outlined with barbed wire to prevent escape, but those wires couldn't contain the sounds from inmates on the yard playing basketball. A cacophony of noises bellowed from the interior through the cavernous hallways of the jail, including the sound of the iron gates shutting before and after every visitor upon entering and exiting.

The waiting areas were always full of women with crying babies, and young children who should have been someplace else doing kid things.

My sister, Donnie, helped my parents raise me while they worked, and Jimmy was absent. We were close enough that I ate stale gum from her mouth if she didn't have more to share. Donnie wore a short afro before it was stylish to wear natural hair. She was the *bald-headed* girl in the neighborhood that women envied and the guys loved because she had a woman's figure as a teenager.

Donnie gave birth to my nephew Tyrone at 19, and decided to leave home when he was still an infant, but not before my mother was able to tell her to leave the baby.

Donnie spent a good portion of her 20s and 30s wrestling with a drug addiction. Her cocaine addiction eventually drove a wedge in her relationship with me, and our mother. It led her in and out of treatment facilities throughout Maryland and Pennsylvania, leaving our mom permanent guardian of Tyrone.

Donnie moved home on several occasions because she couldn't maintain a place of her own. She was a puppet to drugs. She dangled from one lie to another in an attempt to fool my mother into believing she was clean, but her disappearing acts always gave her away. Some weeks my sister was gone for days at a time only to return with a grand story of where she was. She returned one day with one of her machinations after a three-day disappearing act, and my mom was waiting for her at the top of the stairs with the light on. I could hear my sister yelling from the hallway.

"What you hit me for?"

"Cause I see that shit on your nose, so I know you ain't doing nothing but lying. You can pack your shit and go back wherever you just came from!" my mother yelled.

My sister was crying and wiping her nose still playing naive.

"I don't have nothing on my face. What are you talking about? Where am I supposed to go?" she said as she dabbed her nose, taking quick glances at her fingertips.

My mother had reached her limit. She was done debating the issue.

Donnie was in her bedroom thinking of a way to reason, sucking her teeth, sighing and half packing because she thought she could lie her way out of getting put out. Every minute or so, she stopped packing to make another appeal for pity.

"Ma, I don't have anywhere else to go."

"Yeah, well, that is *not* my concern. You should've thought about that while your ass was ripping and running the streets."

"Ma, if you don't believe me you can call—"

"I'm not calling a damn soul and I don't care where you go, but your ass is going out of here tonight! I'm 'bout sick of your shit."

I was starting to believe my sister would lose her battle with her addiction because she was so frail, and we watched her make multiple attempts to get clean, and failing each time. She looked defeated and worn out.

My mother had given my sister many incentives to get clean before washing her hands. My mom finally realized that she needed to let go and allow my sister to make the decision to get clean because she wanted to, not because we asked her to. My mother was only becoming more aggravated and stressed by it. She had already given relentlessly to my sister until it was obvious my sister was abusing my mother's generosity.

At one of my sister's lowest points, she sold some designer suits my mother bought to help her secure a job. We asked for months when she planned to wear the clothes and she gave a variety of reasons why she hadn't worn them before finally admitting she had sold the clothes for drug money.

With just a five-year gap between us, Tyrone and I grew up as brothers. In many ways, it was like my mother had started over raising kids again. She spent hours after work helping Tyrone with homework and other school projects while preparing dinner. Ty and I never got along, which didn't make it any easier for my mom. Because we were so close in age we were always vying for my mother's, his grandmother's, attention. We argued and even had physical fights about everything from who would sit in the front seat of the car to who would get dropped off at school first. We drove my mother crazy. I was acting out because my parents were separated and it showed in my grades. Ty's grades were always hovering around the failing mark, possibly because he was living with us and it was no secret why. He knew his mother was in and out of treatment facilities, and it didn't help that his father was also absent from his life without good reason.

My father moved into an apartment in Randallstown, an upscale community in Baltimore. He was dating a woman whom he eventually moved in. I can't say that I didn't like her nor can I say that I did. Frankly, I didn't care one way or another about her because I didn't live there, so I didn't have to see her every day. My mother, however, was dating a married man, who was at our house every day and I hated it. It was no secret that JB was married. My sister claims his wife sent their oldest son to knock on our front door one day looking for him.

JB lived a few blocks from us with his wife, but he prepared dinner at our house daily before my mother got in from work. *When did he get a key?* I resented that he had a key to our house. Initially, my mother said JB was just a friend helping around the house because he was a self-employed construction worker. I didn't care who he was. I didn't want him around. On snowy days, JB took Ty and me to school in lieu of us taking the bus. I still didn't like him.

I never asked why my parents' relationship was crumbling, and no one volunteered an explanation. Perhaps, they were shielding me from it, but my dad didn't refrain from besmirching my mother. His words and actions told exactly how he felt about the separation. My only concern was a custody battle. I knew I wanted to stay at home with my mother and didn't have a problem voicing that when my father asked what I'd say if a judge asked where I wanted to live.

I was a student at Fallstaff Middle School when my mother noticed my grades slipping, so she told me to sign up for coach classes after school, and she signed Ty up with tutors at Towson State University on Saturday mornings for extra help. Whenever my mother had a day off from work, she took us to school to make impromptu visits with our teachers. She came to my school one morning to speak to my teachers with her hair in a headscarf and hair rollers because she had gone to the hair salon the day before.

"Ma, can you take those rollers out before you come inside?"

"Boy, I ain't thinking about these kids! I just got my hair done and I'm not taking my rollers out."

That same day in ninth period, a girl yelled across the room, "Craig, was that your mother that came up here today with that headscarf on and hair rollers in her hair?" I sat embarrassed as the class erupted with laughter. Embarrassing moments like that reminded me that I had an *older* parent. My mother was past the point of concern for what others thought. I was well aware that my mother was 44 years old and most of the other parents were 20-something.

The younger parents dressed in the latest and drove the finest luxury cars. My mother knew quality, but she wasn't concerned with keeping up with fads. I kept up with most of the new styles, but style wasn't a priority for my mother.

"You're going to school to learn, not for a fashion show," she reminded.

My sister, Donnie, was pregnant with my youngest nephew, Terrell, while still dibbling and dabbling with drugs. She was living with our cousin Shelly, who suffered from mental illness. My mom didn't think she needed to have another baby, considering she wasn't raising Ty, and Donnie wasn't making any plans of taking him in. I was concerned that Terrell would develop birth defects from the drugs, but some of my fears were put to rest when Donnie was arrested for collecting food stamps and working.

My mom was almost 50 years old when Terrell was born, and she became his part-time guardian. He bounced between our house and the temporary places Donnie called home. My mother took custody of Terrell after he returned to us filthy and ravenous one too many times.

My mother felt that my sister needed to bear some responsibility, so she told her to help pay for Terrell's head start. The agreement was to take turns paying the weekly bill on opposite weeks, but Donnie was still up to her old tricks—lying in an effort to get over.

The director at the school stopped my mother one day to ask when someone would pay the outstanding bill. Unbeknownst to my mother, the bill was behind several weeks. It had ballooned to $500. The weeks my sister was supposed to pay reflected the arrears. Apparently, Donnie told the director my mother would pay when she came in to get Terrell.

For weeks, my sister was dodging her turn to pay.

BEAUTIFUL MINDS

My dad broke up with his live-in girlfriend when he purchased a home in Milford Gardens, a suburban community in Baltimore County. He was extremely proud of his home and eager to start his life over.

"If anything happens to me, all of my papers are in here," he said pointing to a metal copper-colored file cabinet. "Everything is going to you Craig. You're my beneficiary."

In addition, my father gave me a key to the house though I never used it. He wanted me to know his home was my home.

My father's next-door neighbor's granddaughter had a crush on me, and wasn't shy about knocking on his door when I was there and when I wasn't. She told me that my father mentioned, after a few drinks, that he didn't think I liked girls. Her eyes searched my face for a reaction and answer, but I didn't blink. I wondered if perhaps my father knew I could possibly be gay and was ok with it.

She, however, couldn't understand why I wasn't interested in her. I didn't know why I was no longer interested in *any* girls since the puppy love I had for a girl who lived near my grandmother. My ex-girlfriend went to school with my cousin Chanel, and was a cheerleader in the marching band that I played drums for. I was attracted to her long, black, silky hair and the tiny Marilyn Monroe beauty mole above her top lip. We spoke on the phone every day for hours about nothing, and I saw her most of the weekends that I went to my grandmother's. That long-distance relationship was my first encounter with love, and I was missing the feeling. Still, I wasn't about to pretend to be interested for my dad or the girl next door. My father may have suspected I was gay, but he never told me.

*****

I was accepted to one of the magnet high schools, Baltimore City College. Many of my middle school friends attended as well, but there were still more kids that I didn't know freshman year than there were that I knew. It was always easier for me to make friends with girls because I was intimidated by the boys. Although my neighborhood friends were mostly boys, it was different because we grew up together. I thought the guys in high school would be standoffish if they suspected I was gay, especially the Black boys. There's an unspoken rule that Black men aren't to befriend gay men.

I had a couple male friends that I spoke to and cut up with in class, but that was the extent of the friendship. We never hung out after school or weekends, and I didn't have any of their phone numbers. Any and all male bonding was with the guys I grew up with. We built clubhouses, went crabbing and swapped sex stories about girls. I exaggerated stories about sex with girls

I knew because no one fesses up about being a virgin, and I didn't need attention pointing to my sexuality.

I was the first of my friends to get a driver's license, which meant venturing further from our neighborhood. We partied at many of the high school parties. They were all interested in meeting girls. I was more interested in driving and finding something fly to wear to the dance.

I was never attracted to any of my male friends, but one in particular often exposed himself, and it made me curious. *Is he just proud of his penis or does he want me to see it?* It was nothing for him to pull his penis out to pee on the street, and he wanted an audience. After he was exposed, he would call one of our names. Once we looked in his direction he'd begin urinating. He thought it was hilarious. I was turned on.

I met Nina through her older sister Jillian when we were sophomores in high school. Jillian was a senior, but City integrated all grade levels, which meant every class was a mixture of freshmen, sophomores, juniors, and seniors.

Jillian and I were in the same chemistry class. At some point we discovered we attended Fallstaff Middle School together, but we didn't know each other there. After Jillian graduated and went to college at Lincoln University in Pennsylvania, Nina and I bonded. Nina and I didn't live on the same bus line, but occasionally I took Nina's route home because we couldn't get enough of each other. We were inseparable, except when I drove to school. Some mornings I took my mom to work to have the luxury of driving.

The foundation of our friendship was never built on support for one another. Nina made unhealthy comparisons in our friendship early on that I tried to ignore. It became virtually impossible when her mother began chiming in whenever I visited their home. There were always random questions about how I was able to buy new clothes and where I bought them. Nina asked why I never shopped at Reisterstown Road Plaza or Mondawmin Mall—a place where shootings had occurred—like everyone else. Her words were laced with jealousy and for good reason. She was one of three children being raised by a single mother, as was I, but she didn't have the same level of parental support from both parents.

Nina wasn't happy for anyone who appeared to have more than she. She threw a fit when a friend of hers got a new leather jacket when we were in high school because she had never owned one.

Strangers passing in luxury cars were also subjects of her vicious tongue that cut deeply, and fair-skinned girls didn't stand a chance. She was quick to label them as *yellow bitches*. Her anger towards light-skinned females stemmed from being labeled a *pretty dark chocolate thing* growing up whom none of the neighborhood boys seemed to ever be interested in.

I refrained from sharing anything great that happened for me because I witnessed how she spoke about her other friends whom she claimed were bragging.

I bought my first car the summer before my senior year in high school. It was an eleven-year-old, Toyota Corolla coupe that was completely rusted on the passenger side. It was a hooptie. The main purpose for having a car was to share in the responsibility of picking up Terrell from daycare. My mother had purchased an abandoned property and she was supervising the renovation after working her full-time job, so it made sense for me to have a car. For Nina, the car meant I would no longer be taking the bus from school with her, and one more *thing* I had that she didn't.

I paid five hundred dollars for the Corolla with money I earned from my summer job. My mom agreed to add me to her car insurance and cover that expense. Nina couldn't believe I had my own money to buy the car without any help from my parents, and she didn't waste time throwing her doubt in my face.

"You tryna tell me you paid for that car by yourself without any help from Ms. Gladys?" she asked with her lips twisted.

"What's so hard to believe? It was *five hundred dollars*. I bought it," I debated.

Needless to say, she wasn't convinced, but I didn't care.

Junior year, our high school participated in a study abroad program with schools in a few foreign countries. Nina and I were French students, and I expressed an interest in going to France. I spoke to my mother about it and she agreed to pay for me to go thus, I made plans to live in Paris for three weeks. My family frequently took vacations when my parents were together, but this was my first trip out of the country.

As I prepared to leave for France, Nina withdrew a bit from our friendship. This was the same person who pondered how my mom could afford to invite her and her sister out to dinner with us, so an international trip perplexed her. I could tell she was having a difficult time with the idea that I was leaving the country.

"Your mom makes about the same amount as my mother. I don't get how she's able to do so much making the same money," she said.

I didn't have the heart to tell her that she failed to realize my father was very much so active in my life though my parents separated, and my mom didn't splurge on take-out food—she cooked most days. On the contrary, Nina's mom was on a bowling league and they sometimes placed bets on their games. She also took frequent trips to Atlantic City to gamble, and they ate out most days.

When I returned from France, she and I never spoke about my trip. She never asked if I enjoyed the trip or to see any of the pictures from my stay, and I didn't dare bring it up.

As we began applying for colleges, Nina told everyone close to us that she wanted to attend Delaware State. I was unsure where I wanted to attend, so I applied to Bowie State in Maryland as a safety net just in case I wasn't accepted to any of the colleges of my choice. I had the grades, but I was paranoid I would be rejected for some reason.

My first choice was Clark Atlanta University followed by North Carolina A&T. At the last minute, I applied to Hampton University and was accepted. I was reluctant to apply to Hampton because the application required all applicants to complete an essay describing *'how are you preparing for a global society?'* My mom suggested that I write about my trip to France, but I was being lazy. I didn't want to write an essay thus, I complained to my high school guidance counselor who was a Hampton alum. Coincidentally, she had an application from the previous year that required a simpler essay, *why do you want to attend Hampton?*

In my essay, I detailed all the things my guidance counselor had shared during her classroom visits encouraging us all to apply to at least one college since our high school was college prep. It obviously worked because I got in.

Nina settled for her second choice, the University of Maryland Eastern Shore because she didn't have the resources to attend Delaware State. The days leading up to graduation were full of questions from everyone, *what schools were you accepted to?* or *where are you going to college?* I hesitated on that question whenever I was in Nina's company. I allowed her to share her *good news* first with whoever was asking, but the moment I said Hampton the energy changed. I could feel Nina shrinking the instant I was congratulated for getting accepted to Hampton, but more importantly that I was actually going. When her sister Jillian found out I was planning to attend Hampton, she told me I'd be back in Baltimore after a year because *Hampton is expensive.*

I became concerned and told my mother that I was nervous she couldn't afford the tuition.

"Don't worry about how the tuition is gonna get paid. I'm taking care of that. You just get down there and do what you're supposed to do," she said.

It was only a matter of time before I would completely withdraw from the *friendship* with Nina. I was close to my limit with her pessimism.

*****

My cousin Lisa was the first in my family to graduate college. My mom had studied at the Community College of Baltimore for a couple years in the nursing program, but Lisa finished at Coppin State College with a BA in Business Administration. Lisa was my favorite cousin, despite the 8-year difference in age.

Lisa grew up in Walbrook Junction off Poplar Grove Street. My cousins Danielle, Chanel, and I spent a few weekends at our Aunt Coretha's because we could stay out long after the street lights came on with Lisa and her siblings, Jill, Sherry, and Keith. Every now and then, we needed the getaway and freedom from all the supervision at my grandmother's.

My taste in music was refined at my Aunt Coretha's because my cousins kept the stereo blasting classics. I know and love music because they exposed me to a myriad of artists and sounds during a time when music genres and artists were more blended. We weren't limited to R&B and Rap. We listened to every-thing—Tears for Fears, Keith Sweat, Hall and Oats, Anita Baker, Culture Club and Loose Ends.

Many of the kids in their neighborhood were rebels. For fun, they hopped on moving trains, and killed people over sneakers and coats to prove a point. It was a completely different world from what I was accustomed to, but they knew everyone in the junction, so I didn't fear being there.

The first time I went to a club was with Lisa. I was still a minor when she snuck me into Odell's in east Baltimore. From there we went to a gay club called Fantasies, but we were only there long enough to get a glimpse of a drag queen that freaked me out. We left after five minutes because the psychedelic flash-ing lights and blaring music were too much for both of us. Lisa sensed I was gay, but encouraged me not to be because people would call me *Craig the fag.*

I tried to tag along with my older cousins whenever I could. I've always been more comfortable with people a bit older than me. I sat in the room under my mom and other adults, sucking up everything they said in conversation until she noticed I was still sitting in the room with my mouth wide open in amazement.

"Wait a minute. Get outta here! He on every word before it

comes outta my mouth."

My precocial behavior led me to get drunk at age 13 with Lisa, her boyfriend Kendal, my cousins Tiffany and Byron, and a few others. They were playing a drinking game called Bullshit. I took swigs from the Red Bull beer cans when I thought no one was watching, but this wasn't my first taste of beer. My Aunt 'Dot' gave me a taste of her Colt 45 from time to time. The only difference was that she sprinkled a little salt in hers for taste.

Before long, I was playing the game. They thought it was hilarious to see me take gulps at a time. I was vomiting before the game was over.

Lisa was blamed after Byron dragged me to my grandmother's, up the stairs and into Mama's bedroom. He startled her when he flipped on the bedroom light. Mama sat straight up with her eyes squinted because of the brightness from the light. She was wearing a nude colored stocking cap that she made from an old cut up pair of pantyhose.

"Get up! Tell her what you did!" Byron screamed.

"What is going on? What in the devil is wrong with him?" my grandmother yelled.

"Tell him Lisa! Cause I told y'all not to let him drink!" he shouted.

"He's fine. His stomach is just a little upset," Lisa said.

"He's not fine, he's drunk! They were 'round there giving him beer Mama."

"What? Now you know better than that! Why in the world

would you do something like that?" Mama asked.

"He didn't have a lot Mama. It was just a couple sips. He'll be ok."

"I don't give a durn! He shouldn't have had no sips. I'm sure gonna tell your mother tomorrow 'cause you know better than to do something like that."

I lay on the floor crying from embarrassment and nausea. My grandmother didn't waste any time making arrangements for my Aunt Arlene to take me home the next morning. When I got home the next day, my mom was furious and relentless in her scolding.

"Get up and take that trash out!" she screamed.

"I can't. My stomach hurts," I moaned.

"Your ass ain't have no business drinking. Get your ass up off that couch and get that trash out of here," she fussed.

Nevertheless, Lisa was the pulse in our family. We all clamored to be around her at holiday dinners at my grandmother's or at other family gatherings. Everyone wanted to sit at the table with Lisa because it was guaranteed comedy. Her laugh was infectious; it forced you to notice her then love her for her wit and sense of humor.

We admired Lisa because she seemed to have it together. She was carrying the dreams so many in our family had for themselves, but somehow let go to settle for mediocrity or to simply live vicariously through her.

She was a full-time college student funding her own education, and a full-time employee as an office administrator. Some pegged Lisa *boughie* because she was well dressed, well spoken, at the hair salon once a week, and unafraid to fling her hair when she had the urge.

Most people change a bit with love, and such was the case with Lisa. Lisa was a virgin when she met her longtime boyfriend, Kendal, who was a few years older than her. Slowly but surely, she went from independent to dependent, on him. Not financially, but emotionally. She lost herself in him and we all noticed it.

Rumors were swirling that Kendal was seeing another woman at his job. Byron, who worked with Kendal, tried to convince her the affair was indeed real, and it was with a girl they worked with. Still, Lisa was in denial until it was out in the open. Lisa and Kendal tried restoring the relationship with an expeditious engagement that may have calmed Lisa's concerns and pulled Kendal from the hot seat, but it couldn't save the relationship.

In the midst of all the madness, Lisa gave birth to their little girl, yet Kendal still left Lisa for the other woman and married her. The two relocated to Virginia, leaving Lisa a single mother with lots of promise, and a new set of problems to sort through. Subsequently, Lisa experienced a nervous breakdown and Kendal's mother became guardian of the baby while Lisa spent a period of her life in and out of the psychiatric ward at Walter P. Carter in Baltimore.

Byron, once again, was vocal. He said in no uncertain words that Kendal was the reason for Lisa's condition. Perhaps Kendal was the start of Lisa's breakdown, but it's possible Lisa was juggling too much and simply burned out.

What I know for sure, *a man is only interested if you're interesting.* Abandoning one's dream or career path to be under someone isn't the way to guarantee forever. I often wonder what Lisa would have accomplished had she mustered the strength to move on with her life after Kendal.

FLIRTING WITH THE LAW

I was never one to cut classes or school, but I certainly cut a few corners along the way. As my insatiable taste for material things intensified, I got crafty to acquire the things I wanted. I went on a shopping spree with some checks I stumbled across from the first bank account I opened after I graduated high school. The account had been closed for several months, but I was sure the checks would still clear the bank. I spent a day shopping at my favorite stores, signing the checks with my left hand with hopes of throwing off handwriting experts who may have been called in to investigate the fraud. I bought everything I could think of. Mainly things I wouldn't spend my own money on because they were outrageously priced. My mother never had a clue because she always believed I had far too many clothes, shoes, and coats for one person, so it was easy for me to integrate the new stuff with the *old* without her noticing.

A few days and a whole wardrobe later, the bank manager contacted me about the bounced checks. I denied any knowledge of the transactions. I told her I had discarded the checks months before.

"Mr. Stewart, we need you to come in to the branch to bring your account current. Although your account was closed, there were some checks written on the account that overdrew it."

36

"Checks?" I said in my best stunned voice.

"Yes, there were several checks that cleared the account."

"I threw those checks in the trash when I closed the account."

"Well, there were some checks that cleared the account."

"Why would your bank allow checks to clear on a closed account?" I argued.

"Mr. Stewart, the account re-opens whenever there's new activity. You should have destroyed the checks once the account was closed to prevent this."

"I threw them away."

"That's not good enough. They should've been destroyed."

"Well, I didn't know so—"

She knew I signed those checks, and didn't refrain from saying so when I had the unmitigated gull to go into the bank to sign affidavits. Still, I was cleared of any wrongdoing. My guess is the bank didn't bother with a full investigation, since the charges didn't exceed $5,000.

*****

JB drove my mother and me to Hampton for early registration for my classes. My nephew Ty came along for the ride, and we needed the extra hands to get the move done quickly and get me settled in my dorm. I liked JB as I got older because I saw just how much he was involved in helping my mother with her business, and he came through for me whenever I needed him. But, even as active as he was in our day-to-day lives, he never stayed a single night at our house.

I arrived on campus three days before classes began with the other incoming freshmen, so once my family left I had a few days of nervousness to move through. I hadn't had enough practice with making friends with guys, and since the girls' dorms were on the other side of campus, I isolated myself. It wasn't that I couldn't bond with any of the guys in James Hall; I just wasn't ready. Video games and weed seemed to be the connection for most of the guys and I wasn't interested in either.

One of the first times the freshman class was all assembled was during the first week for freshman orientation. We met with the Dean of Students in Ogden Hall. He gave us some words to live by that would carry us for the duration of our stay at Hampton.

"Look to your left, look to your right. You're looking at your future husband or wife. Look to your left, look to your right. You're looking at the future godparents of your children. Look to your left, look to your right. Some of these people won't make it to graduation."

His words had a profound effect on me. Not for the literal context, rather, if my sexual curiosity was only a phase, then I shouldn't have any experiences with any of the male students on campus. God forbid I was to get married one day only to return for homecoming years later with my wife and kids, and run into men I slept with when I was a student.

Byron called me to ask that I consider joining Alpha Phi Alpha Fraternity because he pledged as an undergraduate at Morgan State. Instantly, he connected to a brotherhood that promotes academic excellence while providing services in the community. Once Byron crossed, he lived and breathed Alpha. He knew pledging would mean I too would be connected with brothers on campus and friends for life.

"Craig, I know you'll be approached at some point by one of the fraternities on campus. For some reason, I just feel like you might lean towards the Kappas, but before you make a decision I want you to talk to me first."

In all actuality, I never considered joining a fraternity because I didn't want any additional stress of hiding my sexuality. Hell, I didn't apply to Morehouse College, an all-male school, for the exact same reason.

"Byron, I really don't think I want to pledge at all. It doesn't interest me."

"Well, if you change your mind, talk to me first."

Fortunately, all incoming freshmen were paired with a big brother or big sister to make the transition to college life smoother. My big brother was a senior marine biology major from Stockton, CA, and his best female friend became my big sister by default. Instantly, I had a handful of companions once both groups merged.

David was pretty eccentric, and his sparsely furnished off-campus apartment was the first indicator that he was different. Most of the Black kids living off campus lived in fully furnished apartments, even if it meant driving their parents further into debt.

David was extremely proper. He had this valley girl thing going, except he wasn't feminine with it, and his style was that of a White boy. David was usually clad in rugby shirts, tattered jeans, and flip-flops.

Despite his busy class schedule, he always managed to make time to run us to Wal-Mart or on other errands. He and I grew closer than he did with the other freshmen in our group. We spoke on the phone quite a bit in the beginning and I was invited to hang out at his place without the others. I suspected early on that David was gay, but not because he tried to make a move on me. We were strictly friends. There was just something mysterious about him that he wasn't saying. My suspicions were confirmed one weekend when he took me over the bridge to Norfolk to stay the night with some of his friends who were students at Norfolk State University. It was clear that all of these guys were gay.

Before David and I got dressed to return to Hampton the following morning, we were all seated in the living room talking. One of his friends flashed me when no one was looking. He was seated across from me in his boxers opening and closing his legs. I could see his dick growing when he noticed me watching. I looked because I wanted to see, not because I was interested. I wasn't attracted to him, but I did want to see.

I didn't waste any time chewing David out on the drive back for neglecting to tell me his friends were gay. He said he didn't think it mattered because they were friends, but he would never let it happen again. I trusted David, and I knew he wouldn't put me in harm's way. It was just the principle and of course it was my internalized homophobia lashing out at him. David and I continued being friends, but I never saw those friends of his and we never spoke of that weekend again.

Winter was approaching which marked the end of the fall semester of freshman year. I was glad to be moving out of James Hall, and my grades weren't as good as I anticipated. I thought I could get by without studying like I did in high school, but my 2.6 GPA was a clear indication I could not.

Nina and I spoke several times a week when we first moved away for school, and those conversations translated into excessively high phone bills. She told me about everyone from high school who also went to the University of Maryland Eastern Shore with her, and all the new people she met.

Nina and her new roommate were getting along like they had known each other for years. I complained about my roommate, who was up at 5 a.m. every morning to pray because he was Muslim, which meant my sleep was interrupted. My first class was at 11:00 a.m. and it didn't help that he hit the snooze button on his alarm clock every nine minutes for thirty minutes every morning.

I told her about our near fight after I jumped out of my bed one morning to grab his alarm clock, but he beat me to it. After he and I argued, I went to the Dean of Men to complain. The dean told me he couldn't make him move to another room and he rambled on about how a part of the college experience was resolving our own conflicts, so I decided to lie to my former roommate. I knew there was a vacant dorm room in another dorm on campus, so I returned to our dorm and told him the dean gave instruction for him to vacate the room immediately. When he refused to leave I told him the dean said if he didn't move out that same day, he would be charged for two rooms. I left for class and when I returned, his side of the room was empty, leaving space for me to put some of my belongings on his side and in his closet.

Nina and I were eager to get back home for Christmas break to see each other because this was the longest separation since we became friends. However, I enjoyed being away from home because I was exposed to kids from all over the country and world. There was an international house on campus reserved for students from other countries. The amazing part for me was that we were all from different corners of the globe, but somehow convened at Hampton for the same purpose; an education.

I became conscious of how I spoke as a broadcast journalism major because faculty in the department wouldn't allow accents to go unnoticed. The goal of any seasoned journalist worth his salt is to have a Midwestern accent.

A few students laughed when I pronounced words like dog, beige, mother or leather in my Baltimore accent. There was no place for that accent at Hampton or in the Mass Media Arts Department, so I quickly focused on ridding myself of it by the end of the first semester.

During Christmas break, Nina noticed that I had dropped the accent.

"Why you changing the way you talk?"

"Because I take a lot of speech classes in my department and we get graded on how we speak. I can't keep turning it on and off."

"Well, I'm not changing the way I talk just because I'm in college."

"What's the point of going to college if you're not going to grow?"

I could see after one semester that we were growing in completely different directions. Actually, we were always different in most ways. The months apart allowed me the time to see it. I never completely understood why Nina was so negative, but I knew I wasn't willing to deal with it much longer. The spaces in our communication grew larger with each semester of every school year. I refused to apologize for wanting to be better. I was discovering a life outside of Maryland.

As I matriculated in college, I noticed my peers in college had parents who were around the same age as mine, unlike when I was in middle school. Many of the parents were also established and settled enough to be in a position to provide a college education; however, the preponderance of students having financial difficulties had younger parents. It was like middle school all over, except the tables had turned. It wasn't so cool to have the material *stuff* and be unable to pay for books. I was beginning to understand what it meant to have one's priorities in place.

I felt the same adrenaline rush each time I showered in my dormitory that I felt years before when I perused *Black Inches* magazine. I knew there was always a chance to see one of the guys naked in one of the shower stalls when I passed to go into the shower. The pressure from the water against the flimsy curtains often gave me a quick look, but there were also those who didn't draw the curtain completely closed. I sometimes showered on other floors in the dorm for the purpose of sneaking peeks, and I didn't stop there.

Late at night, when no one was in the bathrooms I cut holes in the shower curtains or completely removed them to get a look. I was borderline desperate because I had held myself captive for so long.

There was one guy, on another floor, who wasn't concerned who saw him naked. He always stepped outside of his shower to dry off because he was comfortable being naked. I made a mental note of the times he showered, so I could make plans to go upstairs for my shower to see him.

Periodically, I peeked out of the curtain to see if he was done showering or to get a look at him in plain view. His body was cut and you could see the definition in his muscles because he was smooth, not hairy. He was an even golden-brown complexion. He took his time, leaning down to reach his ankles and toes. My dick got hard watching him pat his dick and ass dry before casually wrapping himself in his towel to exit. I was late to class a few times trying to see this one-man show.

All the major credit card companies were courting the students on the campus, especially us freshmen, to get credit cards. They made every attempt to lure us into debt, offering free key chains, pens, coffee mugs and zero percent interest rates. I chose to use them before they got a chance to use me. I applied for every credit card I thought I could get. Discover was the first to send me a credit card.

Initially, I always paid my credit card bill in full, but this time I intentionally maxed out the credit card on dinner at fancy restaurants, and of course clothes. Once the bill came I called Discover and reported the card stolen. I explained that I hadn't made the charges and they kindly removed them as a courtesy because I was a customer in good standing.

I later applied for Mastercards and Visas to charge up, but my plan was different. Instead of activating the card from my dorm room I activated them from any random office on campus because I knew the card company would check to see where it was activated to determine fraud or not. After charging these cards to the limit I waited for the bills to arrive to call and pretend I never received them. I practiced sounding shocked and angry before calling.

"Hi, I'm calling because I received a statement for a card I never received. I applied for the card, but I never got it. All I have is this bill!"

"So, none of these charges belong to you?"

"No, I never got the card in the mail. Am I...Who's gonna be responsible for this?"

"Well, we have to do an investigation first, sir. Would you verify your mailing address?"

I gave her my campus address and reminded her that I lived in a dormitory and anyone could have intercepted my mail. Once again, the charges were waived and I was issued brand new cards with zero balances. It became so easy that I taught one of my friends and her roommate how to write fraudulent checks—I got in on their shopping sprees too.

I never defrauded the same credit card company twice, unless it was near the Christmas season when they anticipate an increase in fraud, but I applied to new companies for new cards and started all over again.

The times I legitimately shopped were through the mail because there weren't many options in Hampton, VA and everyone shopped at Coliseum Mall. I received so many package deliveries from Banana Republic that the shipping and receiving clerk knew me by name. Occasionally, I'd see him on campus and he'd tell me there was a package at the warehouse for me before I made it to my mailbox back at the dorm.

During my first summer back to Maryland, my friend Chico, whom I grew up with, told me he had a connection to counterfeit money. I trusted him because I had known him for years, and he had taught me how to drive a stick shift after my dad lost his patience after one lesson. Chico was buying fake money from one of his college friends from Philadelphia. I bought $200 worth of counterfeit money for $100 to get started.

The $20 bills looked like real money, but the color was slightly off. The fake bills were lighter in color, so I covered my hands in baby oil and balled each of the bills up in my hands to darken them and give them an aged look. Once I smoothed out the bills they looked like *real* money.

My first stop was Banana Republic, and the Gap in Owings Mills Mall. I changed some of the bills in a few stores along the way, so that I didn't have as much on my person. When I used all of the counterfeit money, I placed a second order and turned my friend Jade on to the scheme.

A month later, I saw a story on the local six o'clock news that there was a rash of fake money in the area. The news mentioned our zip code. Chico called to tell me the Feds had raided his parent's home. He said they turned his room upsidedown, flipping over mattresses in search of counterfeit money. Fortunately, he had gotten rid of all the money he had in his possession. Had they found any, it would have been the end of his college career, and the beginning of a criminal sentence. The news report was enough for me to retire, but I still wasn't done being slick.

I returned to Hampton for my sophomore year. I stayed in Dubois Hall, the coed dormitory. There were no single dwellings in Dubois, so I had to learn to live with a roommate and it was a challenge. I had a mini refrigerator and television that I didn't want to share with my roommate. I was extremely guarded and private. I wasn't too keen on getting too close to any of the guys at school, not even my roommate. I knew if I opened up the gates to a friendship, personal questions would soon follow. I was cold to him because I knew he'd be less likely to make any future attempts to befriend me.

I returned to Hampton the second semester of my sophomore year with a Honda Accord. I got a $15,000 settlement from an accident I was involved in just before my senior year of high school. I drove every chance I could once I got the car, even to the cafeteria on campus if I decided to have a meal there. My meal card was virtually blank because I ate off campus at restaurants in the area more than I did in the cafeteria.

I was relatively popular by sophomore year. My closest friends were Jazz and Ari. It was almost impossible to see one of us without the other two. I had a class with Jazz's roommate, and coincidentally, we had a class together, but didn't know each other. Jazz knew Ari, and introduced me to her.

Most of the students thought the three of us were from rich families because we lived such privileged lives, driving new cars and prancing around campus in designer threads. Even in the rain, we didn't make a habit of dressing down. Our casual clothes were high end, and it was rare to catch any of us in the same thing twice. Ari even toted a cell phone around campus chit chatting in between her classes, and this was before cell phones were commonplace.

We attended all of the cabarets that the fraternities and sororities hosted, ate at all the lavish restaurants in the Tidewater area, and took day trips to Georgetown in DC or Tysons Corner to shop. But, as close as Jazz, Ari, and I were, we never talked about things most personal to each of us, and for me it was whether or not I was gay.

About once a month I made the three and a half hour drive home for the weekend to visit my family and friends, and to quench my thirst at the gay clubs. I felt like I was living a double life. I was sneaking to gay clubs in the middle of the night for the sake of fondling a stripper.

The only gay club I was familiar with was Club Bunns in Baltimore, but I learned of other clubs from the flyers that littered my car at the end of the night. Eventually, I started taking the drive to DC because I was bored with the hole-in-the-wall gay clubs in Baltimore, and after running into one of my neighbor's gay friends at Bunn's I was a bit paranoid that he would run his mouth. He always suspected I was gay, and told a girl I grew up with that he would one day *have* me, but I wasn't going for it.

The first time I saw a drag show was in DC with a male impersonator performing a Luther Vandross song. Unbeknownst to me, it was a lesbian dressed like a man lip-synching the song. I thought she was a he, and I was sure *he* was singing live until the song skipped.

I was never interested in the drag shows no matter how creative they were with the costumes and makeup. I endured the long shows and suffered the long drives from DC to Baltimore at 3 a.m. for the sake of seeing the dancers. I never stopped to consider how I'd explain being in D.C. if something happened on the road in the middle of the night. I just took the chance.

With sophomore year completed, I packed up all of my things in the car to go home for the summer. My partner in crime, Jade, told me her coworker knew an accountant who embezzled money from T. Rowe Price and Price Waterhouse. I knew Jade through a girl I grew up with—Jade detailed my white Honda Accord before she and I became friends.

Jade said we could get in on the cash cow if we turned over our bank information. Of course I wanted in because I was always looking for a come up, and I was feeding a monster I created on campus. I was gaining attention and popularity for how I dressed, and I convinced myself that I had an image to protect since Hampton had a reputation for having an uppity student population. In all honesty, I was using material things to gain popularity to avoid being scrutinized for being gay.

Jade introduced me to her coworker with the connection. He explained that we needed to turn over our ATM cards and pin numbers, and the funds would be transferred to our accounts. Debit cards hadn't been created, so I wasn't leery of turning over my card *after* removing my money from the account. In fact, I gave him two ATM cards—one was connected to my mother's credit union account.

Two days after I turned over my bankcards to Jade, a man called to tell me a deposit was made into my account and I could go into a branch to withdraw $300. I couldn't believe it worked. I was nervous, but not enough to be afraid of going in the bank to withdraw the money.

As I approached the teller I noticed the cameras overhead. I convinced myself that I wasn't committing a crime yet because it was my account that I was making the withdrawal from. The money just wasn't mine. My hands were shaking as I handed the teller the withdrawal slip. I tried desperately to appear calm and casual, but my voice trembled when she asked how my day was going. I was bracing myself as she counted out the money. I raced to the car to call Jade.

"It worked! I withdrew money from the account!"

"Are you for real? Which bank did you go in?"

"The one downtown."

"Oh my motherfucking God. You strolled your important ass in there and cashed and carried," she said laughing hysterically.

"Yes, I was scared as shit too."

I wanted more, and I had another account to work.

"I'mma start calling your ass cash and carry!" she laughed.

"Girl you stupid. Are you going to do it?"

"Yea, I gave him my card today. But wait a minute, guess what Leon asked me?" she said.

"What?" I asked.

"He talking 'bout, 'what's up with your boy? Is he *like that*?'"

Jade and I never discussed my sexuality, but I knew that she knew I was gay because her brother was, and she told me her brother thought I was fine. If she didn't think I was gay, I don't believe she would've told me that.

"I told his ass, 'Craig gets more pussy than he knows what to do with.' With his nosey ass. Nigga go somewhere with all them questions. We tryna cash and carry!" she said.

After a few deposits and withdrawals I had gone through a few thousand dollars, spending money on whatever I wanted.

A homeless mother and her two girls stopped me one night leaving the grocery store. I was in my car preparing to pull off when they walked up to the driver's side window. I didn't hear them approach over the music blasting from the car, so I was startled when I looked up. I was on edge too from all the illegal activity I was involved in at the time.

52

"Oh, I'm sorry. I didn't mean to scare you."

"It's ok," I said looking them up and down.

They had everything they owned with them in plastic trash bags and backpacks.

"I just wanted to know if you could spare a few dollars. We're trying to get a hotel room across the street, and we're like three dollars short."

The three of them were standing huddled close together holding hands. They were filthy, and their hair was scrambled all over their heads like wild women. I knew I didn't have any dollar bills in my pocket. I only had $20 bills, so I pulled one from my pocket and handed it to the mother.

"Maybe you can get something to eat too," I said.

The three of them screamed and jumped up and down hugging each other like they were winning contestants on a game show. I could see tears in the mother's eyes.

"Thank you! Thank you so much," they said in unison.

"You're welcome," I smiled.

They turned and walked across the parking lot towards the rundown hotel. I watched them in the rearview mirror thinking of the countless times I had come across twenty dollars in my life and the comfortable bed I was going home to that I took for granted. I tooted the horn and waved for them to come back.

"Maybe you can stay an extra night."

I handed the woman another $20 bill and like before they jumped in excitement. Perhaps, it was an act of contrition and I was looking to be vindicated in some way for the fraudulent activity I seemed to find myself caught in.

My mother got wind of the bank scam when the credit union contacted her about the account overdrafts because our accounts were connected. The credit union threatened to pull the money from her savings account.

I found out that Jade and I had been scammed in the scam. Her coworker's *insider* didn't work as an accountant. He was a junkie. According to the bank, blank envelopes were being deposited into the account. The computer registered the blank envelopes as legitimate deposits, and credited the account. He, in turn, sent us into the bank to withdraw the funds before a banker verified the funds from the ATM. The day after we withdrew money from inside the branch the account became overdrawn because of the fake deposits.

"Craig! I don't know what you're doing, but you better get that damn money back in that credit union!" she yelled from the kitchen.

I was in my room with $2,500 in cash stashed away.

"If you want to throw your life away you can, but I will not be visiting anymore jails, and you know you can't make it in *nobody's* jail!"

I had just enough money to cover the overdrafts for the credit union account to protect my mother's money. My other bank account would remain negative because I didn't have enough money left to cover both.

By junior year, the guys I grew up with were asking me the same thing, "what are the *bitches* like at Hampton? I know you fucking mad bitches down there." The truth was, I wasn't. Questions were arising from my mother as well about the girls I was or wasn't dating at school. She said a few of her friends asked, "why doesn't he have a girlfriend as good-looking as he is."

"Do you like girls?" my mother asked.

"Yea, I like girls! Why would you ask me something like that?"

"I'm just asking," she laughed. "You don't have to bite my head off. You never talk about any girls you like."

"I'm not worried about dating. I'm focused on school."

"Yea, well that's good. Keep your head in them books."

I was still attracted to girls at the time, but this was bigger than looks. I just wasn't confident approaching them anymore. My feelings were too jumbled up. My urges for guys were intensifying. The only reason I hadn't done something with one of the guys at school was my angst that it was just a phase I was going through.

I think the pressure of my mother asking me about having a girlfriend was weighing on me to find one, anyone. I didn't need more questions surfacing. Besides, my mind didn't seem to wander to thoughts about guys as long as I was in a relationship with a girl.

My friend Monica was a graduate student at Hampton when we met. She worked in the business center in the office where I was originally assigned to do work-study freshman year. Monica worked closely with the recruiters when they came to campus; thus, she helped students create resumes and fine tune their interviewing skills to secure a job after graduation.

Long after my work-study assignment at the career center ended, I was still flocking to Monica's office. There was a girl in Monica's office one day I passed through. She was a sophomore from New York on a full scholarship. Monica told me she spent time in foster care because her mom was on drugs. *Essence* magazine had honored her as a young achiever for overcoming great odds.

There was something that attracted me to Riley, and it wasn't that we both had family members addicted to drugs. I liked her independence. She was essentially putting herself through school. Riley was rough around the edges like most New York women, but there was a softness to her that I liked. I knew I could *clean* her up a bit.

I told Monica that I wanted to take Riley out, and I begged her to put a good word in for me. The only problem was that Riley had a boyfriend. Since Monica didn't really care for Riley's boyfriend she told her for me.

Initially, Riley said we could only be friends because she didn't want to hurt her boyfriend, but after a few dinner dates and phone calls she left him.

Riley told me right away that she didn't want to have sex again until she was married, which left me both disappointed and relieved. I made a promise to myself that I would have sex with a female before *deciding* to be gay because I thought I had something to prove to myself and people, but there was relief in knowing I wouldn't be pressured for sex.

Riley and I got close fast. We met for lunch and dinner at the cafeteria on campus. She wanted to meet for breakfast too, but I wasn't going for the early wake ups since I wasn't an early riser. After dinner, she liked strolling along the waterfront of the campus holding hands and kissing on the benches before I dropped her off at her dorm. Once we got to her dorm, she wanted to sit in the car for another hour. I recognized her clinginess was a symptom of her abandonment issues shining through.

After four months of the same routine, I was feeling smothered and the public displays of affection were embarrassing. She wanted everyone to know we were together. When we met in the cafeteria, she made it her business to lean down to kiss me before she took her seat, and expected me to do the same. It was obvious that I wasn't as in to her as she was in to me. It dawned on me that I was using her to distract *people* while I figured things out.

Breaking up with Riley was tough because I knew she had left her boyfriend for me, and I was about to leave her. I pondered the decision for weeks, dragging it out because I didn't want to hurt her, nor did I want to tell her during midterms. I didn't want to be responsible for a drop in her grades. I made every excuse why it wasn't the perfect time to tell her and began avoiding her on campus.

She cried and begged for a chance to give me the space I needed, but I refused. I couldn't give her any more false hope that things could be different though we had sat on the benches along the waterfront for hours fantasizing about a life together with children, but there was a piece of me that wasn't as convinced it would ever happen. I was holding a secret that she wasn't privy to. It hurt me to see her in pain, but it would hurt more if I continued to delay the inevitable truth.

I never ran into Riley at the cafeteria after we broke up. I found out that she was taking her lunch and dinner out to avoid me. I saw her from across campus one afternoon, but I avoided her. I couldn't face her. If I knew then what I know now, I would have told her that it had nothing to do with her and everything to do with me.

DREAM CHASING

I dreaded the thought of having to write a thesis to graduate and the anxiety plagued me from freshman year to senior year. I couldn't wrap my brain around the idea of writing a paper that had to be a minimum of twenty-five pages.

I was stuck with Dr. Peyton for senior thesis, a thin Black woman with chinky eyes whose primary residence was in New Jersey, but lived in Hampton Roads during the week to teach at HU.

Dr. Peyton had a reputation of being a snooty tyrant in the Mass Media Arts Department because it was obvious to us students that she had money, and she was so cold. She didn't tolerate excuses and if you thought it was ok to skip her class, and still turn in an assignment, you were sadly mistaken. The way she saw it, there wasn't anything else you had to do with your time other than be in attendance at her class. Dr. Peyton wasn't interested in being well-liked by her students nor was she keen on developing any sort of rapport with students outside of her classroom.

Dr. Peyton didn't play favorites with any of us—she expected excellence from everyone. She wasn't in the business of overlooking our tendencies to be lazy either. She was one of the few instructors that wouldn't tolerate colloquialisms or broken English in her class or in passing on the campus.

Most of the Mass Media students thought Dr. Peyton was arrogant because she refused to answer if we didn't use proper grammar or speak clearly when speaking to her. She simply batted her eyes at you in an "I don't speak that language" kind of way until you rephrased the question. That was part of the reason students feared her—she had a standard and she held us to it. My only desire was to stay out of her way so she would in turn get out of the way of my diploma and me.

Dr. Peyton scheduled private sessions with each of us students in her office after we outlined the scope of our thesis. I witnessed some leaving her office in tears after she ripped apart topics brought to her for approval. She put the fear of God in us.

In lieu of class, she gave us the time to write our papers once we had our topics selected and approved, but I continued visiting Dr. Peyton's office once a week to get feedback along the way. I was unable to take thesis first semester because all of the classes were full before my chance to pre-register rolled around. I had to pass this class the first time if I wanted to graduate on time. The only other option would've been to return the next year for one semester just to take thesis all over again.

I chose to write about the increasing teen pregnancy rate in Baltimore, and luckily Dr. Peyton found it interesting. After a few meetings, Dr. Peyton began venturing into more personal conversations with me, much to my surprise.

"What are your plans after graduation?" she asked with her legs crossed and her chin resting on her fist.

She actually looked absorbed in what I was going to say. Normally, she rifled through papers on her desk, appearing too busy for small talk. This time she was tuned in.

"I'm moving to Atlanta to write music."

Dr. Peyton's office was pretty empty because my senior year would be her last year teaching at Hampton, so apparently she had already begun packing. The only furniture in her office was a desk and a single chair—for herself of course. It was her way of keeping us from staying too long.

"What makes you the cat's pajamas?" she asked.

"What does that mean?" I chuckled.

"You would have to think your music is pretty good if you're moving there with aspirations of writing music," she said smiling and fluttering her eyes.

This was one of the first times I had seen Dr. Peyton smile. Hell, it may have been the first time I saw her teeth because she kept her lips pursed at all times.

"Yea, I think so," I said.

"What do your peers think of you?" she quizzed.

"Huh?" I asked grinning.

"What do your peers think of you?" she said batting her eyes.

"I don't know. They like me I guess," I said shrugging my shoulders.

I was slightly embarrassed and it showed. I wasn't sure if she was about to broach the subject of me being gay or not.

"You're not like them. You're different, even in the way that you dress," she said looking me up and down. "Is that suede?"

"Yes."

I was wearing an ivory colored suede blazer. The suede was so plush that ostensibly it appeared to be cream velvet.

"May I touch it?" she asked standing to her feet.

Dr. Peyton was leaning over her desk to feel the sleeve before I could answer.

"Yes," I said.

"That's beautiful," she said.

"Thank you."

I was officially embarrassed.

*****

In 1998, Atlanta was home to three of the biggest recording labels in R&B music, and it was becoming the gay mecca of the world, of which I was completely unaware. LaFace Records, So So Def and Dallas Austin Recording Projects, Inc. collectively had a hand in the success of artists like Toni Braxton, TLC, Usher and Outkast. LaFace, in particular, was the resident label for those artists and in many ways was revered as the modern day Motown, and a staple in Atlanta for those signed to or employed by the label. My plan was to get on staff as a songwriter at one of the three.

Dream Chasing

My first visit to Atlanta was during spring break of my senior year in college. The original plan was to vacation on the Cayman Islands with Jazz and a few other friends, but I knew I needed to get serious about this move because graduation was imminent, and I had played enough during my college years. I needed to find a job, and fast. It was already March.

My plans quickly changed from lying on the beach to visiting Atlanta to plot out my move immediately following graduation since there was no way I was returning to Baltimore for an extended period. I hadn't lived in my hometown for more than four years. I didn't move away for college only to have to return after graduation.

To secure a place to stay, I reconnected with a girl I knew from high school who was living in Atlanta. Once Heather gave me the ok to crash at her apartment for the week, I booked my flight and a rental car. When I arrived in town, Heather was still at work, so I took the time to tour the city.

I drove from the airport through downtown on Peachtree Street to Buckhead in search of LaFace Records. I just had to see it, but it wasn't visible from the street. It was tucked away in a high rise with a few other businesses unrelated to music. That evening, I met Heather at Phipps Plaza and followed her back to her apartment on the south side of the city.

After I got settled in at her place we mapped out plans to hit 112—a club located behind the Tara movie theater on Cheshire Bridge. The next night, we partied at the infamous Atlanta Live, which later became disco Kroger at Piedmont and Peachtree Roads. This city was calling my name. I had to make it my home. It was refreshing to see so many young, Black, educated working professionals.

I had a cousin who was a senior level VP at Coca~Cola who set up an interview for me the week I visited with a staffing agency called Talent Tree. They were located in Midtown on Peachtree Street, just south of the Amtrak station, but north of the Alliance Theater.

Talent Tree staffed all new contract employees for Coca~Cola as well as some other major corporations in the city. I was hired the day I interviewed. The woman who interviewed me gave me the name of an apartment locator to find a place. She suggested I consider Vinings, a little quiet, but diverse, community that borders the city and Cobb County.

I returned to Virginia to complete the remainder of the school year and contacted Promove, the apartment locator, who in turn sent me a stack of photos of a variety of apartments. The agent I worked with did a search for apartments in the city based on the amenities I wanted, cost, and areas of town I outlined.

I opted for a one-bedroom apartment in Vinings about two miles from Cumberland Mall. I couldn't believe I was about to lease an apartment sight unseen. The photos they sent me were shots from the outside of the property. I had no idea what the inside of the unit looked like, but it was a chance I was willing to take. My parents deposited enough money in my account to cover the security deposit and application fee to secure the apartment.

The last thing to do was turn in my thesis. It was finally done, and I had more than twenty-five pages. The only question left was what my grade would be. Dr. Peyton scheduled times for us to come to her office individually for our final grade. We were only allowed to see the paper because once it was turned in it became the property of the university.

Dr. Peyton's office door was closed when I arrived for my appointment, but I knocked anyway.

"Come in."

"Hi Dr. Peyton."

"I guess you're here for your grade," she said rhetorically.

"Yes," I said nervously.

My heart pounded. This grade was the only thing that stood between graduation and me. I knew it was possible to fail. I had heard a myriad of stories from seniors who weren't allowed to walk at graduation because they failed one class—in this case senior thesis. And if that wasn't bad enough, they were forced to write an entirely new paper on a different subject the next school year.

She handed me the paper with the same ease as when she reached to feel my suede jacket a few weeks before. "A-" was scrawled on the top in red ink.

I smiled, flipping through my paper. I was speechless. I tried to make out the comments she had marked in the margins, but I didn't care what they said. I had an A-.

"I have something else for you," she said reaching into her briefcase. "I thought about you and cut this out of the paper."

She handed me a newspaper clipping. It was a story from the local newspaper about the flourishing music industry in Atlanta. The article mentioned songwriters and producers that were responsible for many of the hits coming out of Atlanta.

"Thank you. I appreciate this," I said.

"Well, I figured you should see this since you're going there. Atlanta is definitely the place it's happening."

There was a person behind the cold veneer that Dr. Peyton was most famous for displaying. I began to make sense of her. Dr. Peyton wanted to be an example for students, not a friend.

"You know this is my last year teaching at Hampton."

"Yes, I know."

"So, I have a generous offer for you. If you'd like, you're welcome to have my bed and mattress at my apartment. It's practically brand new. As you know, I'm only here on weekends. The only thing, you'll have to come get it the Friday before graduation because I want to have everything out of the unit by five."

"Ok, I need to speak to my parents first, but I will let you know soon."

Dr. Peyton scribbled her number on a piece of paper for me to contact her about the bed, and of course, in true Dr. Peyton fashion, advised me not to share her telephone number with anyone.

After graduation, my parents, grandmother, two aunts, and I were preparing to head back to Baltimore. We decided against dinner following the graduation ceremony since we celebrated over dinner when everyone arrived in Hampton on Friday. Instead, we opted to grab something fast to eat on the road.

As my family filed in line to place to-go orders at Burger King, I fled to my friend Justice's place across the street in the Hampton Harbors apartments. I was really good friends with Justice's roommate, who was a student in the Mass Media Arts Department also. Justice and I bonded after she confided in me about a tempestuous relationship she was involved in with a guy her mom called *an intelligent loser* because he should've graduated semesters before we arrived on campus. Justice knew he was dating some of the incoming freshmen women, and using her car at times to do so.

Justice knew I was leaving for Baltimore immediately after graduation, so she reminded me at least two times that day that her mom had *something* for me. Her parents and older sister Tracy were watching television when I walked into the apartment.

"There you are! I'm so glad you came. I have something for you," said Mrs. Marshall.

"Congratulations!" Tracy yelled.

"Thank you. Hello everybody," I said.

"I'll be right back," said Mrs. Marshall before she dashed to Justice's bedroom.

I couldn't imagine what she had to give me that was so important. This was only my third time meeting Mrs. Marshall. I answered the phone at Justice's apartment a few times when her mom called, and we usually exchanged a few words before I gave Justice the phone, but I didn't think I left much of an impression.

The first time I met Mrs. Marshall in person was in passing on campus, and the second time was during Parent's weekend when she took a few of Justice's friends to brunch. At brunch, Mrs. Marshall asked us all what our plans after graduation were and I told her I was moving to Atlanta to write music. After brunch, Justice told me her mom spoke highly of me.

"Craig, my mom said, 'there's something really special about him. He's gonna be somebody one day. That's someone you need to stay in touch with,'" Justice recalled.

Mrs. Marshall emerged from Justice's room holding a sealed envelope.

"There isn't much in here, but it's the perfect card. I read many cards before I found this one and if one word was out of place I put it back. This is the card for you," she said, holding the card close to her chest.

"Ok," I smiled as I started opening the envelope.

Normally, I would've waited to open a gift in private, but she wanted to be there as I opened it.

"Now, remember it's not much in it, but pay attention to the words," she reminded.

"Ok, I'll appreciate whatever's in here," I said.

I stood alone in the kitchen reading the card as Justice's family congregated in the living room talking and watching television. I opened the envelope and found a beautiful Hallmark card. There were countless yellow candles photographed on the front of the card. Each candle was burning and the text was written from the black soot emitting from the candles.

If I could give you ANYTHING as you graduate from college, I would give you A CANDLE that burns as BRIGHTLY as the light within you, the light YOU ARE...I would tell you to KEEP IT BURNING, No matter what. I would say don't let the WELL-INTENTIONED extinguish it. Don't let the MEAN-SPIRITED blow it out. Don't let your light flicker AND FADE because of everyday CHALLENGES and concerns.

I could feel my bottom lip trembling as a rush of warm tears began sliding down my face. When I opened the card I found the $25 Mrs. Marshall tucked inside. I backed further into the kitchen to lean against the wall by the fridge to finish reading the card.

The world is large, and NO ONE can illuminate it alone, but it is amazing how A single candle, BURNING BRIGHTLY, can light so many others. The world NEEDS your light. Hold your candle high.

"Awww, he's crying," Tracy screamed.

Mrs. Marshall turned, and ran to me with Justice and Tracy. The four of us stood huddled in the kitchen hugging as I sobbed.

"Oh, Craig Stewart," Justice said.

This was the first card to ever bring me to tears. It finally sunk in that I was leaving the place that nurtured me from irresponsible teenager to adult. I was leaving friends who knew the person I grew to be, and one they helped shape. These were the people I promised I'd always stay in touch with, but in that instance I knew there was a possibility we might lose touch because life happens and people often grow apart especially with distance between them. *This could very well be the last time I ever see them again.*

More importantly, how did Mrs. Marshall see so much in me from such brief encounters? We said our last goodbyes and I left to meet my family for the four-hour drive to Maryland.

I left Hampton with the senior superlative award for best-dressed male, a degree in Mass Media Arts and more inquisitiveness about my sexuality. My curiosity was boiling over.

My car was packed with everything I accumulated over the previous four years that was going with me to Atlanta. The only belongings that didn't get packed away were my toothbrush and enough clothes for the two days leading up to my move.

I hired a car transport company to pick up my car up from my mother's house to be delivered to my apartment in Atlanta. Everything else was packed in the car with my dad and me.

It was in the wee hours of the morning on Wednesday, May 12, 1998, that my father and I drove from Baltimore to Atlanta. My father decided we would leave at 1 a.m. to avoid possible traffic on 95 South.

"Go to sleep, *Slim*. I got it. I took a nap," he said.

My father always called me *Slim* because of my height and lean frame.

I've never been able to sleep in a car while someone else is driving, especially after a near accident in college with a few friends. Five of us were sandwiched in a Volkswagen Jetta leaving a club one night, and fortunately I was in the front seat. Everyone, except me, drifted to sleep—including the driver—as we veered towards a utility pole. When I grabbed the wheel they woke up screaming.

Since I was awake for the ten-hour drive, I tried to pinpoint when my relationship with my dad changed. He was rambling about something as we merged onto 95 South, but my attention was divided. A series of memories dawned on me. My parents' divorce was finalized when I was a freshman in high school, but my father continued to play an integral part in my life despite it.

He was the one who consistently told me I could be and do anything I put my mind to because I was smart.

"You can go further than your mother and I did. Get your education and the sky is the limit. No matter what happened between your mother and me, we'll always be here for you because we love you."

I never forgot that, but apparently he had for a short time during his 8-year marriage to JoAnne. My dad remarried the summer before my freshman year in college. He and JoAnne married and honeymooned in Montego Bay, Jamaica, the same summer I traveled back to Montreuil, France, for a second visit with the exchange family I lived with junior year of high school. This trip was a high school graduation gift from my mom.

My mom told me after I returned from Europe that my dad had been sending child support. I found out after I came across the divorce papers that my father had been sending money every month since my ninth grade year, which explained why I had everything I needed, and most of what I wanted, including the car insurance for the Corolla I bought in twelfth grade. My mother told me she would start depositing the child support check into my account each month to cover my expenses once I left for college.

"The check comes around the fifteenth. Sometimes it's early, and sometimes it's a little late so I suggest you make it stretch, but do not call me for anything. I'm paying the tuition and the phone bill only," she warned in the way only a Black mother can.

That money was my livelihood and the reason I didn't have to work a part-time job to survive like many of my college friends, but for whatever reason my father couldn't seem to believe my mother was depositing the full amount into my checking account each month. He questioned me to see if my mother really told me the correct amount. Even after I confirmed the amount, he griped about being *required* to send it to her first. Instead, he said he wanted to send it to me directly. His feelings about sending the money changed after he remarried, and his wife was the reason for his suspicion. It had never been a problem for him to send it until he and JoAnne shared a joint checking account.

Fortunately, my mother was savvy enough to add a clause in their divorce papers that enforced the child support payments until I turned 22 years old or finished college—whichever came first. My father obviously hadn't paid much attention to the document since the divorce because he called just before my eighteenth birthday to *tell* my mother he wouldn't be sending the check any longer.

"Craig is turning 18 in May, so that will be my last check!"

My mother politely advised he turn to page seven, clause 11 of the divorce decree that stated he had an additional four years of payments to make. Furious, my father hung up the phone.

I was so deep in thought my father kept asking if I was asleep.

"What you thinking about? You awfully quiet."

I looked at him, debating if this was the time to address the things that devastated our relationship. I could hear my mother's voice, "think about what you're gonna say before you say it." That advice was something she often reminded me of because I had a habit of saying things however they came out without regard to the delivery, especially if what I was saying was the truth. This time I took more time to think.

"Just thinking," I said.

For Christmas during my freshman year, I asked my father for a word processor that I planned to use to complete my college papers. I wanted the word processor with the monitor that resembled a computer because it would be easier completing the many papers I'd be assigned as a Mass Media Arts major. Instead, I asked for the one that resembled a typewriter with the flip up screen that only showed 3-4 lines at a time because *he is sending child support* I reminded myself. I became increasingly conscious that my child support was a burden to my father, so I graciously asked for the least expensive word processor of the two. Once I learned my father was sending child support, I became reluctant to ask him for anything because like a reflex, his systematic response was, "ask your mother. I'm sending child support."

After Christmas, as with every Christmas, there was an after Christmas sale in stores. I was at my father's house flipping through the newspaper and noticed the word processor I originally wanted was on sale, and it was only $50 more than the one I had received for Christmas. I called my mother first to discuss the possibility of exchanging it. I figured I should ask her to cover the difference in cost because it would've been ungrateful to ask my dad to exchange it and pay the additional amount. My mom agreed to cover the difference if my father didn't mind exchanging it.

I hung up the phone and found my father milling around in the kitchen. I told him what my mother and I discussed and surprisingly he was okay with the idea. I wasn't shocked that he agreed to let me exchange it, rather, he didn't use this as an opportunity to say no to my mother.

"JoAnne has the receipt. Ask her for it and we can run to the store to exchange it," he said.

Up to this point, JoAnne and I were beyond cordial. Most times when I called my father's to speak to him, she and I would talk instead. My father and JoAnne met as neighbors—her home was two doors from his. She worked from home as a self-employed day-care provider, so she often saw my dad coming and going to work. When they married, JoAnne retained her home to continue the business there, and moved into my dad's home. I never trusted that decision. I always felt it was her safety net in case their marriage dissolved.

When I got to JoAnne's house she was working with the children in the daycare, so I got straight to the point.

"Hi JoAnne, my father said you have the receipt for the word processor. Can I have it please?"

She had a puzzled look on her face.

"What's the problem?"

"Nothing, I found another one on sale that I want to exchange it for."

Not only did she look disgusted, but she looked agitated too.

"Well, why can't you keep the one you have? A friend of mine did me a favor and got that with her discount."

I couldn't believe she was bothered. *What did that have to do with me exchanging it?*

"The one I really wanted is on sale and it's only $50 more, so I'm exchanging it for that one."

"Well, at this point I think you should just keep the one you have 'cause you're starting to sound ungrateful!"

"I didn't ask you or my father to pay the difference. My mother said she would. Can I have the receipt?"

She handed me the crumpled paper and I walked out. Our relationship changed forever that day, and all because of a 10% discount that barely covered the state tax. Perhaps, my choice of words weren't the best or maybe I could've handled myself differently, but I was eighteen. I wonder how the scenario would have played out had my father retrieved the receipt instead.

Nevertheless, that would be the last Christmas she would chip in on a gift for my ungrateful ass.

Every Christmas after that year, she relished in giving Christmas presents to everyone in the family except me. Any stranger would have been fooled to think there were small children living in the house because the Christmas tree would be surrounded by gifts. There were multiple gifts for everyone in the family: JoAnne, my dad, my grandparents, JoAnne's adult children, and their spouses or significant others, but not a single present for me. I pretended to be unphased as she intentionally and very noticeably passed gifts over me to other family members, but my feelings were hurt.

"Craig, pass this to your grandmother."

"Do you like it?"

"I remember you saying you wanted—"

Once all the presents were handed out I looked at my father and grandparents waiting for someone to question why there weren't any gifts for me, but no one ever said a word. Not only did I feel betrayed by them, I began to believe they too were in on it. My father's only movement was to the bedroom to get a Christmas card for me autographed with his lonely signature at the bottom with $50 enclosed. JoAnne never signed the card. My only revenge was to not eat her Christmas dinner. Everyone would be seated at the table that she carefully set with gold plated flatware, her best china, and a complete spread in the center.

"Craig, you're not eating?" she asked.

"No, I'm gonna wait to eat at my mother's house," I said with a half smile.

All I had was juice.

Looking back I realized my criminal activity stemmed from the money woes imposed on me surrounding the child support, and my father was acting out of hurt and anger towards my mother as a result of the divorce, but his actions were impacting us severely. Memories continued to resurface like someone awakening from a coma remembering little by little at a time.

I noticed when I first began receiving the child support money that he and JoAnne shared a checking account that he wrote the checks from, until she expressed concerns about helping him pay my child support. He later sent the money written on checks from a different bank that only listed his name.

The most disturbing detail—JoAnne replaced me on his life insurance policy and the deed to his house because she told him I would be entitled to more should something happen to him. Oddly enough, my father wasn't listed on the deed to her home—her children were. I never could understand how a parent could put a relationship before their children, and to think my father had done the same thing to me, his only child.

My father became more ornery about sending child support to *my mother* after she started her business. The abandoned property that she bought in downtown Baltimore was finally renovated and opened as an assisted-living home for patients suffering from mental illness. It was my father's belief that he was co-sponsoring my mother's business venture.

Our conversations shifted to quizzes on how she could afford to buy and renovate the property. He wanted to know how many residents were in the house and where it was located. My father's concern was whether or not she was now earning more money than he, and if so then why was he still required to send her money. My father and I stopped communicating for several months because our conversations were limited to money and attacks on my mother leaving me no choice but to defend her since she wasn't present for his slanderous remarks. He even made some of his dirty remarks in front of JoAnne.

The father I once knew, who was always eager to support everything I did, had vanished. I remembered him leading me with a flashlight to my parents' bedroom as a kid to show me money he left me for school shopping. He was the one who said I could never let him down and here he was letting me down.

I believe a woman's love is the closest we'll get to unconditional love in our lifetime because when a woman loves you she'll do everything in her power to support you—even if there's no evidence she should. She'll sacrifice to keep you from suffering even if she suffers a bit in the process. No matter how many times the man she loves lets her down or makes her cry, once she loves you, she loves you for life and that couldn't be truer of my mother. During the fraction of time that my father and I didn't speak, my mother consistently prodded me to call him, but each time I refused. I didn't understand why she cared especially given my father's newfound persona.

"You should call your father."

"He's the parent," I responded.

My father called my mom a month later to say he was diagnosed with prostate cancer and would be unable to send the child support until he returned to work. My mother understood his condition and told him not to worry about sending the money until he was in a position to do so. She was also aware that he had recently purchased his home, and didn't want to see him lose the house, so she agreed to forego the child support payments. I was skeptical because I had witnessed my mother make repeated phone calls to the divorce attorney because previous payments were behind, so I opted to believe this was yet another ploy to get out of paying. I wasn't convinced until my mother told me the date he was scheduled for surgery. Once again, she pushed me to call him.

"You should really call your father. Something could happen to him during surgery."

My feelings of betrayal and years of practice with stubbornness wouldn't allow me to make the phone call. Fortunately, my dad recovered and we got the opportunity to mend our relationship enough to move past some of the things that had transpired.

I shared with him everything I remembered. I never imagined my father apologizing for many of the things I referenced. Things I believed he chose to overlook or simply dismissed. In turn, my dad recounted an incident that happened when I was in high school. My car got a flat tire and he said I called him for help with changing the tire, but as he was leaving the house to meet me, JoAnne stopped him.

"Where are you going?" she asked.

"To help Craig. He caught a flat down on Belvedere," he replied.

"I need to go to the store," she said.

Instead of coming to help me, he chose to take her to the store. JoAnne didn't drive, so he was responsible for taking her to the places she needed or wanted to go, and at that exact moment that I was stranded she wanted to go to the store. My dad said I called a family friend to send AAA to assist because he was a no show. I flashed back to that day, remembering every detail the way he explained except calling him first for help. I guess at some point I suppressed that memory in the way I had become accustomed to suppressing my sexuality. My dad was sniffling. He hit the steering wheel, snapping me back to reality.

"I let her turn me around! I was coming for you Craig."

I sat in silence looking out the window staring at the *Welcome to Virginia* sign at the state line. He confessed that JoAnne was part of the reason he questioned if I was getting the child support checks or if my mother was spending the money on herself. My disdain for her amplified the more he spoke. I was glad I hadn't invited her to my college graduation. Our journey to

Atlanta turned out to be a much-needed counseling session, except there was no therapist present, just my dad and me.

We arrived in Atlanta early afternoon. I was exhausted from the drive, and I still hadn't recovered from the move from Hampton. My Aunt Gloria worked at a shipping and receiving facility, so she agreed to ship my winter clothes, coats, and large items from her job to save us on the expense. Besides, it was almost summer and I wouldn't need any of those things for a while. As a graduation gift, my parents agreed to pay the rent for the first two months, stock the refrigerator and freezer with groceries, and furnish my apartment, so we decided against Dr. Peyton's offer.

My dad and I spent the first day and a half in Atlanta looking for furniture, so when my mom arrived we could get everything else I would need from silverware to coasters.

On Friday, my mom flew in for the weekend to pick up where my father left off. My car was delivered shortly after I took my father's car to pick my mom up from the airport. He took a nap since he was heading back to Maryland late that night, and she helped me settle in when my dad made the drive back to Maryland. The timing of everything couldn't have been better. The move was completely seamless.

A friend of mine and Nina's called me after I moved to tell me Nina and her sister Jillian were predicting how long it would be before I returned to Baltimore. The saddest part was that they were calculating my bills and guesstimating how much I had left after I paid all of my bills. Nina was most vocal.

"What makes him think he can move there and just start writing?"

"He'll be back in a year."

"He thinks Ms. Gladys is gonna take care of him."

There was always built up resentment towards me when something great happened for me, and this was more than enough for me to sever ties with her completely.

My job at the Coca~Cola Company began one month after I moved to the city. I was hired to work on the Coca~Cola cash card promotion, and I hated the job. There was nothing enjoyable at all. My team was held hostage in a room Coca~Cola called a call center. There were no windows, and there was one door to enter and exit through. I just knew Coca~Cola had to be violating a fire code.

All day long I answered inbound phone calls about a promotion that was expiring in the weeks to come. The job felt pointless, and my instincts assured me I wouldn't be at this job for long.

I was fired before I had the opportunity to quit. The day I was *excused,* I had begun plotting my departure in my head. I was seated in the outdoor courtyard watching the hundreds of people pass through the glass corridors that connected the two towers. I sat thinking, *I'm not the only person unhappy working here. Many of these people are here because they have to be. They have families, mortgages, and debt. I don't.*

I had money saved from graduation gifts and my rent was paid for another month. I could quit if I wanted because jobs were plentiful in Atlanta. When I got home that evening, I was met with a voice message from someone at Talent Tree advising that I didn't need to report back to work on Monday. Fear snatched the air from my lungs for just a moment, but I remembered my purpose in Atlanta. I was there to write music. The way I saw things, there was more time for me to create and network. Coca~Cola was in the way of my dreams. I was no longer employed after one short month.

I spent the remainder of the summer writing for a theater company, *The Freddie Hendricks Youth Ensemble of Atlanta* (YEA), and making cameos at the Martini Bar on Crescent Ave. YEA didn't pay, but I was happy. My mother told me I needed a real job with benefits.

"You can write any time. That's a hobby. You need a job with a 401k and some benefits."

I knew I'd have to prove to her and a few others that writing was my job. I just hadn't been paid to write, but it would come soon enough.

THE OTHERSIDE

I accepted a job at MARTA, Atlanta's transit company, working as a customer information operator. It was another call center position, but it offered variety because each caller was looking for directions to a different destination, and I learned my way around the city because of it.

I became close with a female coworker that I trained with at my new job. I saw Daphne as a close friend, but she developed a crush that was encouraging her to leave her husband for me. She told me she couldn't stop thinking about me, and no longer craved intimacy from her husband because she found herself caught in fantasies about me. She started sleeping in their guest bedroom because she was having dreams about me, leaving her husband lonely and perplexed in their bed.

Lust cajoled her to my apartment late one night begging that I seduce her. With tears in her eyes she pleaded unapologetically as she unbuttoned her blouse. I gave her every reason why she needed to go home and why I couldn't. Mostly for the sake of her marriage and their 3 year-old little girl. I never uttered a word about my attraction for men. She left my place with her conscience clean, and a handful of disappointment.

I was tired of being single. I wanted companionship since I hadn't made any real connections in years. Before internet hook up sites there were free, voice-activated lines that allowed callers to listen and record messages containing their physical descriptions, sexual position, and what they desired sexually. There was something strangely familiar yet eerie about this to me. Familiar because on a few occasions when I was in college I received a few anonymous phone calls from a male caller whispering sexual suggestions that titillated my sexual curiosity. Eerie because it provoked me to think of how empty sex with a stranger would be.

Nevertheless, I recorded a message with hopes of meeting someone in the ballpark of sane, attractive, intelligent and gainfully employed. I wasn't looking for sex, yet. I still wasn't ready to cross that bridge.

Eventually, I graduated to phone conversations with a guy I met on the chat line. We found ourselves at Eats on Ponce de Leon Ave. Not only was the food bland, he was equally uninteresting to me. He seemed to be smitten and called a few times after, but I never saw or spoke to him again, nor did I entertain the chat line.

I was 22 and only knew three people when I moved to Atlanta, but once I started writing for YEA I met people quickly. Naturally, most of the guys in the theater company were gay. I shied away from the obvious ones because I didn't want anyone to get the *wrong* idea about me nor did I want any of the gay company members to pick up on any notion that I was like them. I barely spoke to any of them because I thought any association with them meant I too was gay.

There was one guy in particular, Skyler, whose gaze reeked *I know who you really are.* His glare met me at every rehearsal and it was always accompanied by a half smile that made me increasingly uncomfortable. Whenever our eyes met, I quickly looked in a different direction. I didn't want to leave a door open for him to think it was ok to talk to me about anything. I never believed he was attracted to me in a sexual way, rather, in a kindred kind of way. I've compared that look to one I've received when traveling abroad in a foreign country and being the only Black person before finally connecting with another Black person.

My reaction to Skyler was classic internalized homophobia. My insecurity then is similar to that of men I encounter now that live heterosexual lives and lies, but enjoy the company of a man too. They're as uneasy around me as I was with Skyler. If a man is anxious around a gay man, he's unsure of himself and he's probably hiding a secret that only a gay man can uncover.

One of the girls in the theater company connected me to a guy named Marcel that had been a part of the theater company before moving away for college. Marcel had just moved back to Atlanta after graduating from film school in Ithaca, NY. She thought he and I would make a great writing team and should collaborate.

From the moment Marcel and I spoke on the phone I knew he was gay. He didn't sound gay. His voice wasn't high pitched and it was devoid of the gay lisp and typical gay slang, but his tone and phrasing gave it away. I just knew from the seductive tone he used when we spoke.

Marcel and I decided to meet after a rehearsal. He showed up with his best friend Kristina, and together they insisted on taking me to a gay club. He was openly gay, but not *clockable*. Marcel looked straight, so it was easy for me to consider hanging out with him because, for the most part, he was the opposite of everything I thought I knew about gay people. He simply wasn't the flamboyant stereotype on the surface.

Marcel claimed to be bisexual because he dated women at some point, but hadn't most of us? In the span of time in which I knew him, he hadn't dated any women. For several months, Marcel attempted to show me around Atlanta because I was new to the city, far from family and friends, and instinctively he knew I was gay.

Marcel showed up at my apartment one night unannounced. I was sleeping when I heard a knock on the door. This couldn't possibly be another noise complaint from the nagging ass neighbor upstairs because I was sound asleep. I opened the door, and Marcel walked in before I could invite him in or question why he was at my place so late.

"What are you doing here?" I asked.

"We're going out. Put some clothes on," he replied.

I was standing there dumfounded wearing my glasses and a plush white bathrobe I had stunted from Banana Republic.

"I'm taking you out 'cause I know you're tired of hanging with those YEA kids. Come on. Get dressed."

"Where are we going?" I asked.

"To a club," he replied.

"What kind of club?" I asked.

"A gay club! Get dressed," he insisted.

"Why do you want to take me to a gay club?" I questioned.

"You're gay, aren't you?" he quipped.

There was a pregnant pause. I hadn't *acted* on the feelings nor had anyone ever *told* me I was gay. I had been asked, but never told.

"No!" I said.

"Well, I am. Actually, I'm bisexual," he remarked casually.

There was a freedom in his voice that I wished for, but hadn't managed to find. Before I knew it, I was dressed and we were seated on the patio of The Otherside. This was the same club that had been bombed a couple years before as a result of a hate crime. The club was seated on the cusp of Midtown and Buckhead on Piedmont Road. Its clientele was balanced between gay men and lesbians. It was cozy and sexy all at once. In the wintertime it boasted its fireplace and in the spring and summer months the club showed off its patio, complete with pool tables and sun deck. I was in love with this place. I tried to appear uninterested, but the number of beautiful Black men who didn't *look* gay intrigued me.

I returned to the club a week later, but this time I went solo. I wasn't ready to tell Marcel that I enjoyed going to gay bars. As far as I was concerned, I was ok with him thinking I had never been to a gay club before he took me.

That night, I saw the first guy that I considered dating. I spied him from across the room long before he noticed me. The only other guy I thought I could make an attempt to date was in college and he was supposedly straight. He was fair skinned with a swimmer's build, curly hair, hazel eyes and pretty pink full lips—and he was an upperclassman. There was no way he was 100% straight and my suspicions were confirmed when he appeared in a school fashion show dressed as a girl. To see someone else that I was drawn to was huge.

He was wearing a cutoff shirt, blue jeans with a hole in the knee, and Timberland boots. His body was ripped. *If he says anything to me, I'm giving him my number.* Before I had time to really enjoy the thought of getting to know *him,* some other character came drifting over to me to talk. About what, I don't recall. It was insignificant. I was trying to keep my eye on *him* as he bobbed and weaved through the crowded club.

I tried paying attention to the guy I was talking to, but I noticed *the guy* sitting just behind the dude that was detaining me. He was trying to get my attention.

"Are you with him?" he whispered.

I smiled and shook my head *no* the first chance I got without looking obvious. I quickly wrapped up the conversation, but not before dude asked for my number. Unfortunately, I hadn't mastered the art of politely declining someone I wasn't interested in. I was ready to send him on his way, so I obliged. The moment he walked away, the other guy took his seat as if we were speed dating. He was bold. Not shy at all. He sat really close to me. My heart was throbbing. I was excited I got to this moment after watching him from across the room hoping to make contact, but it also meant I would be taking a step I was still unsure I wanted to make. Up to this point, I thought I could suppress *the feelings*. I had done a great job doing so for the first 22 years of my life.

"How you doing?" he asked.

"Hi, how are you?"

"I'm Farrell. What's your name?"

"I'm Craig."

He was wearing hazel colored contacts and he had a texturizer in his hair. Normally, I would've been turned off, but his body was incredible. He knew right away that I was new to the scene.

"I've never seen you before."

"I just moved here."

I've since learned you're more appealing if no one recognizes you on the scene because you're less likely to be jaded from dating. Conversely, it's some sort of indicator you've gotten around sexually if you're too visible.

"It's too loud in here to talk. You wanna go to my car?"

"Yea, that's cool."

We walked outside to a SUV and got in. We crammed everything we wanted to know about each other in the few moments we sat in his truck—birthday, age, number of siblings, profession, and the most important question of all, "how long have you been single?"

When I disclosed that I had never dated a guy before he paused. Such was the case when I told him I had only been in Atlanta a few months. Because there are so many *options* and opportunities to sew ones oats in Atlanta it's almost an unspoken rule that no one dates a gay man that's lived in the city less than a year.

"Why was I so lucky to be the first to meet you?" he asked.

"I don't know. I'm really picky," I answered.

I could see his mind working behind the question.

"I need to go because I have to work in the morning. You wanna catch a movie on Friday?

"Yea, that's cool. We can do that."

"Ok, I'll give you a call tomorrow. Be safe going home."

"You too. Have a good night."

Shortly after I got home, I heard my telephone ringing.

"I just called to make sure you got home ok."

I've been getting home by myself all these years without you checking on me. This is game.

"Yea, I just walked in," I said.

"Ok, have a good night."

Two days later, I was getting dressed for my first date *with a man. What am I doing? I have a date on a Friday night with another man. Is this really what I want to do?*

I took one last look at myself in the mirror before I left my place. I was consciencious of my appearance, but it didn't feel normal to be concerned with how I looked to meet up with another man. I thought about my friends and what they would think as I sped up Piedmont Road to Lenox Mall for dinner and a movie with Farrell—*a man.* I was anxious.

It didn't feel like the dates I had with women. Everything was in the reverse, but I kept driving. *Am I supposed to open the door for him? Who should pay? Is he the girl in the relationship?* Falling into a role wasn't an option for me.

He was standing outside the box office with the movie tickets in his hand when I arrived. *I wonder if people think we are on a date.* I analyzed things I wouldn't have had I been with a woman. I questioned everything. *Is he gonna sit right beside me in the movie?* The most obvious sign two guys are on a date, but hope to throw onlookers off, is to leave the obligatory gay seat between them open. He sat beside me and I was uncomfortable. I leaned towards the other armrest.

We headed across the street to Bennigan's after the movie. As we were leaving the restaurant, there was a feeling that neither of us wanted the *date* to end.

"You wanna come to my place to watch a movie?" he asked.

We had just seen a movie, but I couldn't bring myself to say it out loud.

"Yea, that's cool," I said.

It was almost eleven o'clock and I lived in Vinings, a twenty-minute drive from his Norcross address. I decided to go anyway. We got to his place and it was evident he didn't live alone. He had a roommate. I was slightly turned off. This was how he afforded the BMW and all the labels he wore.

By the middle of the video I was sleepy and stretched out on his bed. My contacts were burning my eyes because they were dry and had been in my eyes over twelve hours.

"You want to stay the night?"

"Where you gonna sleep?"

I may have been a beginner, but I wasn't thirsty.

"I can sleep on the couch," he said.

I knew he hadn't anticipated sleeping on the couch since I had come back to *his* place.

"Yea, I'll stay," I said.

"Can I have a kiss?" he asked.

I froze. I wasn't expecting it so soon.

"Why didn't you just do it?" I asked.

He shrugged his shoulders. It wasn't that I didn't want to kiss him. I couldn't rationalize agreeing to it.

"Now, I'm thinking about it," I said.

The looming thought of playing *Truth or Dare* arose. Should I play again, I could never honestly declare I had never kissed a man before. That question always found its way in the game. He stole a kiss as I pondered. I felt an extreme sense of grief and guilt overtake me like when someone dies, and it was visible to him.

"Are you ok?" he asked.

That kiss was the threshold to homosexuality.

"No," I said.

If someone I know walks in this room... He lay looking at me a few moments before going to the living room. I didn't see him again until the morning.

The next morning Farrell came in the bedroom to ask what I wanted for breakfast. He slipped on a pair of jogging pants and laced up his sneakers as I placed my order.

"Where you going?" I asked.

"To the store to get it. I don't have any of that stuff," he said.

He was out the door in five minutes en route to the grocery store. I left immediately after I ate because I had to work and I didn't want things to become awkward.

I didn't know if I would ever call him again because he was far more seasoned than I. He was ready for things I had only thought, and dreamed of in wet dreams. A day passed without communication, but on the second day, he called and left a message.

"I guess you decided not to be gay because I haven't heard from you. This is Farrell, call me back."

I was speechless. *What if someone was here with me when I played the message back?* I snatched the receiver from the phone as if someone else was in the room with me listening. I couldn't dial his number fast enough.

"Hello."

"Don't leave messages like that on my phone!"

"Like what?"

"Like the one you left. Someone could've been here when I played that message."

"Oh, I'm sorry."

I was extremely protective of my personal information as I acclimated to dating men. I had heard horror stories of crazy exes outing old boyfriends, so it was a rarity for me to give out my cell number. I generally only gave out my home number until I concluded a person was mentally stable. I didn't need any stalkers. I witnessed many of my friends giving out their home, cell, and work numbers on day one.

Once I *knew* Farrell for some time I invited him over to stay the night and this time I gave him my bed. His first visit would be his last visit because he got upset that I wouldn't sleep in the bed with him.

"Craig, would you come get in this bed. This is ridiculous."

"No, go to sleep. I'm not coming in there!" I shouted from the couch.

He was used to moving at a fast pace and I wasn't interested in being coaxed. Farrell sometimes went to the gym twice a day, so his body commanded attention and that made it easy for him to get sex, but I wasn't looking for just sex.

"I'm going home," he said.

"Bye."

The next sound I heard was the door closing behind him.

Daphne hadn't given up on her quest of sleeping with me. She had progressed to eavesdropping on my phone calls when I was on break.

"Are you gay? I heard you talking to a man! I heard you say his name."

"What? What are you talking about? And why are you listening to my phone calls?"

"You lied to me!"

"No, I didn't say anything at all."

"Why are you gay? You're not gay! It's wrong."

"Daphne, I'm not talking about this."

Daphne requested a shift change to make it easier to avoid me. The bigger tragedy would've been leaving her family only to discover later that I was gay.

Farrell lived fifteen minutes from my job at MARTA headquarters. We made plans to meet at his place after work. He rarely locked the door to his apartment, so I walked in when I got there. Farrell's roommate Sidney was a nurse, so he spent long hours working. I may have seen Sidney three times the entire time Farrell and I dated. Sidney told me he and Farrell dated before becoming roommates. In fact, they became roommates after the relationship fell apart.

"Why did you break up?" I asked.

"Farrell plays too many games. He has guys in and out of here all the time."

Farrell and I weren't exclusive, but it still didn't sit well with me.

When Farrell got home I was still in the kitchen with Sidney. When I went into the room, he was lying across the bed watching television

"Hey, what's up?" he asked.

"Nothing much. How are you?" I asked.

"Pretty good. How was work?" he said.

"It was alright," I said.

"You can sit down. Get comfortable," he suggested smiling.

I took my shoes off and lay across the bed. I wanted something to happen, but I didn't want to initiate it. I didn't know what was ok and what was off limits because I had only known straight men. Touching another man sexually never happened except at the strip club. I needed to follow his lead, so when he leaned in for a kiss I ran my hand from his outer thigh to the inside of his leg. I reached under his bathrobe and started fondling him. I massaged his dick and slipped my tongue in his mouth. I felt it getting bigger and I could feel his body relaxing when I opened his legs to slide my finger inside him. He moaned as I fondled him. He handed me a bottle of lube from his nightstand beside his bed. I covered my middle finger with the gel and slid it back inside him. He lifted his legs and held both of his thighs up as I slowly moved my finger in and out of him.

"Give me a condom," I said.

"Why you wanna fuck me?" he asked.

There was a long pause as I searched for an answer. Farrell lowered his legs and exhaled as he lay there with his eyes closed. I crawled back up on the bed to lie beside him. He rolled over to suck on my nipples and reached down to stroke my dick. When he felt it rising he moved lower to lick and suck on my nuts before he put my dick in his mouth. Farrell sucked and licked repeatedly while staring down at it. Every now and then he looked up at me.

When my body became limp he lifted my legs to lick inside me. I put my face in the pillow as he ate ravenously. *His tongue is in my ass.* I tried not to scream, but I couldn't help but make noises. His tongue was wet and warm on my ass. He inserted his tongue in and out. It moved along the area between my nuts and my ass to the crevices between my thighs. I didn't want him to kiss me afterwards, so I kept my face planted in the pillow when he tried to kiss me.

I squeezed more lube into the palm of my hand and in his so we could jerk off. He was kneeling in front of me stroking his dick with his head back and his eyes closed. His breathing became rapid. He was panting. I felt the warm explosion on my stomach. He exhaled and collapsed on the bed bedside me.

I never got comfortable with the idea of being gay during the time Farrell and I dated so it caused a huge strain on things. Not to mention, I didn't trust him. I was annoyed by his angst to move quickly while he was agitated with my hang-ups, so we ended things.

The turning point came when I made a surprise visit to a birthday party for his best friend that he co-hosted. We were no longer dating, but he said he still wanted me to come to the party. On the day of the party, we both had to work. He told me he would fax the directions to my job. I must have checked the fax machine four times. The directions never came.

Nevertheless, I went to the barbershop after work just in case he called with the details. Before long, I knew this was a game. What he didn't know was that I intended to win. An idle mind is a dangerous mind. As I sat on my couch in my favorite bathrobe I pondered how I could get directions to this party on my own. I dialed 411 and gave his best friend's full name with hopes they could provide the telephone number. When the operator told me it was unlisted I got antsy and more determined to find the party. The operator must have sensed the urgency in my voice because she suggested I call the police for non-emergency assistance since I knew the street name. So I hung up and dialed them right away. I gave the operator my address and the name of his best friend's street name.

"Fortunately, there's only one Horseshoe Bend. It's in Powder Springs. Do you have a pen and paper for the directions?" she asked.

The operator gave me directions from my front door to the party. When I hung up the phone, the clock read 11:30 p.m. I jumped up, showered, got dressed, and snatched a bottle of wine from my wine rack on my way out the door.

"I'm gonna get there by midnight and if he's there with someone it'll be a new day," I mumbled to myself.

I pulled onto the street with no idea which house I was going to until I saw a brigade of guys huddled outside the house. As I approached, I heard someone from the crowd whisper, "who is this?" Everyone in the crowd looked my way as I approached the walkway. I was first day of school clean—wearing a black leather pea coat, black velvet pants, black boots and a crisp white collared shirt.

"Hello," I said as I made my way through the crowd.

"Can I holler at you for a minute?" someone asked as I passed by.

"I'm meeting someone," I said.

When I walked in, Farrell's best friend was standing in the kitchen. He had a puzzled look on his face when he saw me. I knew then that he knew the fax machine story.

"Hey, what you doing here?" he asked.

"Where's Farrell?" I said.

I wasn't in the mood for small talk and he knew it.

"I'll go get him," he said.

He slinked passed me and headed to the back of the house. Farrell emerged from a back room looking like he saw a ghost.

"How did you find it?"

I couldn't believe those were his first words like this was some kind of game of hide and seek.

"A better question is 'why didn't you send the directions?'"

He stood looking as foolish as I felt going back and forth to the fax machine earlier that day. I handed him the bottle of wine.

"Who are you here with?" I asked.

"What do you mean?" he asked.

"There must be a reason you didn't want me to come," I remarked.

"I don't know everybody here," he replied.

"Why did you tell me you were sending the directions when you know you weren't?" I quizzed.

"How did you find it," he asked.

"I'm not telling you, but just know I'm always a step ahead of you," I said as I turned to leave the party.

For me, showing up was about proving to him that he could be outsmarted and that I wasn't a game he would play and win nor was it necessary for him to lie. I had the last laugh that night.

"Call me to let me know you made it home," he said following me to my car.

"Call you for what? I'm done. You can delete my number."

When I got in the car, my first instinct was to turn the cd player on. I was hooked on Faith Evans' *Keep the Faith* album, but I opted to drive home in silence because I didn't want any song to remind me of that night or him, ever.

I immediately blocked his home number. Farrell must have tried calling me from that number first because he called me from the gym. He had never called me from the gym before. I blocked all of his numbers—work, cell, home, and gym.

Because I was new to Atlanta, I didn't know many people, which meant I didn't receive many phone calls. Blocking his numbers meant sitting in the quiet of loneliness. I lay in bed the next morning sulking because I was slightly humiliated and crushed with no one to vent to because no one *knew* I was gay. I was still closeted. There was no one I could tell.

My phone rang. It was Monica calling from New York. She had taken a job in New York when I was a senior at Hampton, but we never lost touch. Even she was left in the dark about my sexuality.

"Hello," I said.

"What's wrong with you?" she asked.

I frowned. "I just woke up," I said.

"But you sound *turrble*," she continued.

She made an attempt to mock the Baltimore accent I had when I first entered Hampton that some of our friends failed to relinquish in college, but it just wasn't funny to me this time. I knew exactly what she was referring to. I sounded like someone in mourning.

"Something I was hoping would happen isn't gonna happen now."

"Something happened with the music?" she asked.

"No, it's not about the music. It's personal. I don't wanna talk about it."

"What is it?! You sound awful."

"It's about a relationship!"

"Well, what happened?"

"Monica, I was seeing someone and it didn't work out!"

I was careful with my choice of words. I never said *he* or *him,* instead I used *them* or *they.*

"Well, who is she?"

"It's a man!"

The silence on the phone was loud.

"No!"

I heard her sniffling.

"What do you mean? You can't be. You're one of the good ones. You're supposed to get married and have kids. How do you know?"

I didn't know how to reply. Monica had introduced me to my last girlfriend. My ex-girlfriend and I spoke a few times about what it would be like to have a family and those conversations triggered thoughts of juggling a married life and a secret life. Deep down I knew I couldn't live with myself carrying around such a secret. It was an existence my conscience wouldn't allow.

I was moved that Monica considered me 'one of the good ones' but I also felt liberated to have finally said it out loud to someone. I was keeping such a daunting secret from the people closest to me. Monica was like a sister to me. She took monthly trips to Atlanta so we could go to concerts and eat at all the new restaurants that popped up around the city. She traveled out of the country with my family and me to Byron's wedding. Monica knew everything about me except that I was gay, but she became the first person I uttered those words to. No one else had that bit of knowledge I was guarding with the most care.

"But it's wrong," she whispered.

"Monica, the Bible has been rewritten and at one time was used to justify slavery," I said.

"How do you know this isn't a phase?"

"It's not a phase. I've always known."

"It'll never work."

"How do you know I wasn't put in your life to change your views about gay people because you love me?"

"How do you know I wasn't put in your life to tell you it's wrong?"

"Look, I'm not gonna debate about this. I think you should take a few days and think about this before we speak again because I don't wanna have this conversation every time we talk. If that's what it's gonna be, then we can stop talking now."

"Ok," she said softly.

We hung up.

We spoke the next day and our friendship didn't skip a beat. I was clear as I began opening up to the people closest to me that I didn't want to be *'Craig, my gay friend in Atlanta'* because being gay didn't define me. It was simply a part of who I was.

Heartache has enough power to bring us to our knees, and this one forced me to communicate the words *I'm gay* after years of containing it because I needed help carrying the weight of the pain. When the time came to nurse my wounds, Skyler was there. The person I shunned and practically ignored because he was feminine. My 'breakup' with Farrell was the impetus for my friendship with Skyler, and my journey of self-affirmation and my eventual acceptance of gay men—despite their level of flamboyance.

I asked Skyler why he overlooked my coldness and continued being nice to me.

"I knew you needed time," he said.

"But, how did you know I was gay?" I asked.

"Because a rose can smell a rose," he said.

I smiled and left well enough alone.

I felt trapped between two worlds, the new friends who knew I was gay and the old ones who I had yet to tell. Kepri was one I debated telling. I met Kepri at the end of our junior year of college at our friend Natalie's. Everyone called Natalie's place *Cheers*, after the television show, because all we did was drink

106

and party there. Kepri and I clicked immediately much to her surprise because she's never been one to call someone a friend as quickly as she did with me.

I remembered Kepri from an African American history class we took freshman year. She sat in the front of the class and was as outspoken as most opinionated New Yorkers. Her Queens accent was thick and mixed with a tinge of a Caribbean accent she borrowed from her mother's Trinidadian roots.

New York women have an edge to them, and the same was true of Kepri, but there was a loftiness that I liked about her. She wasn't as rough around the edges—she had class. Kepri often rocked big gold hoop earrings and she stayed in a sick shoe, designer sunglasses, and her hair was always bouncing and behaving like she just left the Dominican shop whenever I saw her on campus.

We spoke just about every day once she moved back to New York after we graduated. I knew if she had a toothache—that's how close we were. We both love hard and we love *love* in the same way, so I knew she would relate to how I felt about Farrell. I didn't love Farrell, but I knew Kepri would understand my disappointment, even if it meant I had to tell her I was gay.

I had reservations about telling her after the outcome I had with Monica. I knew Kepri loved me because she showed it, and said it at the end of every phone call. She was the first person I was accustomed to saying "I love you" to.

I called Kepri at work.

"There's something I want to tell you," I began nervously.

"Ok."

I stalled because I knew I was running the risk of our friends from college finding out. Kepri and I shared many secrets, but this one could've been the one that was too big to keep.

"What do you think I'm gonna say?" I asked.

"I don't know, but just go ahead and say it."

"You *know* what I wanna say Kepri."

"No, I don't, but why can't you just say it?"

It sounded simple enough, but I still had never said the words *I'm gay* out loud to anyone.

"Listen, there is nothing you can tell me that can make me stop loving you or make me less of a friend to you."

"I'm gay or whatever," I said nervously.

There was a brief silence; then I heard her sniffling through the phone.

"I'm crying because I'm honored that you thought enough of me and our friendship to share that with me."

I could feel my heartbeat slowing down. It was relief, and a bit emotional for me. A cloud that hovered over me had finally dissipated. I was able to peel back a layer without fear of being too exposed.

"I don't want to be your gay friend in Atlanta. I'm still me."

"You won't be. You're my friend first. Craig, I've told you, you're my 'there's no other friend *like you*' friend."

I could always take Kepri at her word because she had always been fiercely loyal in her friendships. This was the same girl who got into a physical altercation while we were in Coliseum Mall in Hampton. A local girl got into it with one of Kepri's friends, and she jumped in. Mall security came and cuffed her and the rest of the girls. I stood there embarrassed. Kepri came dangerously close to being expelled during the first semester of our senior year.

"You know niggas at school used to always ask me, 'yo, what's up with your boy Craig? Is he gay?' And, I'd tell them, 'I don't know if he is or isn't, but I'm not asking him shit. I never asked you if you were straight, so I'm not asking him if he's gay.'"

"Who used to ask you?" I quizzed.

"Them niggas Otis and Keith. They both were like, 'come on...look at how he's dressed. He's always impeccably dressed. You tryna tell me that nigga ain't gay?' They used to make me so mad with that shit. I told them, 'just because you motherfuckers walk around campus in baggy pants, Timberlands and bubble coats, and that nigga rocking tailored pants and wool pea coats from fucking Banana Republic doesn't mean he's gay.'"

Much of my concern was who thought I was gay before I acknowledged it. I was offended whenever someone said, "Oh, I knew you were gay" because I thought they were really saying, "because you're flamboyant." But, I concluded femininity in a gay man or masculinity in a lesbian woman isn't the only indication he or she is gay. A friend told me that when people care about you, they pay attention to you, and the things that you think you're doing a good job of hiding are the things most obvious about you.

"Well, it wasn't so easy telling Monica. She didn't take it well," I said.

"What she say?"

"That it's wrong and she wanted me to be married with kids."

"Oh shut the fuck up Monica! I'm happy for you."

I was relieved when we got off the phone. I felt lighter.

LIFE OUTSIDE THE CLOSET

My ego was bruised by what would've been my first relationship. I dated aimlessly in search of a real connection. Marcel introduced me to friends and I met guys at clubs, but nothing worthwhile materialized. The hardest part about dating was determining who to date and who to place in the *just friends* category because the lines are blurred because we are all men.

My eagerness to meet someone led me to the chat line. A switch had been activated in me and I was suddenly in a hurry to gain a sexual experience because things fell apart with Farrell before we had sex. Honestly, I should have done more soul searching to allow my feelings to catch up with my thoughts. I was acting on unresolved feelings. I was looking for a connection, but was still unsure how I felt about being gay.

I was more than halfway through my first lease at my apartment when I started receiving noise complaints from the upstairs neighbor. He consistently complained to the property manager about the volume of my stereo, day and night. The apartments were so poorly constructed that I could actually hear him urinating and flushing his toilet.

When the property manager contacted me to advise me I was *"disturbing the peaceful enjoyment of his apartment."* I told her he should have purchased a home if he didn't want to hear any neighbor noise. She politely informed me they would not be renewing my lease when it ended in May. That was my first nice nasty reminder that my Black ass was in Cobb County and not Atlanta with the rest of the Blacks. I was adjusting well to the city so I wasn't bothered. I had more friends, so finding a place to move wouldn't be problematic. The dilemma was getting all the furniture moved.

Not long after Marcel took me to The Otherside he introduced me to Club Fusion. All of my preconceived ideas of gay men were challenged and confirmed in one night. These men looked like *real* men. They were dressed like straight men. I honestly thought I had died and gone to heaven. It was hard to wrap my brain around the idea that these men were all gay or bisexual, but the drag show forced me to believe. I felt more in place than I did at The Otherside, but I still didn't tell Marcel.

After about an hour at the club, Marcel was ready to leave so we walked to the exit. I stole a few more looks as I paced myself to the door. I had to think of a way to prolong our departure until I remembered we came to the club separately. Once Marcel got in his car and pulled off I got out of my car and went back inside.

I got a call from Marcel the next day.

"How late did you stay?" he asked casually.

"Stay where?" I asked.

"At Fusion. I drove back through the parking lot and saw your car was still there hours later," he said.

Marcel was careful not to persecute me. He knew I was still uncomfortable with my sexuality and people knowing about it. Marcel's approach made it easy for me to be honest with him because his question wasn't laced with judgment.

"Oh, I was there until they closed," I confessed.

"I just don't understand how so many beautiful Black men can be in one place and not one of them asked for my number and I know I'm not the only one who feels that way. That's why I left," he said.

I hadn't experienced his level of angst to get a number. Sure, there were guys I was interested in, but if we didn't exchange numbers, I figured it was God's way of protecting me from something—not rejection.

"Why can't you enjoy yourself even if no one asks for your number?" I asked.

"Because no one goes just to dance or listen to the music. I can listen to music at my house, " he said.

"I don't have the guts to approach."

"I don't know why not. You approach these music industry people all the time. Now, that's something I can't do. But think about it—if you never approach the people you want, you're left with those who come to you, and the pickings are already slim," he said.

One of the things I liked most about him was his brilliant way of thinking and rationalizing things. Marcel and I were attending a monthly discussion group for young Black gay men

18-24 called My Brother's Keeper (MBK) that he introduced me to after I finally accepted that I was gay. He also introduced me to another monthly discussion group called Second Sundays, and they met every second Sunday of the month at the Gay and Lesbian Center. Marcel could always, so eloquently verbalize how he felt as a gay man and I admired that about him.

The topics were all things central and of interest to Black gay men: what it means to be gay, relationships, being gay and Black, sex, coming out and HIV. I wondered how effective this group could've been if more of us had chosen to utilize an outlet like this. Most of the Black men that needed this group were the very ones missing from the room because they were too closeted to show up or they simply lacked interest.

I left the Second Sunday group to attend MBK exclusively because I was annoyed with the flirting and note passing that took place at the Second Sunday meetings. The older brothers didn't seem to have any more solutions or answers than we had.

The personalities in MBK were enormous. We were all in search of our identities in the community while making every attempt to affirm ourselves, and galvanize our beliefs about being strong, gay men. No one in MBK was originally from Atlanta and the same was true for many of the people I met in Atlanta. It was like everyone I met had moved to Atlanta for college or to be gay.

I gravitated to one of the quieter personalities in the room, a guy named Neequaye from New Jersey. Neequaye was a loner, and didn't say much in the group. He moved to Atlanta with his family while still in high school, and his mom passed away just before we met when he was 19. He and his younger siblings moved into his brother's three-bedroom apartment immediately after his mom passed. A few months later, Neequaye moved into his own apartment because the living quarters were cramped, and the Social Security money only benefitted the two kids under 18.

Neequaye was fiercely private when we met, and the only practicing Muslim I knew who celebrated Thanksgiving and accepted Christmas gifts. I could never read what he was thinking, and it didn't help that he lived in the center of Midtown, the gayest section of Atlanta, at 710 Peachtree, also known as Vaseline towers.

710 Peachtree was a high-rise apartment building known for sex parties, and long dark corridors where anything could happen en route to an apartment from the elevators. I heard many tales from Marcel who was propositioned for and accepted sex when he lived there.

Neequaye disappeared a few times after our phone calls. I called him back a few times moments after hanging up with him, but got no answer. When I asked where he was, he'd claim he was home the entire time, so I stopped asking.

Neequaye had a calm about him. Nothing seemed to ever get him stirred up, even if the walls appeared to be closing in on him. He never flinched, even though he didn't have much family to call on if he was in some sort of financial bind.

When I unexpectedly lost my job, Neequaye gave me $250 on his own volition. He came to my place to meet for the gym. I left my sneakers in the living room while I was changing clothes in my bedroom. When I slipped my foot in my sneaker, I felt the wad of money in my shoe.

"What's this in my shoe? Did you put something—"

"Huh?"

"Oh my God."

Neequaye wouldn't look at me.

"Thank you! I appreciate this. You didn't have to do this."

"Uh huh, you're welcome. Just a little something."

More times than not, Neequaye participated in side conversations—at the MBK meetings— about the topic with whomever he sat next to for the day. When the conversation shifted to my move from Vinings to Buckhead, he was the first to offer a hand. With Neequaye and Marcel's help, I moved to my second apartment, but this time within the city of Atlanta. The new place was on 26th Street off Peachtree, and seven minutes from Neequaye's apartment.

I reserved a U-Haul and we loaded everything from my one-bedroom apartment in it. We were able to transport everything in a single trip. After we got everything in the new apartment, I ordered pizzas.

Marcel stopped going to the MBK meetings, but Neequaye and I were regulars when we met Chance. Chance was from Brooklyn, New York, but had relocated from Buffalo, New

York. He seemed to be the only other rational thinking personality in the group. He was introduced to MBK by one of the other members he met at Outwrite, the gay bookstore. Chance only spoke in his mezzo-soprano octave and every other sentence started with *"you girls"* or *"y'all hoes."*

Chance was gay and offered no apologies to anyone for it. He was the queen's queen. I could have never imagined being so close to him a year before, but there was an energy and vivaciousness that drew me in. He was the first person that got away with calling me *girl* or *bitch* without backlash from me.

Chance layered his lips with Mac's signature *lip glass*, and his jeans were always skin tight—they barely left room for him to lotion his legs. There was something courageous, adventurous, and progressive about him. He spoke openly about issues he encountered when he tried dating Black men, and even more candidly about the perks of dating White men because Black men didn't offer the same level of stability or longevity. As he put it, "y'all girls have too many issues. Everybody wants to be a top."

Not to mention, he was too comfortable for most Black men he met because he was unabashed when it came to his sexuality.

Chance told me he had a break up as recent as his move to Atlanta. He dated an older White guy named John whom he lived with in Buffalo, but after it fell apart he moved to Georgia.

John was in his early fifties and Chance was twenty-three years old, roughly half of John's age. Chance said the relationship was toxic. John was living with AIDS and guilted Chance into staying with him. He made Chance believe it was virtually impossible for him to move on because of the disease. John said no one else would love him. I also believe Chance stayed because he was dependent on John financially, in addition to simply being lonely. Whichever the case, Chance stayed in the relationship longer than he intended. Eventually, Chance saved enough money from his dog-grooming job in Buffalo to move south.

Chance was fortunate to find a grooming job at a swanky dog groomer operated by two White girls that opened in Buckhead. They got along famously until he realized he was working the longest hours and every weekend, and was the reason business was running smoothly.

Chance came out before he was a teenager. Let him tell it, he was sucking dick in middle school while most of us were still too scared to play jump rope with the girls.

Neequaye, Chance, and I became inseparable, and collectively we pulled away from the MBK crew to speed through the streets of Atlanta listening to *The Miseducation of Lauryn Hill*. I bought a new gold Honda Accord EX after the white one was stolen. My mother thought I had arranged for it to be taken to get the insurance check since I was quite the miscreant, but truth be told I didn't. It was stolen from the parking lot outside my job.

The three of us spent hours on three-way calls that often ended with Chance falling to sleep on us. He'd call the next day full of energy, completely forgetting that he had fallen asleep on the phone the night before.

"Bitch, I did not! I said I was going to sleep!" Chance shouted.

"No you didn't, bitch," Neequaye giggled.

"All we heard was your TV," I said.

"Oh, well mama was tired."

We all had things in common. Neequaye and Chance had a friendship separate from me, as did Chance and I. Together they explored bathhouses, but never invited me because they knew I had no interest. Neequaye and I were both getting into fitness, so we often worked out together. And every weekend, Chance and I were together in Lenox Mall or Phipps Plaza looking for something to wear to the club.

Chance called one Saturday asking me to pick him up to go to the mall, but I had laundry to do.

"Girl, drop that shit off at the wash and fold and let's punch it! We got places to go and people to see."

"The wash and fold? What is that?"

"It's the place over here by me, girl, where the Mexicans will wash and fold your panties for you."

"How much that shit cost?"

"I don't know. I just drop it off and pick it up. I don't ask all them questions. They barely speak English over there, girl. They just better not fuck up my stuff or somebody getting fucked up!"

I packed my dirty laundry in the car and dropped it off en route to Chance's apartment. His roommate was a guy he met on Craigslist. I couldn't imagine living with a complete stranger from the internet, but he had no issue with doing so. He hated his roommate once he moved in because he also used Craigslist to find sex. Chance's roommate had a new guy over just about every day.

I was in front of Chance's place honking the horn within the hour.

"Ok bitch! A girl ain't deaf! Stop pressing on that got damn horn! This is *Buckhead* girl!"

"This seedy ass neighborhood. You're used to it with all this salsa music 'round here," I said.

Chance lived in Buckhead, but it was a noisy Hispanic enclave in Lindbergh.

"You talk to Antandra today?" he asked stepping into the car.

We started calling Neequaye *Antandra* after the three of us fell in love with the Lifetime movie *Jackie's Back.*

"No, not today."

"Call that girl up and see what she doing today. She probably went *swimming* knowing her. She's the only girl I know that goes to the bathhouse just to swim. She ain't fooling nobody."

Neequaye was no stranger to the bathhouse, and he wasn't ashamed to say he enjoyed going. I called him a few times in the past, but he was unavailable because he was at Flex swimming.

Neequaye worked multiple jobs, so he rarely had afternoons or weekends free to run the streets with us. The three of us had a Monday ritual of going to the Monday night drag show at Traxx to see the Stars of the Century.

The only job Neequaye spoke of was the one at Ticketmaster, but he was a busboy at Mansion also. He could never seem to get tickets for any of the shows that Chance and I wanted to see, but every time we looked up he had tickets for himself to see Alvin Ailey at the Fox Theater.

Chance and I headed to Lenox Mall. He always got stares from people, but he either ignored the looks and comments or was completely oblivious. I saw and heard them all because I was still preoccupied with what people thought.

I was most embarrassed when he came racing in my direction, switching and waving clothes in the air "girl, did you see this top? She'd be cute on you 'cause you got body and stuff."

Ironically, he was always referring to men's clothes.

I was surrounded by gay men who had already come to terms with who they were, but I was still searching for me, the gay me. In some ways I was mimicking what I saw them doing. I went from one extreme to another. I bought clothes that fit a bit more snug. I even dyed my hair platinum blond, but that wasn't me. I found a balance after a few experiments, but Chance was single handedly pulling me further from the closet without me realizing it.

JUST CALL IT LOVE

I met Saleem in August 1999, sitting on a wall outside Traxx nightclub in Atlanta. Leslie and I were in my car watching everyone going in and coming out of the club. I noticed Leslie staring, in somewhat of a trance.

"Who you looking at?"

"That *thing* sitting right there. He is fine," he muttered without blinking an eye.

"Who...him right there with the plaid shirt on?" I grimaced.

"Mmm hmm."

"He's alright," I said.

"No, *he* is fine."

"Let me pull up so I can see him."

I put the car in gear and eased closer. Saleem watched us getting closer, but he didn't move. His eyes shifted from us to the club to the cars passing by, and back to us again. He was squatting down on a short brick wall with both elbows resting on his knees, and his hands clasped in front of him.

"Oh, he *is* fine," I said.

"Your mother might be old, but she can still see," Leslie said.

Leslie referred to *himself* as my mother because he had unofficially taken me under his wing. Typically, Leslie and I had completely different taste when it came to men, but there was something about Saleem that grabbed my attention too.

"I need to talk to him," I said.

"Nah, I saw him first!" Leslie laughed.

"Yea, but I always *let* you get them when we go out. I want this one," I said.

Leslie usually beat me to the punch when it came to approaching someone because I was still relatively green when it came to dating men, and still shy about approaching anyone. I let them come to me, but this time would be different.

*****

Leslie was a fast talker from Pittsburgh. He knew many of the movers and shakers in Atlanta because he floated in and out of the hair industry MCing hair and fashion shows.

Leslie and I met seven months earlier inside this same club we were camping out in front of. He stopped me as we passed each other on the staircase. I was going up to the hip-hop floor, Leslie was going down to the house music level. He was wearing a *Paddington Bear* styled hat that was pulled down over his eyes. I thought there was something attractive about him until he lifted his hat. After a quick glance under the light I could see he was worn. I got a glimpse of his eyes—they looked aged. I knew we would be nothing more than friends because he was much older.

The first couple of months, Leslie made relentless attempts to date, but I refused. It wasn't just a lack of attraction. My instincts wouldn't allow it and I had learned to be more in tune with my spirit. Leslie was too anxious to have sex and once we solidified our friendship, he told me he was only trying to have sex.

Soon after, Leslie asked me to help him write a stage play about the things that go on within the gay community, but I categorically said no and dismissed the idea each time he asked.

Leslie was 13 years older, HIV positive and a recovering drug addict. He resided in a government-subsidized efficiency apartment for people living with mental or chronic illnesses like HIV/AIDS.

Most of Leslie's life existed in the fast lane and it showed. He preyed on young boys, his new *high*, since he was now sober. Sex was an adrenaline rush for him, especially if he attracted and fucked naturally masculine men because he was inherently feminine, but masqueraded as masculine. Leslie frequented sex parties, novelty shops, gay bookstores, and spent hours on the chat line.

Whenever we were out together, he was good for pointing out guys that allowed him to penetrate them with or without a condom. Morehouse College was a playground for him. Leslie bypassed security to lurk the all-male college campus in the middle of the night looking for someone to hook up with. He was even bold enough to venture into the bathrooms in the dormitories to cruise the showers for a nut. The risk of being caught and escorted from the campus didn't deter him. For him, it was worth the reward of making it back to a college boy's room to fuck.

He had sex with one of the students while the roommate was asleep in the room. I couldn't help but think of the countless gifted, young Morehouse men he fucked raw. Sadly, these young men had the ambition to pursue an education, but lacked the common sense to require safe sex, thus, possibly leaving college with an education and HIV at the hands of a sexual predator. I'm not at all suggesting that people living with HIV have the burden of broaching the subject of safe sex because the responsibility is shared, but Leslie was ruthless.

I asked if he ever disclosed his status before having sex with someone, and he said most don't ask if he's positive or not.

"Most of these kids just say *'are you ok?'* or *'you good?'* If they aren't man enough to ask *'are you HIV positive?'* they don't care. If they gonna let me go up in them or take my cookies without a condom in this day and age they probably already got it and could be trying to give it to me."

Befriending Leslie was a blessing and a curse because he indirectly taught me all the games played. On one hand, it raised my level of awareness and it kept me on my toes. On the other, it made me increasingly suspicious of every gay man, making it almost impossible for me to trust anyone.

*****

"What's up man?" Leslie asked in his deepest voice.

"What's up?" Saleem responded looking at me.

"He is nice looking," I whispered.

Saleem appeared to be about 6'2". His plaid shirt didn't look so bad with his denim shorts and high top sneakers. I knew he wasn't from the south by the way he was dressed. He was definitely from up top—Maryland, DC, Philly or Jersey.

"You may have seen him first, but I'm gonna get him," I said stepping out of the car.

"May the best *girl* win!" Leslie laughed as he unfastened his seatbelt.

I took a seat next to Saleem on the wall. Leslie leaned against the passenger side of the car.

"Where you from," I asked.

His build almost fooled me into believing he was a country boy. Saleem's arms and shoulders were naturally solid, but I knew he didn't work out because he wasn't sinewy.

"Philly," he said.

"What brought you to Atlanta?" I asked.

"Stupidity," he said with a slight smirk.

"Oh, a relationship," I surmised.

"No, stupidity," he said again.

He smiled and looked up the street as if he was expecting someone to show up. He was beautiful up close. His dark, creamy clear skin looked like melted chocolate. His hair was manicured and cut close. His eyes were almond shaped with long curly eyelashes. Saleem's lips were full and his teeth were flawless. I was so lost in conversation that I forgot Leslie was with me. He knew he didn't stand a chance with Saleem once I started talking, so Leslie retired to the car and lit a cigarette.

Saleem was waiting for friends who were still inside the club. He asked if I would wait while he went to see if they were ready to leave. When Saleem disappeared, Leslie asked if I was ready to go. I could tell he was pissed, but I was driving so he had no choice but to wait until I was done. I hadn't gotten Saleem's number yet, so I definitely wasn't ready to leave.

"I'm almost ready. He asked me to wait til he comes back," I said.

After ten minutes, I walked over to the car to leave because I was ready to go. I could see Saleem coming down the street towards me.

"You have a pen and a piece of paper?" he asked.

I reached in the car for a pen and grabbed a napkin from the glove compartment. He leaned on the roof of the car to scribble his name and number on the napkin.

"What is that?" I asked rhetorically.

"That's my pager number," he said reluctantly.

I knew from the first three digits that it wasn't a home number.

"I don't do pager numbers," I said.

A pager number was the first clue he was living with someone, and the first red flag.

"What am I supposed to do with this?" I asked.

"When you page me I'll call you back," he reasoned.

"How will you know it's me?" I quizzed.

"Use #1," he said.

He explained like I had never paged someone before. It sounded like game, and every negative thing I believed about gay men flashed in my mind. Not to mention, I witnessed most of this firsthand through Leslie. This was shit he said and did.

"I'll give you my number 'cause I don't do pager numbers," I said.

I tore off a piece of the napkin and wrote down my number. I got in the car and pulled off. Saleem called the next morning, but I wasn't home so he left a message with his home number.

Saleem told me he moved from Philadelphia to Atlanta to be with his ex Wayne, with whom he was still living. Wayne saw Saleem in some wedding pictures a mutual friend of theirs had, and got in touch with Saleem through the friend. After a few visits and a couple months of long-distance dating, Saleem moved to Atlanta.

"I found out the week I got down here that he was an alcoholic. He was going to AA meetings every Tuesday. And the week after that, I caught him at the house with some other guy. They were on the couch messing around when I walked in. I beat the boy up."

"Why'd you beat him up? It wasn't his fault."

"I don't know."

"So, why didn't you leave then?"

"Stupid. I was embarrassed to go back home. Plus, I wanted to stay down here. I was tired of Philly. But, when I started doing my thing, he couldn't handle it. He was jealous and shit."

Saleem said he was looking to move into a place of his own once he completed his hours at a cosmetology school, and secured a job. He already had enough on his plate.

"Why did you give me your number if you're still together?" I asked.

"We're not together. We sleep in separate rooms," he explained.

"As long as you're living there, you're still together," I reminded.

He said they barely spoke when they saw each other because the relationship had become contentious. Nevertheless, I told myself not to get attached to him because he was only rebounding. I figured I would just have fun until something better came along.

Saleem never tried to keep me a secret from Wayne. We spent a lot of time together and on the phone. He didn't have a car, so I drove to Decatur a few times to pick him up from the house. One day I knocked on the door and Wayne answered.

"Hi, is Saleem here?"

"Saleem, your little boyfriend is here," he yelled.

Wayne didn't look anything like I expected. Saleem was settling. Wayne was an average looking guy with a slight belly.

I heard a dog barking in the garage, so I got back in the car to wait for Saleem. I didn't need Wayne sending a dog after me. A German shepherd attacked me when I was fourteen, and I have the keloids to prove it. I wasn't looking for a repeat of that.

Some days I picked Saleem up from Five Points train station downtown depending upon where we were going. The more time we spent together, the more eager I became to see more of him. I knew I was falling in love with him, even though I said I wouldn't. Wayne noticed the increase in time we spent and became pretty vocal in the background during one of our phone conversations, *"Why don't you go stay with him? You're always with him or on the phone!"* Saleem laughed, trying to ignore him.

Wayne picked up the phone and refused to hang up because he claimed to need the phone. He remained on the phone for the duration of the call. I could tell Saleem was embarrassed. It was one of the first indications that things were becoming progressively worse between them. I knew it wouldn't be long before Wayne evicted him; thus, I told Saleem to be prepared if it happened.

"I've already checked with the county. He hasn't filed any papers. He can't just put me out. I know my rights," Saleem said.

I couldn't understand why Wayne was so malicious to Saleem. The person I knew was genuine, and had a heart that he didn't mind sharing, despite the collapse of his previous relationship. I respected Saleem more because he never stayed the night at my place out of respect and as a courtesy to Wayne. He said he wouldn't stay until he moved out.

I dropped Saleem off at home one afternoon, and normally I would've left right away, but something told me to wait for him to get in. I couldn't tell from the car what was actually happening, but it didn't appear that Saleem could get in the house. I parked and walked up to the front of the house.

"That bastard changed the locks," he said.

I had seen in the weeks before how desperate Saleem was to escape the dramatics that increasingly escalated with each passing week. Although, I was sympathetic I wasn't motivated to allow him to move into my place after only knowing him two months.

Saleem raced to the back of the house and tried the key for the back door and it worked. Wayne had only changed the lock on the front door. Saleem grabbed a screwdriver from one of the drawers in the kitchen, and removed the lock on the front door and called the police.

"You can go. I'm good. I'll call you later," he said.

*****

Saleem and I found a routine and fell in, but still I anticipated bigger storms on the horizon. Weeks passed before the next wave of Wayne's antics. I was working 11:00 a.m. to 8:00 p.m. for Hewlett Packard in Kennesaw, GA. Saleem called me at work like clockwork each day. The first call always came between 11:00 a.m. and 11:30 a.m. during his lunch break at school. The second call, between 1:30 and 3:00 when his class took a break, and the last call just as he caught the 4:45 bus to head home.

My supervisor told me that my personal calls were excessive, and they were. He showed me a call log with multiple calls from Chance, Neequaye, my mother and Saleem. I never knew who was calling until I answered because my work phone wasn't equipped with caller ID, otherwise I could've screened the calls before answering. I set my work phone up to send all external calls to voicemail after one ring.

Chance never really wanted anything when he called except to play.

"HP, this is Craig."

"*HP this is Craig*? Girl, what does the HP stand for, Hot Pussy?"

"Chance, what do you want? I'm working."

"Oh, excuse me girl. You all busy and stuff at your lil desk. You can call me back."

And if that wasn't enough, Neequaye took the liberty of saying *hot pussy* incessantly. He even saved hot pussy in his cell phone by my number in lieu of my name, so naturally it flashed on the screen whenever I called him.

October 1, 1999 changed both Saleem's life and mine. Something felt off, but I couldn't manage to figure out what it was exactly. It dawned on me about 12 o'clock that I hadn't heard from Saleem. Saleem knew to leave a message when he got the voicemail, and to call back five minutes later to give me time to take the block off the outside calls, but this time he hadn't called at all.

Finally, around 2:30 p.m., I saw the flashing red light on the phone indicating I had a message:

"Hey, it's me. I'm just waking up. You don't have to call me back. I got a few errands to run before I go to school. I'll call you later."

It was Saleem's voice, but he didn't sound like himself. He sounded exhausted. His voice was gravelly and somber.

Saleem called again and left a second message later that afternoon:

"It's me. I made it to school. I'll call you back later."

His evasiveness was somehow tied to Wayne and I was determined to get the answer face-to-face. I didn't return any of Saleem's calls because I knew my boss was watching my calls. Saleem called again around 6:00 p.m. and I answered—my boss was gone for the day.

"Where you been?" I asked.

"I had some errands to run then I went to school and came home," he answered.

"So, what's going on?"

"Nothing," he mumbled.

I could hear the television playing in the background and a hint of melancholy in his voice.

"I had the worst day today," I said hoping to open up the conversation.

"I did too," he said softly.

"What happened with you?"

"You go first," he offered.

"Just stuff at work. There's something wrong and you're not telling me. I get off in two hours. Meet me at my house," I said.

"I already told my friends from Philly I would meet them. They're not gonna take no for an answer," he said.

"Come after you're done with them," I said.

"It's gonna be too late," he said.

"I don't care how late it is. I need you to come to my house when you're done."

His line beeped. Someone was clicking in on his second line.

"Hold on," he said.

I could hear him moving to look at the caller ID.

"That's them calling now. Hold on," he said.

Why is he avoiding me? Wayne had done everything to try to make Saleem's life miserable. *What was left to do that he hadn't already tried?* I knew instantly what *it* was.

"Hello?"

"Yea," I said.

"I have to go. They're on their way to pick me up," he said.

"Saleem, come to my house when you're done with them."

"Ok."

"I'm not playing. You better be there."

"Ok," he whined. "I gotta go."

I couldn't concentrate for the last two hours at work. My mind vacillated between whether he would come to my house

134

and what was really troubling him.

I got home at 8:30 and found some busy work to preoccupy myself. I was changing the sheets on my bed when I heard a knock on my front door about 9:10.

My front door was a sliding glass door, so when I opened the vertical blinds I jumped. Saleem's head was pressed against the glass.

"You scared the shit out of me," I said as I opened the door.

He was wearing a navy blue sweatshirt, blue jeans, black Timberland boots and a navy baseball cap that was propped on his head. He looked exhausted. His eyes were bloodshot like he hadn't slept much in the past day or so. Saleem followed me to my room as I continued making the bed.

The weather in Atlanta was just beginning to turn cold, and all I wanted to concentrate on was bundling up under my 800 thread count sheets and down comforter. I tried thinking of the good sleep I usually got with clean sheets on the bed as I was smoothing them out on the bed, but the tension in the room fore-shadowed a sleepless night.

Saleem stood on the threshold looking at the floor.

"I feel like I keep letting you down," he said.

Saleem referenced past troubles we managed to hurdle. Leslie made it his business to report back to me everything he heard about Saleem's past with hopes that I'd stop seeing him.

I looked up at him. He wiped one of his eyes. I couldn't tell if he was just rubbing his eye or trying to catch a falling tear.

"What happened?" I asked.

"I don't wanna talk about it."

"I already know what it is."

"I still don't wanna talk about it."

"Why are we talking around it?" I asked.

"Cause I don't wanna talk about it."

He began fidgeting from nervousness. He walked back into the living room and sat on the couch. This time I followed him.

"But, we both know what we're talking about," I pressured. "Not saying it won't make it go away, so we may as well say it."

"Don't say it," he pleaded.

"HIV. We're talking about HIV," I said bluntly.

He dropped his head.

"Tell me what happened," I said as I took a seat next to him.

"We got into a fight last night. I couldn't take it no more. He came home drunk again, and he was trying to pick a fight with me, so I grabbed a knife so he would leave me alone, and he said 'you need to get tested.'"

"That's how he said it?" I asked.

"Yea."

"What were his exact words Saleem?"

"He said he had it and I need to go get a test," he mumbled as he fought back tears.

"So, that was the errand you had to run? You went to get an HIV test?"

He nodded. I couldn't hold back my tears.

"I don't know if he gave it to me or if I gave it to him. He just found out first," he whispered.

"You don't even know if you have it."

"I do. I can see it in my face and when I went home last month my mother said I looked different."

Saleem and I almost had sex the previous weekend and the only reason we didn't was because he insisted we wait. He said he liked the way I did things. I wasn't in a rush to have sex in the way he had with other people before me. If we had had sex, I would've been paranoid about seroconverting, though we would've used a condom.

"Stop crying. It's ok. I've already cried for me. I'm crying for all the things I can never have with you," he said.

"It's not ok! This can't be happening to you," I cried.

"I wasn't gonna tell you since we never did anything. I was just gonna stop calling," he said.

"Why would you do that? Then I would've been wondering what happened."

"You would've got over me...I know how you feel about it. You already told me you wouldn't date someone with it."

"But that was before I fell in love with you," I mumbled.

"You're not in love with me. You just feel sorry for me."

"I do love you."

"I'm at a point that I love you more than I love myself. I wouldn't be able to live with myself if I gave it to you."

"This is why it's not worth all the games people play. It

seems fun to sleep with all these niggas, but no one stops to think about this shit," I cried. "Everybody thinks it's cool to just fuck. That shit ain't cool and when they end up sick they wonder how it happened."

"That's true," he said.

"It's not fair. I feel like I found a needle in a haystack...I'm not gonna let go."

"You don't have a choice. I'm not gonna do that to you," he said.

"I could get with someone else who has it. What's the difference?"

"Well, that's on them and their conscience. You're not gonna talk me into it, so stop," he said as if he was talking to a recalcitrant ten-year old.

"You don't even know if you are positive or not. You talking like you know. When will you know?"

"I won't know 'til Tuesday."

Rapid testing was few and far between at the time, and blood tests were sent off to labs. The results usually returned in three days.

"Saleem, you're thoughts create your destiny. If you believe you have it then you do. You're already giving up and you won't get the results 'til Tuesday," I said.

We sat in silence. He stared off into space. I stared at him while praying to myself for a miracle. Saleem got up to turn on the stereo, and returned to the couch to lie down. I didn't recognize the piano intro of the song he played, but I recognized the voice. It was Yolanda Adams.

"I know that there are times in your life. When the wheels just seem to turn, and uncertainties about your tomorrow seem to grow and grow and grow. One thing you should remember and you should always know. That out of everyone who loves you, I your Father I love you the most. For I am just a prayer away..."

It was my Yolanda Adams, *Live in Washington* cd, but I had never listened to it before. Saleem was lying on his back sobbing softly as she sang.

"...and when you cry at night, I'll wipe the tears away..."

His sobs got louder. I sat beside him and hugged him. I cried with him.

"...I am just one simple prayer away. Stop calling everybody else and start calling Me with your heart, and yes I'll hear you..."

His head rocked back and forth, possibly, in disbelief and anger with himself for allowing it to happen.

"...ya never, you should never, you should never think that I'm not bothered about what goes on in your life. Everything that has something to do with you concerns Me! If you're crying tears I wanna wipe them away..."

When the song finished he skipped to "I'll Always Remember" then to "The Battle is Not Yours." In some way I felt he was torturing himself, but I allowed him to deal in the way he knew how.

That night Saleem stayed over for the first time. He slept on top of the covers, completely dressed except his baseball cap and Timbs. We stayed up most of the night talking and crying. By the next morning, I had a headache and my eye sockets were throbbing. Every time I looked at him, tears streamed down my face. He didn't deserve this. No one did.

"You look awful," he said with a faint laugh.

"That's ok, you know what I'm capable of," I smiled.

The next morning we drove around East Point and College Park looking for apartments for Saleem to rent. This was his final straw. He couldn't continue living under Wayne's roof, and he was determined to remain in Atlanta. Going back to Philly would have been a sign of giving up.

Every apartment we visited was out of his price range or a complete dump. He was frustrated and I was restless, so we headed to Blockbuster video to rent *Beaches* and *Claudine,* two of his favorite movies. I had never seen either movie. Saleem cried watching *Claudine* when Diahann Carroll's daughter learns she's pregnant and fears contracting VD.

"Why are you crying," I asked.

"That's all they had to worry about back then," he said.

With each day, Saleem's demeanor changed unpredictably. I could always tell when he was thinking about being positive. Whenever I tried to kiss him, he'd turn his head so I could only kiss his cheek.

"Why do you keep doing that?" I asked.

"Cause, I don't want you to get it," he said.

"Stop being ridiculous! If that was the case everybody would have the shit. It's not like we haven't already kissed," I said.

"Well, they don't know everything. I'm not taking any chances with you," he said.

"You're being silly," I insisted.

On Tuesday, Saleem called with his test results.

"Hey!" he said.

There was such brightness in his voice that I hadn't heard in weeks.

"It was negative?" I asked.

"I started to play a real cruel joke on you—"

"What?" I asked.

"Say it came back negative," he chuckled.

All I heard was *negative*.

"It was negative?" I asked.

"No, it was—"

I couldn't believe my ears. I had prayed. He prayed. We prayed together.

"No," I heard my voice tremble. "Where are you? You want me to meet you?" I asked.

"Yea, you can. I'm off Covington Highway," he said.

THERE'S NO GLUE

Saleem wanted to prepare Thanksgiving dinner at my place since he was still living with Wayne. The only hitch was my mom was also planning to spend Thanksgiving with me for my first Thanksgiving in Atlanta, and I still hadn't told her I was gay.

"Let's have Thanksgiving together. Are you gonna be in town?"

"Yea, but my mom is coming down for Thanksgiving."

"So, we could just be friends. She doesn't have to know about us," he said blithely.

"Unh-onh, my mother is not crazy. She'll know something is up. Even if we didn't touch she would pick up on body language. I'll just tell her," I said.

"No, don't tell her. You shouldn't force it on her. Plus, she's gonna automatically hate me 'cause I'm the first boyfriend she meets," he reasoned.

"No she's not."

I knew my mother better than Saleem. What I knew was she would be cordial to him if they met, but she wouldn't be ok with me dating someone living with HIV. That was the only detail I planned to keep secret.

I chose to call my mother from work to break the news just in case the conversation got too heavy. It would be easy to make an excuse to get off the phone with her because I had *work* to do. When my mom picked up, I made small talk before getting to the crux of why I called.

"I have something to tell you."

There was a hush over the phone.

"I hope it's not about that job," she sighed.

I was fired from MARTA a few months earlier while in the process of being promoted. My manager and supervisor selected me as the evening supervisor, but the director of the department hired someone outside the company for an internal position. Subsequently, I appealed the decision and was fired when the director questioned how I learned the other candidate wasn't an employee at MARTA. When I refused to tell him, I was terminated. I filed a lawsuit against MARTA for wrongful termination and took a job at Hewlett Packard while the case was pending.

"No, it's not about this job," I said.

"Is it personal or professional?" she asked.

"Personal," I replied.

"Is it about a man?" she guessed.

I almost dropped the phone.

"No! Why would you ask that?!" I snapped. "Well, yeah it is," I said before she could guess again.

"I knew it," she said.

The phone was silent again with the exception of a sigh.

A mother always knows if her child is gay or not. I've had countless conversations with grown men who have never been married or fathered a child who believed their mother didn't suspect they were gay because they never broached the subject. Even is she never mentions it or you decide against telling her, a mother knows.

"I was hoping, wishing, and praying you weren't," she said.

"I have too for 22 years. I hoped, wished, and prayed it would go away, but it didn't."

"We're ok. Nothing's gonna change," she said.

Before we hung up, I told her about Saleem and Thanksgiving dinner.

"Mmm hmm," she said glossing over it.

For two weeks, my mother and I played phone tag. She strategically called when she knew I would be working to simply leave a message on the same answering machine Farrell had left the infamous *"I guess you decided not to be gay"* message on a few months prior. She wasn't ready to face me—to face it.

When I returned her calls, she was always too busy or exhausted to talk. Either she was about to have dinner, clean up the kitchen after dinner, take a shower or get ready for bed. I had to accept that she wasn't ready to deal with it in my time. More importantly, I had to allow her adequate time to process it. After all, it had taken me 22 years to be ok with me. I couldn't possibly expect her to be comfortable in two weeks.

One evening Saleem cooked dinner for Chance, Neequaye,

and me at my place. Before we sat down for dinner my mother called. When I saw her phone number on the caller ID I picked up right away.

"Hey, what's up?"

I hadn't spoken to her in a few days, which was different because we were in the habit of speaking daily once I moved further from home.

"*Hey?* What do you mean 'hey'?" she snapped.

I knew we were about to have *the* conversation.

"Look, this is not sitting with me as well as I thought, and you need to decide what you want to do for Thanksgiving because I don't want to meet any of those people!" she said.

I got up from the couch and went into the kitchen where Saleem was prepping the food. When our eyes connected I whispered, "it's my mother."

My face must have given away that we were discussing him.

"It's about me?" Saleem whispered.

I nodded.

"Ma, what do you mean *those* people? I'm one of those people."

Saleem looked at me suddenly. His eyes were stretched like I had cursed. He knew the conversation was heating up. He laughed quietly at me trying to diffuse it.

"Shut up!" I whispered with a smile.

"I told you," he said.

"Look, you can either spend time with family or them, but I

don't wanna be with any of those people so you can just tell me now what you wanna do 'cause I can stay in Baltimore," she grumbled.

"Who are those people?" I asked.

"Those people!" she fired back.

"Well, I'm one of those people."

"Like I said, do you want to have dinner with family or them? You can tell me right now 'cause I can save my money and stay home."

"Ma, you just want me to choose, so you can have a reason to be mad. You can come. I don't have to have Thanksgiving with my friends."

I couldn't help but look at Saleem. I could tell from his body language his feelings were now hurt.

"Well, I'm telling you now, I don't want to meet any of them. You can try to be slick if you want and have them show up, but you will not like it!"

"Ma, if you're coming, come. Book your flight and I'll see you when you get here."

"We can talk about this when I get there," she said.

The moment I got off the phone, Saleem looked at me.

"I told you not to tell her," he said.

"Shut up. Is the food ready?"

My mother and Ty visited for Thanksgiving, but not one word was spoken about me being gay and I was relieved. I expected tension, but there wasn't. Everything felt normal. Two weeks after my mom returned to Baltimore I called her to face the obvious. I asked her why she was so upset if she knew I was gay already. She explained she was fearful that I would become HIV positive because everyone she knew who was gay contracted it or died as a result. And, it's one thing to believe something—it's another for it to be confirmed. The reality of me being gay pained her because she could never pretend not to know again.

"Have you cried about it since I told you?" I asked.

"No, I haven't cried, but I pray every night that it goes away," she explained.

"Ma, I can pray every day for the rest of my life to wake up one day as a White man, and that will never happen. Not because prayer doesn't work, but because we have to adjust to the life God gives us," I said.

"I just don't understand why you pretended to like all those girls you were with," she exclaimed.

"I wasn't pretending. I did like them, but I was also trying to understand what was going on with me too. Ma, if I was straight I wouldn't have to make an announcement that I was straight. I only told you because we're close, not because I had to. You should be glad I'm telling you. You know how many people live in secret and because of it they're strung out on drugs or are suicidal because they keep it bottled up? It takes a strong person to live this truth. I've already dealt with the thoughts that are bothering you. You're worried about what your friends will think, and what our family will say. I'm past that."

She listened intently and I could tell I was getting through to her.

"I'll always love you 'cause you're my son. It's just hard hearing it."

I decided on that call that HIV wouldn't be my fate. It was an unspoken promise I made to my mother.

It would take time for my mom to warm up to this new reality, but I was patient and never force-fed her. Soon, she began asking about all of my friends, including Saleem.

"Well, has *he* been tested?" she asked.

"Yes, he has," I said nervously.

"Well?"

"Ma, he can be negative today, but that doesn't mean he'll always be, so I have to protect myself."

I didn't lie, but I certainly wasn't about to tell her the whole truth.

*****

I was extremely careful not to share Saleem's status with anyone that knew him because once a secret is released, we have no control where it goes. I did, however, tell my cousin Tiffany who lived in Ohio. I felt comfortable telling her because she lived in another state and I knew she would probably never meet him. Also, I couldn't carry the weight of this secret alone. I needed an outlet.

Before I told Tiffany I was gay, she periodically gave hints that she would be ok with me being gay. I remember most vividly her saying, "find someone to love. I don't care who it is. Just find someone. You deserve love."

Once I found Saleem, and told her his status she couldn't understand why I would risk being with someone living with HIV. At times I was confused about why I wanted to stay with him, but I couldn't bring myself to let go because he was positive. She told me to be patient because I would find someone else, but I was more afraid I wouldn't make another connection because quality is scarce. Saleem was the person I grew to love without sex confusing lust for love. And, I didn't believe love was about cashing in one's chips and walking away once you find out something less than favorable about the person. Love is knowing everything about a person and loving them in spite of it.

Saleem reminisced on his adventures of risky sex in previous years. He recounted stories of threesomes, sex parties, one-night stands and trips to Atlanta from Philadelphia for hook ups in Piedmont Park. Behind his smile was a splash of shame. His smile slowly dissolved to a pitiful grin. It dawned on him how he arrived at this point. His past had finally caught up with him.

"Was it worth it?" I asked.

"I think all of us [gay men] believe it's gonna happen to us at some point," he muttered.

"I've never thought that," I said softly.

Christmas was just around the corner, and Saleem was becoming inconsistent. He was fickle at best. He wouldn't always return my calls and he rarely kept his word when we made plans. More times than not he was often a no-show or called to cancel moments before we were to meet. He and I were supposed to have dinner with Chance and John, but Saleem cancelled moments before dinner was to be served. He said Wayne had pissed him off, but he had pissed me off.

I started attending HIV/AIDS workshops to learn the dos and don'ts of being with someone HIV positive. I wanted to show Saleem we could still be together despite the virus. We couldn't let it win, but the more I learned the further he pulled away. I knew more about the medications than he was willing to learn. He refused to take the medications when he was first diagnosed. When he started staying at my place for the weekend he intentionally left his medication at home to avoid taking it, so I suggested he keep a supply at my apartment. His concern was that one of my nosey friends would find it in the medicine cabinet while in the bathroom.

"What if somebody sees it?" he exclaimed.

"I'll hide it in my bedroom," I said.

The only task was getting Saleem to take the medicine on schedule.

I got a call from the headhunter that hired me for Hewlett Packard informing me I was no longer employed. My manager wanted me terminated because my personal calls continued to spike after Saleem was diagnosed. The stress from everything going on with Saleem affected my work, and my personal phone calls at work were still a concern, much to the dissatisfaction of my manager. I couldn't ignore his calls.

I had been fired before, but the difference this time was I had no backup plan or money saved. I couldn't tell my mother I was fired again because she was relieved I found this job after being terminated from MARTA. Plus, I had just told her I was gay.

Saleem was receiving unemployment when we met, so I called him to vent and he told me the process to get an unemployment check. I could've gotten unemployment after I was fired from MARTA, but didn't know to apply. Saleem told me which forms to ask for when I went to the Department of Labor, and what explanation to give on paper because I was clueless.

"You're gonna get a brown envelope in the mail. That's gonna be the check," he said.

Saleem was certain I would receive benefits, but my nervousness wouldn't allow me to be as confident. A few weeks later, there was an orange colored envelope in the stack of junk mail. It was my first check including the retroactive pay from the past weeks.

Saleem was the first person I called.

"I got the check!" I beamed.

"I told you," he said.

To celebrate, I had a tree trimming party at my place. I invited several friends to my Christmas party. Neequaye and Chance came with ornaments for the tree I bought. You could smell fresh pine the moment you entered the front door.

At the height of the party, Saleem called me into the bedroom. He sat down at the foot of the bed, and I took a seat next to him. We were facing the mirror on the dresser. We took turns looking at each other in the mirror and face-to-face.

"I want you to find someone that's not sick. Eventually, you're gonna want to have sex and I wouldn't be able to live with myself if you came home one day to tell me that I gave it to you," he said.

I knew from the look in his eyes there was nothing I could say to make him waiver this time, but I tried anyway.

"You're not sick."

"I am sick."

"There's nothing wrong with you."

"You know what I mean."

His almond shaped eyes were dreary and it wasn't from the buzz from his cocktail. Maybe I was in denial because he didn't look sick. Had I seen him walking on the street in the dark denim jacket and pants, and black ribbed turtleneck sweater I wouldn't have known he was HIV positive. He was the new healthy face of HIV.

"Saleem, one in three has it. Who's to say I won't meet someone after you that has it? What's the difference?" I reasoned.

"It won't be me."

"We don't have to have sex. We can do other things."

There's No Glue

"You're not gonna change my mind. You're just starting out. I can't do that to you. That wouldn't be fair to you," he said.

My eyes were tearing up. I heard a few of my friends calling me from the other room. I heard someone mumble, "what they doing *having* in there? They sure been in there a long time."

"You need to go back in there with your friends. You're being rude," he said.

"They'll be ok," I responded.

"Come on. Let's go back out there. I'm about to leave anyway," he said.

"Look, I'm not begging you to stay this time. If you leave I'm done," I said trying to scare him into staying.

"Ok, good. That's what I want."

He got up and started towards the living room. I sat on the bed watching him. I couldn't think of anything else to say. He made the decision to walk away never to look back except for my friendship.

Originally, I was only planning to stay in Maryland for three days, but decided to stay a week because I needed to escape this new world that was causing me difficulty. The extra time at home would help me remember the person I was before I moved to Atlanta.

I drove to the airport to change my return ticket. I slipped Yolanda Adams' *Live in Washington* cd in the changer, and skipped to "Just a Prayer Away." I replayed everything that happened in my mind. I couldn't contain the feelings. I was afraid Saleem would never find love again because some are so unforgiving when a person becomes infected. And, I was scared of starting over with someone new.

I thought about the shame that might follow him when he was put in the position to disclose his status. Saleem said he would never get in another relationship to avoid that, but I knew better. He was only feeling that way because that was the space he was in. I imagined him dying because people still die from AIDS, despite advancements in medicine. I cried all the way to the airport.

When I parked, I gained my composure long enough to go to the ticket counter to change my flight. The moment I got back in the car to return home, the tears began falling again.

I arrived in Maryland days later. My mother asked why I looked so skinny. I couldn't tell her I lost weight and sleep because Saleem had HIV, so I shrugged and hoped she wouldn't ask again.

I didn't get a chance to see some of my family on that visit because time wouldn't allow. After I returned to Atlanta, I was sorting through mail and came across a letter addressed from my Aunt Coretha. I had no idea what she could be sending me. I had never received mail from her before.

It was a floral envelope with matching stationery. I was standing in the living room when I opened it, still pondering what she needed to say in a letter. *Why didn't she just call?*

Hey Dirt,

I tried to catch you before you went back to Hotlanta. We as a family love you, in spite of what some may not understand. To hell with the others.

Love,

Aunt Coretha

My eyes filled with tears. After everything I had been through with coming out to Monica, my mom and losing Saleem, I needed to hear those words. I stashed the letter with all of the cards that meant something to me, including the one Mrs. Marshall gave me after graduation.

A WHOLE NEW WORLD

Although Chance was working at a thriving dog grooming business, he was still struggling to make ends meet. He debated taking on a part-time job to survive. Chance didn't have much experience dating Black men, although he too was Black. Chance lived in Buffalo, New York, where the small Black gay population left him with very few options. Chance was burdened in Atlanta because he didn't believe Black gay men were attracted to him. No matter where we were, and as Black and gay as Atlanta is, White men always gravitated to him.

Chance called to tell me he and John were back together, but I knew it was coming after he and John invited Saleem and me to dinner a few weeks before. Chance was lonely, and since John was familiar and offered to help Chance get on his feet, it made sense to him.

Chance and I were both involved with men living with the same disease. I wanted someone, anyone, to assure me that it was ok to date Saleem because I couldn't reconcile it with being HIV negative, and Chance did that for me.

"Do you think I should let him go?"

"Girl, you just have to be safe and use protection. You can't be having no slip ups! Talking 'bout *oops*."

"No, there won't be any slip ups. Do you and John *always* use protection?"

"I mean, we have had times that we didn't in the past because he doesn't like the way condoms feel, and I didn't wanna make him feel bad by asking him to use them. That was during a time that I didn't really care about myself. I suffer from severe depression. I didn't really find myself attractive, but I'm not playing them kinda games no more, girl. If he wants some from momma he gonna have to use them."

The things Chance told me saddened me, but his admission was true for many of the gay men I met. He was in great company with a league of men who found it difficult to love themselves, and ironically or not, many were HIV positive. I believe the connection between gay men and HIV has more to do with low self-esteem than it has to do with our sexual habits, and that connection is tied into the way in which society denigrates us as a community.

Ostensibly, Chance was a person with lots of self-esteem, but tucked away behind the effervescence was a person who didn't love himself like I thought. Chance's self-esteem was so damaged that he put John's wants before his own health. The most disturbing thing was that John allowed Chance to have unprotected sex with him knowing he had AIDS. I was no longer convinced that Chance was still HIV negative.

John offered to lease an apartment for Chance because he was fed up with living with his roommate and the strangers he continued to meet online for sex. According to Chance, his roommate had plenty of traffic coming in and out of their apartment at all hours of the night.

"If you let John cosign for an apartment for you, make sure it's one you can afford by yourself just in case you break up," I urged.

"Oh, yea, yea. Of course, girl," he said.

But of course Chance opted for an apartment in Buckhead that he could not afford alone. When the relationship began to implode John stopped paying the rent, and he urinated on and sliced up furniture he bought for Chance.

After a few short months, Chance was planning to move back to New York after his rekindled long-distance relationship with John fell apart a second time. I was left with memories from our first and only New Years Eve together, and the many lessons he taught me without knowing he was teaching me.

As quick as Chance, Neequaye, and I bonded, Chance was gone with the same speed back to New York.

I attended programs throughout Atlanta, and facilitated a few workshops at AID Atlanta with Saleem in mind. Although Saleem and I were no longer together, I invited him with me hoping he would gain the knowledge he needed to cope. Each invitation I extended was met with a firm '*no*'. His concern was his anonymity.

"I don't want people all in my business," he said.

"But, I'm going too. People could think I'm positive," I said.

158

"But the difference is you know you're not," he argued.

The attendees were health care providers and those infected and affected by HIV, but Saleem still wasn't interested. He struggled to pay for his medication each month rather than going to a center to get it free because he didn't want to be seen going or coming.

Once the phone calls started tapering off with Saleem, I began to feel empty without him, and now Chance. I couldn't stop talking about the effects the break up had on me. Everyone assumed Saleem cheated because I refused to disclose the reason we split. They couldn't understand why I wouldn't reconcile with him since I was lonely without him, but it wasn't so simple. Chance and Neequaye were the only two who knew what really happened between Saleem and me.

Although Leslie was HIV positive, he was the last person I wanted to tell about Saleem. Leslie was most negative about the break up, mostly because he wanted Saleem for himself in the beginning. He often said gay men couldn't commit because they where whores and there was no need to commit because sex is too readily available to be monogamous.

I was beginning to think everyone I met, platonic or otherwise, was HIV positive. I couldn't go to a party, club or event without wondering how many people in the room were HIV positive.

Neequaye and I started working out several days a week, and I completely submerged myself with writing music to escape the residual pain that comes with a broken heart. I began writing for local artists who were looking for recording deals and producers who were signed to production deals, but needed lyrics for their tracks. I was building a catalog of songs for my publishing company, Impeccable Works, LLC.

I was in a recording studio every night writing or recording to make up for lost time. I moved to Atlanta to write music, but somehow I was sidetracked with being gay. Every Monday night I was at the drag show with Chance and Neequaye followed by many nights at *thugged* out Tuesdays, Bulldogs on Thursdays, The Palace on Fridays, and random house parties given by people we didn't know on Saturdays. There was something to do every day or night of the week.

Not only had I misplaced my purpose, I was forgetting my roots. The further along that I matriculated into the *life,* the more removed I became from my personal values, belief system, and identity—the things that were instilled in me. I temporarily abandoned what my family had given me because it seemed the people I met within the subculture did things differently with respect to sex and relationships. I gradually became ok with casual sex.

I collected unemployment for the entire six months allotted to me. I calculated the date of my last check, so I wouldn't be taken by surprise. As the date for the last check approached, I got nervous because I hadn't looked for work, though I told the Department of Labor otherwise. I was counting on my case against the transit company I worked for to settle. I called the attorney weekly for an update.

I went to a birthday party in Louisville, Kentucky, with two friends and I called to claim my last check before I left town. The night before we returned to Atlanta I got a call from the attorney.

"Mr. Stewart, we settled your case. They have to pay you 14 months back pay including salary increases that occurred while you were gone plus your vacation days, and you get your job back," she said.

"Really?" I said. I couldn't believe the timing of it all. "I don't want the job back. I just want my money," I said.

"Well, you have to go back. That was part of the deal. But listen, once you get your check you can do whatever you want," she said.

"I'm only going back long enough to get my check. Thanks for all your help," I said.

I returned to work the following week. I received one lump sum payment after two weeks plus my first paycheck. I resigned after I accepted a job at IBM.

I was starting over with a clean slate and the same was true for my sister. My mother called to tell me my sister checked herself into a drug treatment center in Philadelphia. Donnie remained in the program for six months and decided to start a new life in Philadelphia after treatment to avoid the triggers in Baltimore that may have caused a relapse. She was finally clean and this time it was for good.

One of my co-workers at IBM found out that I was a song-writer and thought it would be a good idea to meet her cousin Tweet after hearing a song I recorded. Tweet was an aspiring singer visiting from Rochester, NY. April told me Tweet was having a difficult time breaking into music as a singer, so she was trying to convince her to give up music and settle down in Atlanta at a job. Tweet worked with Missy Elliott and one of the guys from Jodeci previously, but nothing ever panned out.

April arranged for me to meet Tweet because I had some tracks I was writing to and I needed a singer to record them. Tweet sang for me over the phone before we met, but she was extremely shy in person.

"How do you sing for Missy and all these people, but are scared to sing in front of me?"

She nervously shrugged and looked away. She was beautiful. Her face was flawless without makeup and her hair was natural. She had it brushed back into an afro puff.

I gave her a copy of the lyrics and the track to practice the song without me until she was comfortable singing in front of me. Before I left, Tweet played a video of herself and two other girls singing a song she wrote called "Hotel." I loved the breathy and raspy qualities in her voice, so I made plans to meet her at the end of the week.

Before we got a second meeting, Missy sent a plane ticket for

Tweet. A car picked her up days after our first and only meeting. Tweet flew to LA to write and record her debut album, *Southern Hummingbird*. Again, I was close, but still so far away.

I was promoted to another division at work and the position paid well, but it didn't challenge me because I had very little responsibility. I was becoming bored again. My new job offered lots of flexibility, which meant I was able to schedule studio time with singers, producers, and other writers when I was supposed to be at work. I was late to work every day and had the gall to leave early every day. I took the new job for granted because there was no structure.

I was en route to work the morning of September 11th when the World Trade Center was attacked. I was listening to cds in the car because radio stations consistently play the same six songs, so I had no knowledge of what happened in New York before I arrived at work.

When I got to the office it was empty. Someone working on the same floor told me everyone was watching television upstairs. When I got upstairs, the replays of the planes crashing were on. I walked over to Karyn—the only person I spoke to outside of work.

"What happened?"

"There was a terrorist attack in New York at the World Trade Center. If the plane had hit this building you would've been the only survivor 'cause your ass is always late," she said.

THE HETTABRINKS

Some people come into our lives to be a bridge to other people. I met Miles through a guy I dated briefly and Miles connected me to my core group of friends. He visited one day and coincidentally he knew one of my neighbors—a guy named Brent. Although Brent's apartment was directly across the parking lot from mine, we had never seen each other before.

Brent was born in Trinidad, but raised in New York by his Trinidadian grandparents. We got along famously because I grew up with West Indian friends—mostly Jamaicans or Trinidadians. He couldn't believe how familiar I was with Caribbean foods outside of curry and jerk chicken.

Brent went to college in Virginia and relocated to Atlanta after graduation as I had, but he still wasn't out to his family. He still had plans of dating women again and having children because he felt men played too many games to take any of his relationships seriously. And, Brent's grandparents were vocal about wanting him to give them some great-grandchildren. Personally, I couldn't understand how they were unaware Brent was gay. Not because he was overly feminine, but because there were many things that pointed to his sexuality—he permed and colored his grandmother's hair.

Brent and I had plenty in common including our addiction to clothes and shoes. He worked part time for a clothing retailer, so I had everything the store carried including the home accessories.

Miles also introduced Brent to another friend of his named Devon who was in the process of moving to Atlanta from New York. The first time I met Devon, Miles came to my place with him and a guy named Elden in the car. The four of us drove to Alon's Bakery in Virginia Highlands and to the Wal-Mart in Douglasville.

Elden was a bit soft spoken and somber as he spoke mostly about his relationship that was ending. He and his ex were settling into separate apartments after being together about five years. Elden was still in love, but he couldn't get past his ex's internet cravings. Apparently, his boyfriend was using a webcam to entertain men online when Elden was away from home.

Elden and his college roommate, Wendell, rented a place five minutes from Brent and me on Collier Road. Elden was from Texas, and was employed by a technology-consulting firm with aspirations of launching an interior design firm. His roommate Wendell was from Michigan, and his career path was unclear to him and us.

Devon returned to New York to finalize plans to move as Elden continued piecing his life back together. It was several months before we all reconnected, but Brent and I forged a friendship right away.

Devon was supposed to crash at Miles' apartment while he saved money for his own place, but he stayed at Brent's instead. Brent offered Devon his couch, which made perfect sense because he was always with us, and Miles was gay one day and uncertain the next. Plus, Brent was tired of taking Devon back and forth to Miles' place for clothes and other random things he may have forgotten there. Eventually, we phased out our friendship with Miles.

Initially, Elden and I didn't get along when he emerged. He said I had a really strong personality and I was used to being the leader in the group. Part of me resented him for saying it, but I also knew he was right. My mother told me plenty of times growing up that I was bossy and controlling, so this wasn't unfamiliar. Elden's roommate disagreed. Wendell figured I said the things everyone thought, but was too afraid to say. Elden went on to say that Devon and Brent didn't have a mind of their own and did whatever I wanted to do. Nevertheless, he and I found our rhythm and became more like brothers than friends.

Elden introduced us to his friend Julian, whom he met at Morehouse College. Julian left Morehouse after his freshmen year and finished school back home in North Carolina at East Carolina State University. Julian moved back to Atlanta and was working for a clinical research laboratory.

I gladly welcomed the new friendships since Neequaye moved to Washington, DC when his job at one of the credit bureaus moved out of the states. His move to DC was also an excuse for him to see if things would work out with a guy he met at the gay pride event we attended the previous Memorial Day weekend.

Brent always had a story about one of his coworkers, especially a character named DJ. DJ had an interest in Brent, but Brent only saw him as a friend. Brent invited DJ to a party with us, and DJ showed up at our apartment complex with his best friend Twiggy. As soon as DJ stepped out of his *vintage* green Mercedes I recognized him.

"We've met before," he said.

"Yea, I remember. Do you remember where?" I said laughing.

"I came up to you on the dance floor at the Palace tryna dance with you and you turned your back on me," he chuckled.

"Yep! I can't believe you remember that," I said laughing.

Twiggy was quietly observing with the exception of a nervous jingle from his key ring that reminded us he was standing there.

DJ was from Philly and Twiggy was from Elizabeth, NJ. Seemed all the gay boys I met were Morehouse men. DJ and Twiggy also met in undergrad at Morehouse College. I may have applied to Morehouse had I known there was such a large gay presence on campus, but I avoided it for obvious reasons.

We were all single when we met, and it became obvious that we all wanted to be in relationships. I pegged us *The Hettabrinks* after the sisters from the television show, *Amen* because we, like the sisters, had a lot going for us except a good man. We were all degreed, gainfully employed, independent, Black gay men, and single without any decent prospects.

The six of us were practically inseparable. Some were closer than others, but we were a family away from our families. We celebrated each other's birthdays, exchanged Christmas gifts, and shared our most personal secrets on three way phone calls. There wasn't anything that could happen to one of us without everyone knowing—not even a headache.

We took turns hosting potlucks at our apartments, but we had no problem crashing a party or standing around the pool table together at Club Colours. If you saw one, you saw at least two of us at a time. To most, it appeared that we were dating within our group because we danced with each other or stood clustered together, possibly preventing anyone from approaching us. And if any of us met someone while we were out, we made sure someone in the group knew whom we were with, and where we were going as a safety precaution. I was quick to jot down a license plate number.

I adored my friends. The times that I traveled home to Maryland became quick turnaround trips because I was always anxious to get back to Atlanta—my new home. My mother was offended because my trips were so brief, and when I was home I spent most of my time on the phone with one of my friends in Atlanta or racing through the streets of Baltimore with old friends.

We had a special bond that we all were protective of and rarely allowed anyone new to penetrate. No one was more apprehensive of inviting new friends in the group than DJ. He screened any and all new *potential* friends.

"Child, who is that girl?"

"Where is she from?"

"How you meet her?"

"Is she saved?"

But, as cautious as we thought we were, elements would slowly erode our bond with time.

SETTING THE STAGE

Karyn and I were fired from our software development jobs. For years, I told people I was laid off because of 9/11, but Karyn and I knew the truth. Our salaries were cut after the economy went into a frenzy, so we took it upon ourselves to make up the difference in pay by selling the company software on the side. Unfortunately for us, the software developer that we propositioned reported us to the company, but not before we made some money first.

Karyn was escorted out of the building first after we were caught. She tried to text me to alert me, but our supervisor had already tapped me on my shoulder to confiscate my badge and directed me to leave the property.

Meanwhile, Leslie was still prodding me about writing a play that focused on the gay community, and since I had no desire to look for another job I agreed. My experience with Saleem increased my interest in writing the show. The information I gathered at the HIV workshops I attended during the time he and I dated became the backdrop for the show.

It was time to do something different because I had lost every job I worked. I began to see that I lost those jobs because I was off course. I was no longer on the path God had planned for my life, so He snatched the rug from underneath me to gain my attention. I began writing the first scenes for *A Day in the Life* two days after I was terminated, and I didn't think it was a coincidence that I lost that job on Saleem's birthday—March 9, 2002.

Leslie attended an HIV convention in Atlanta—the weekend before I was fired—where he met Percy, who had an extensive theater background. The three of us met on a Wednesday night at Starbucks on Peachtree Street.

Percy was a short dark skinned older man, and he looked unkempt. He wore old reading glasses that had tape on the hinge, and a kufi on his balding head. He consistently raked his bushy beard with his fingers. Percy was always costumed in a pair of shorts he cut from a pair of old pants, so they were tattered at the end. Nappy salt and pepper chest hair spewed from his tank top undershirt. At first glance, one might assume Percy was a little off his rocker, but he was more than intelligent and he spoke eloquently.

"Where's the script?" he asked.

"We just started talking about doing it," I rebutted.

"I want to see the first three scenes by Friday."

"Friday?"

"Yes it's here, right?" he asked pointing to his head. "You just have to put it on paper."

I was intrigued by the challenge and excited that he lit a fire under me. By Friday, I had more than three scenes done—I had five scenes completed.

Leslie was living with his mother—almost thirty minutes from the city. The commute on public transportation each day to my Brookwood Village apartment was impeding the writing process. I spent many nights writing and rewriting scenes without him. There were plenty of nights I was pulled from my sleep to write. By the time he arrived at my place, I was done writing for the day. He was simply reading what I had written that day and night before.

The script was filled with everything I didn't fully understand about the gay community though I was now a part of the subculture. The storyline centered around six characters that I believe represent the persona found within the community: the queen, overly feminine guy who was kicked out of his home as a teenager because of it; the transgender, who believes she was born in a stranger's body and isn't accepted by gay or heterosexual people; the Minister of music at the church, who can't reconcile his religious beliefs with his sexuality; the closeted professional, who has a long-term partner, yet, none of his family or peers know he's gay; the progressive gay man, who comes from a supportive family that embraces his sexuality, but can't seem to find love; and the DL man who has sex with men, but refuses to believe he's gay because he has a girlfriend and doesn't move in gay circles.

Percy was first to acknowledge that I was writing the play alone. He pulled me aside to offer words I would never forget.

"This is your shit. You and Leslie need to figure out what role he'll play when this thing gets bigger. There's something really special about what you're writing, baby. Fifty years after you're dead some little gay boy should be able to go into a library and pull this script from the shelf to read about what it was like for us. He should be able to see exactly what we were going through."

I felt the power of his words. I was twenty-six years old writing a story that could live years beyond me. I could see in Percy's eyes that he sincerely meant what he was saying and I knew I was charged with being thoughtful, honest, and sensitive with each word I chose.

We decided Leslie should spend a few nights a week at my place to participate in the writing process, but Leslie had other plans for his time at my place. One night I woke to sounds coming from my living room. I couldn't tell from the bedroom if the mumbling was coming from the television or a conversation Leslie may have been having with someone on the telephone.

As I approached the living room, the only light flickering was from the television. When I walked into the living room, Leslie and a stranger were wrapped in my down comforter on the living room floor. I couldn't see either of their faces, just movement under the comforter.

"What are you doing?" I asked.

Leslie threw the covers back.

"Who is this?" I asked.

173

"A friend. We're just watching a little TV," he said.

"He has to go."

Leslie was getting too comfortable at my place. He got in the practice of helping himself to my clothes when I wasn't home, and as fast as I brought groceries in the house he was eating them up and not contributing. Remember, I was unemployed, so I couldn't afford to feed his grown ass.

Leslie became the topic of many of my conversations with the Hettabrinks. With them, I was able to vent my frustration with putting up the show and his brief stay with me. There were a slew of things to do before the show opened and Leslie seemed unphased by it. The script was incomplete, we needed a web page and flyers designed, and most importantly we still hadn't garnered any funding. Leslie only seemed concerned with gallivanting around the city dressed like he was still in his twenties for the sake of getting a nut. The consensus of the Hettabrinks was that he was juvenile and had no sense of how to take anything seriously. Without a doubt, if no one else showed up in the audience for the play when it opened the Hettabrinks would to shield me from any embarrassment.

I wrote a proposal, with help from one of the board members, to solicit funding for the show. I sent proposals to pharmaceutical companies that manufactured HIV drugs, as well as small businesses and HIV/AIDS organizations.

The first wave of support received was in kind. An Atlanta based non-profit organization covered the cost of postage so the proposals could be mailed. The Atlanta Gay & Lesbian Center donated the rehearsal space, and Glaxo Smith Kline covered the costs for a staged reading at Park Tavern. Agouron pharmaceuticals and Bristol Myers Squibb were the only companies to donate money. I faced the harsh reality that HIV drug companies weren't in the business of supporting projects that spoke of prevention because they make money in caring for those infected by manufacturing the drugs.

Because I grew up in the *Support Black Business* era, I assumed Black business owners would be first to jump onboard to support the play. I personally targeted Black owned businesses, hoping for sponsorship since my intent was to bring awareness to HIV in the Black community. Sadly, the first wave of monetary support came from White business owners, and the proposal clearly stated the show was geared to bringing awareness to HIV/AIDS in the African-American community.

Once money began trickling in, I secured the 14th Street Playhouse with a deposit, and I began paying stipends to the cast we assembled. The leftover money was used to pay the utilities that Leslie and I ran up at my apartment.

One of the board members gave us use of his cabin in Elijay, GA, for a mountain getaway for the cast. We took the cast for the weekend to bond before rehearsals because we thought it was important for the actors to get an understanding of the characters they were playing.

Leslie and I were optimistic that more funding would come in to fund the project and some of our living expenses; thus, we began looking for two-bedroom apartments in the city to live and work from.

We decided on a new complex that was still under construction, but his stunts continued so I backed out of the plan. Leslie used our growing popularity as a tool to have sex. We made a promotion schedule listing days and times we would go out to the clubs to promote the play because we couldn't afford a street team to do it for us. Instead of passing out flyers, Leslie gave out his number to pick up dates.

I called a meeting with the team we assembled to help with financial decisions for the show. I shared with them what was happening and made it clear I was no longer interested in living with him. Leslie sat listening, unable to deny the truth.

"We can't live together. He's meeting people on the number line and bringing them to my house. If he's doing it at my place, I know he'll do it if his name is on the lease."

"So, where will you live? Isn't your lease up?" one of the board members asked.

"I'm still gonna move to the new place. It'll be a one bedroom, not a two."

There was movement in the room. They were visibly uncomfortable with what I said. All at once they exchanged glances with one another.

"Well, that's not what we agreed to. That money's not to secure a place to pay your rent."

"There would be no script or proposal to discuss had I not written them. And the business account, holding the money, belongs to me. I'm not asking for permission to move. I'm telling you that's what I'm doing."

Again, there were looks across the room, but this time no one spoke. Clearly, they had forgotten I was the only one with access to the script.

"Well, how much is the rent?"

"Nine hundred."

"That's just too much to pay for rent."

"But, it wasn't a problem to pay two thousand a month when we were gonna be roommates," I said.

I realized it wasn't such a good idea to form a team comprised of Leslie's friends because naturally they would side with him. But, it didn't matter what they decided because I owned Impeccable Works, the publishing company, and I retained all of the records pertaining to the show, including the contract with the theater. I was simply making an attempt to be diplomatic.

Eventually, they saw things my way. The day I moved in I ran into Leslie's friend Cris, a hairstylist at an upscale salon that catered to the players of Atlanta's flourishing entertainment industry.

I met her at the salon with Leslie when we started promoting the play. Cris moved into the same complex a few weeks before.

I was taking a load of clothes up to my apartment when she spotted me in passing.

"Hey, you moving in?" she shouted from her white Benz.

Her hair was cut in a short bob with Chinese bangs. She was a typical DC girl, but refined. She was always stylish and made no exception when she went to work at the salon. Cris was glammed every day dressed, in high-end designer labels like Badgley Mischka or Christian Louboutin to cut, color, and curl hair.

"Hey, yea. You live here?" I asked.

"Yea, I just moved in a few weeks ago. I live in that building right there," she said pointing to the back of the complex. "You need some help?"

"Yea!"

Cris followed me to my old apartment, which was on the same street and less than five-minutes away. She grabbed some trash bags and sliced them open to lay a rack of clothes inside them with the hangers still in the clothes. She tied the ends of the bags and together we moved the clothes in one trip.

"Cause you'll be all day carrying a few hangers at a time," she said. "This way they can go from the car right to your closet and already on the hanger."

Because my apartment was at the front of the complex, Cris made a habit of stopping by on her way out or back in. Usually, she had a bottle of champagne or wine for us to enjoy under the moon by the pool.

Cris was accustomed to living the good life. She was engaged to Mike Tyson for a period of time and eventually married a professional basketball player who played overseas, but they divorced before she and I met. Cris wanted to find love again, and that was what we talked most about. The one thing we had in common was men who failed to love us the way we needed to be loved—unconditionally.

To Leslie's credit, he was instrumental and most effective with fundraising, but he was not a writer by any means. His contacts in the hair industry came through with funding that allowed us to pay the balance on the 14th Street Playhouse, secure insurance on the venue, and the sound and light technician fees.

I was shy when it came to public speaking, so I wasn't vocal at our fundraisers. Before the show was casted, we held readings. We invited people we knew and assigned each of them to a character to read so we could hear the lines out loud to identify what worked and what didn't. And it was also a way to determine what else needed to be said in the script. At each of the readings I allowed Leslie to do most of the talking and the same was true for our radio interviews.

At the radio interviews, he classified himself as a storyteller because he couldn't publicly claim to be doing any writing. Several of the cast members occasionally asked why I allowed Leslie to control things because they knew he wasn't writing any of the script.

"We know he ain't writing none of this script. His ass can barely read it!" one of the cast members said. "When are we gonna get the rest of the script?"

"I don't know. It hasn't come to me yet."

For months we ran the same scenes. I didn't finish writing the script until a week before the show opened, which meant the cast had to cram the lines, but they were excited to get the ending.

"Ooooh, you had *wrote* the shit outta this baby!"

Leslie was within earshot and left rehearsal early that night.

One of the actors was Tyler Perry's personal trainer at the time. He told Tyler about the play, and the subject matter. Tyler in turn told him he would come to a rehearsal. I didn't believe it until Tyler showed up in a white Phantom.

Tyler and I were attending New Beginning Full Gospel Baptist church when I began writing the script and soliciting funding for the show, but I never approached him. I didn't feel it was appropriate to do so at church, and I didn't believe he would support this kind of show. Not to mention, I hadn't finished writing the script when I ran into him. The coincidence of one of the actors training him was proof positive that what's meant to be, will be.

When Tyler arrived at the rehearsal, we were preparing to go home. He came dressed casually in a t-shirt, a pair of nylon sweatpants, and some athletic flip-flops.

"What's the show about?" he asked.

I rambled off the details of the show with a full description of each of the characters.

"Wow, you're covering some really heavy stuff. I hope you do it justice. When is the show?"

"Labor Day weekend."

Leslie and I decided on Labor Day weekend because Atlanta hosts gay pride weekend. We figured if we got the support of In The Life Atlanta, the gay pride planning committee, we would have a trapped audience attending.

"If I'm in town when you do your show I'll come," he said.

With the strain from the things that happened when Leslie moved into my place, and the feelings I had of doing most of the work meant we were barely talking to one another when the cast and crew loaded into 14th Street Playhouse. Several of the cast members questioned why I kept him around. Sure, I had written the play alone, but I wasn't sure I could handle all of the logistics involved. My confidence hadn't quite caught up with my talent, so I thought I needed Leslie.

Two days before opening night, the lighting tech asked Leslie to call the show which requires one to know lighting and sound cues in technical terms so the effects happen when and where they need to. Tension on the set was mounting because we were days away from our debut and the cast was still learning lines, trying to remember the blocking, and I was still writing music.

Leslie had boasted of an extensive theater background when we started, but when *his* moment arrived he was unable to do it.

181

Instead of admitting he didn't know how to call the show, he told me to.

"Craig, they need you to call the show."

"I don't know how to call the show."

"You have to call the show."

"You call it. I don't know how to do that."

"Craig, get up there and call the damn show!"

"What the fuck did I just tell you? I don't know how to call no fucking show!" I yelled.

The cast dispersed from the stage grabbing all their belongings, as I got closer to Leslie.

"I will fuck you up!" I yelled.

"Child, let's go. I could've stayed at choir rehearsal if I knew it was gonna be all this," someone from the cast mumbled.

A guy that I was dating pulled me downstairs and someone else kept Leslie in the control room. Rehearsal was officially over with two hours left for that night and two days before curtain call.

Leslie had already bumped heads with several of the cast members and it was finally our turn. It seemed everything was falling apart because everything that could go wrong went wrong.

I was left with no choice but to call Percy to assist with calling the show. I had dismissed Percy from the production weeks after production started. We found out Percy was a recovering drug addict and had relapsed during production. There was no room for his antics after he got drunk at one of our production meetings, and Leslie and I deemed it necessary for him to focus on his recovery.

"Percy, Leslie and I just got into it. I don't know how to call the show. Can you come to rehearsal tomorrow?"

My nerves were shot. I couldn't stop shaking after my argument with Leslie.

"Yea baby, I'll be there. What time is rehearsal tomorrow?"

"Six. I really appreciate you doing this," I said.

"No problem, baby. I'll see you tomorrow. Go in a good way."

I was glad I hadn't been insensitive to Percy's addiction when I let him go. This would've been the perfect opportunity for him to leave me in a jam, but he didn't. Percy showed up to rehearsal the next day as did Leslie with a messenger bag slung over his shoulder. He was still mad though, he tried to appear unbothered. He was forcing laughter with cast members he had previous run-ins with because he knew it was now *us* against him.

*****

Tyler's assistant called me the day of the last show requesting tickets for the evening show.

"Can I get six tickets for Tyler?"

"Sure, they're $30 each."

"Oh, you don't have comp tickets you can leave at the door?"

"No, the show is selling out. You'll have to pay for them."

"How much are the tickets again?"

"Thirty dollars."

The Hettabrinks hadn't even asked for free tickets, and they were all there to support me opening night. I couldn't fathom giving away tickets to a millionaire.

"Ok, I'll pick them up at the theater," he said.

When I arrived at the theater, the lobby was full of people, including Tyler and Saleem. I didn't know if I was more excited that Tyler was going to be in the audience or that Saleem would get to see the show.

After the show, we received a rousing standing ovation. Leslie and I went backstage and stood outside the dressing rooms preparing to go to the lobby for a meet and greet when Tyler came backstage.

"I wanna help. I wanna give you $1,000 because I know what it's like to do your first show and I'm sure you're in debt," he said.

Leslie and I looked at each other then back at Tyler. Leslie knew his time to be the spokesperson for *A Day in the Life* was over.

"Ok," I said.

What Tyler didn't know was this was our second show that sold out, so there wasn't any debt. Nevertheless, I wasn't about to turn down the money. More importantly, I wanted a meeting with him.

"The show was great," he continued.

"Thank you." I smiled.

"Call me tomorrow. You can come to the house to get the money. Make sure you call early because I'm leaving town tomorrow evening."

"Ok, I will," I said.

Leslie and I hadn't mended wounds from our near fight or from the board meeting fiasco, so he knew not to ask to take the trip to Tyler's house with me.

The next afternoon, I called Tyler's assistant for directions. Tyler lived in Fairburn, GA, about 45 minutes outside Atlanta. I noticed the house was still under construction when I arrived. There was a dirt plot in the front of the house where the fountain would be installed. On the backside there were plots for the swimming pool and tennis court that were to be completed also. Tyler's assistant met me at the cul de sac.

"Did you have trouble finding it?"

"No, the directions were perfect."

As we approached the staircase Tyler appeared.

"Come on in," he said.

The house looked like a museum from the outside.

"I apologize for it being so hot in here. I didn't have on the air on this side of the house. I've been on the other side."

The house was massive, so I understood the need for multiple air conditioning units. It wasn't completely furnished, but the woodwork was incredible. The architects used wood and metal in ways I had never seen before to construct the spiral staircase that led upstairs to a catwalk that overlooked the living area. Below was a sunken living room with columns and floor to ceiling windows. Tyler said he designed the house himself. The completed home was featured years later in his first motion picture *Diary of a Mad Black Woman.*

"Here's the money as promised," he said leading me into his office.

Tyler handed me ten $100 bills.

"Thank you," I said smiling uncontrollably.

"Have a seat. You mind if I give you a little constructive criticism?"

"No, not at all."

I figured his feedback wouldn't be too harsh since he invited me to his home and gave me a thousand dollars.

"I thought about the show last night, and this morning when I woke up. I couldn't get it outta my mind."

I had never seen a Tyler Perry show, but I knew this was a huge compliment despite what critics said about the caliber of his work.

"I don't know how you did it. I couldn't get 30 people in that theater the entire weekend when I did my first show there."

Tyler was genuinely impressed with the show.

"I don't know how you wrote some of what you wrote. The writing was so strong that your actors were unable to deliver some of the lines because they aren't professionals, but if you cast that show with professional actors, and I know you didn't have the budget, the show could be really amazing. On a scale from one to ten, it was a ten," Tyler said.

I couldn't believe he was speaking so highly about something I had written, and had only produced once. There were so many things I wanted to improve on and yet he thought the show was brilliant.

"Wow, thank you," I said.

"There were a few wrinkles that need to be ironed out. The first half was a lot longer than the second. You could move some of the scenes to the second act," he said.

"Ok, anything else?" I asked.

"I didn't like the guy who played the therapist, but that 'Tj' was something," he added. "You had a lot of actors. How many actors did you have?"

"There were 13 actors, " I said.

"Some of them could've played double parts. When you start to travel the show, you wanna cut down on your travel expenses."

"Ok, I can see that."

"But other than that, it was brilliant."

"Would you put me in touch with a promoter?"

He looked away in thought.

"Yea, I can do that. I'll put you in contact with a guy named Wayman Thompson."

Tyler gave me a tour of the house and I left because it appeared from his half-packed Louis Vuitton luggage that he still had some packing to do for his evening flight.

There was an eviction notice on my front door two months after the meeting with Tyler. I was attempting to put together a budget to tour *A Day in the Life.* There were so many factors to consider for the budget—which cities were ideal, venues and transportation. I couldn't figure out where to start to prep the show for a tour, so I called Tyler for advice.

"I'm trying to figure out which cities to hit first and how to get the cast there," I said.

"I don't play small venues so I wouldn't know," he said.

I looked at the phone because this didn't sound like the same person that was previously willing to offer his help.

"Ok, can you tell me what transportation company to use or how to go about getting a deal for the accommodations?"

"You just get them there any way you can. Even if you have to rent cars or vans just get them there."

He sensed my aggravation with his disposition.

"What? What are you thinking?" he quizzed.

"I'm thinking you haven't helped me. I'm thinking you're telling me what I already know. I'm calling because you've been in my position, so I was hoping you could help me navigate around some of the pitfalls you may have encountered along the way."

"I don't think a promoter would pick up your show. It's too controversial. I believe God put me here to make people laugh," he said.

"Tyler, when I was writing my show, you and I attended the same church. I never stopped you to ask for help because I thought it was inappropriate to do so at church, and I knew you wouldn't help because your primary audience is Black church women. I thought you'd be too afraid to touch my show, but you found out about my show and came to the rehearsal. And when the show went up, you came back stage on your own volition and volunteered your help. Why wouldn't you want others to get from my show what you obviously got from it?"

Tyler debated that there is so much misery and sadness in the gay community that it couldn't be right as he witnessed the unhappiness on the faces of many gay men. I knew the discontent he spoke of all too well because I was discouraged by the culture at times. Many of the gay people I came across deemed short-lived relationships as proof that it's wrong to be gay. Still, I contended it was the stress placed on a community of people by the community at large that caused the greatest part of the discontentment felt by many of us.

This was supposed to be a discussion of how to get my show on tour, but we were debating whether it was right or wrong to be gay.

"I think God is processing you," he said.

"Tyler, I've already been processed! I have an eviction notice on my door. I have no idea how I'm gonna pay my rent next month," I said.

"Let me read something to you."

"What do you want to read to me?" I asked sarcastically.

"Hold on. Let me find it."

Tyler was celebrating ten years in the business and wanted to read a passage from his book. The part he read described how he moved to Atlanta with $12,000 and lost it all by investing in his first show that flopped. He continued to read to the point in the story he was living in a shelter when his first show sold out.

"Tyler, that's where I am now."

"You're not gonna be homeless. You're gonna make it. God is gonna use you in ways you can't even imagine right now. I can see so much of myself in you. The only difference is I didn't have someone in my position I could call, but you do. Call me whenever you need to talk."

I didn't respond.

"I know you wanna cuss me out," he said with laughter in his voice.

"No, I don't wanna cuss you out," I said.

The truth, Tyler knocked the wind out of me in one statement, "I don't think a promoter would pick up your show." I was reminded why I preferred playing touch football to tackle as a kid. When I was a teenager I was hit in a game of football. I couldn't feel anything. I lay on the grass gasping for air with my friends arguing overhead with the guy on the opposing team responsible for the blow. That day on the field my pride was bruised and the same was true after my conversation with Tyler. A piece of my dream crumbled on that call. In so many words, he was telling me my show couldn't go any further than a 200-seat theater in Atlanta.

"You can call me whenever you need to talk," he said.

I contacted Tyler's assistant to get tickets for his shows in Atlanta, but secretly I was hoping Tyler would take me under his wings, and show me the ropes. I stopped calling for free tickets when I saw he wasn't going to help me reach my dream of producing my show on a national stage.

I didn't end up getting evicted from my apartment because my mother deposited enough money in my account to cover the rent and the late fees assessed. That month was the first of a series she would deposit money into my account and there was no proof that things would turn around for me.

I was in a woe is me, feel sorry for myself kind of space. I had done the work. I needed a boost. I was angry with Tyler for not connecting me to a promoter. I even asked if he would contract me as a writer on some of his projects and his answer was a flat out no. I saw Tyler as my only option, but it wasn't his responsibility to help me, even if he thought I was talented and my show was brilliant. *A Day in the Life* was my vision and I couldn't be upset because he wouldn't buy into my cause, but it took years for me to release the bitterness I harbored.

LOVE IS IN THE AIR

Elden and Julian went to a birthday dinner at Après Diem while I was in New York for the weekend attending an HIV/AIDS workshop with a small non-profit I was working for. When I returned, Elden bloviated about a guy named Carrington who was also at the dinner. Elden mentioned that he was a dentist and supposedly so cute. One of the reasons our friendship worked was because we all had different tastes, and Elden's was always questionable. His definition of cute wasn't mine. Julian and I often teased Elden because he seemed to only date guys with certain job titles or status. He hated that we called him a resume dater.

"Did you get his number," I asked casually.

"No, he has a boyfriend," Elden replied.

We were like brothers, and that was true for all the Hettabrinks, but more times than not someone was saying, *"where's your sister?", "that's my sister, child!"* or *"have you talked to your sister today?"*

Somewhere along the way Elden, Julian and I were pegged *The Angels*—Charlie's Angels. Julian programmed the theme song for *Charlie's Angels* as his ringtone for Elden and me when we called.

We were so different from the typical gay guys we knew. Not better, just different. We weren't into threesomes, sex parties, drugs or any of the other vices that so many find themselves caught in. We wanted long-term, monogamous relationships, and until we found that we enjoyed our friendship with one another.

*****

The one-year anniversary of *A Day in the Life* was approaching fast. I had begun some initial planning for the show, but was feeling a bit reticent because the second production was a complete flop.

Leslie and I rushed to do the show two months after the debut. The 1000-seat venue was almost empty. I hadn't quite gotten over the embarrassment and humiliation of coming onto a stage with only a handful of people in the audience. And even worse, I didn't have the money to pay the cast that time. My instincts told me not to produce the show so soon, but I ignored it and moved forward because I was stopped by so many who said they heard about the show, but missed it because they were out of town for the holiday weekend. We decided on a three-day run during the week of Thanksgiving, and the show tanked. The promoter lost money, as did my mother who invested the second time around.

Again, I didn't feel the timing of an anniversary show was right, and Leslie and I weren't as close as we once were. My focus had become a line of greeting cards I was busy writing. Nevertheless, I proceeded with plans to do the play.

Julian, Elden and I went to a Pisces party given by some of Julian's friends and a few other Pisceans. On the way to the party I asked Julian why he kept his other friends from us. He spoke of other friends, but we hadn't met any of them.

"Are any of them decent?" I drilled.

"Girl, what do you mean? I'm not keeping anything from anybody," he lashed back.

"He's so secretive," Elden chimed in.

"He still ain't answered my damn question," I said.

"Well, y'all bitches will meet them tonight. How's that?" he said smugly.

We finally arrived at the party in Buford, GA. Julian knocked on the door, and much to Elden's surprise Carrington opened the door. He was ok. I couldn't see what impressed Elden so much. Julian re-introduced Elden before introducing me. The homeowner was a friend of Carrington's, which explained why he opened the door.

It was a beautiful home with pea soup-green walls and contemporary furniture. Seemed every party I went to at someone's place at that time boasted the same paint colors—pea soup-green and crimson. Everything about the home was great, except the location. It was too far outside the city. As we moved through the party towards the bar, Elden and I realized we didn't know any of the people there so we kept to ourselves.

Two months later, Julian and I went to a fiesta style party one weekend Elden went home to Texas. The party was Mexican inspired from the décor to the food, and the cocktail of the hour was margaritas. We sipped margaritas and ate taquitos, burritos, and tacos drizzled with salsa and guacamole.

I was dressed in true Maryland/DC style—a pair of butter Timberland boots, blue jeans and a black cut off shirt, and corn-rows.

"Carrington's here," Julian said as we pulled up.

"How do you know?"

"That's his car," he said pointing to a Silver Mercedes Benz CLK parked in the driveway.

There were people out on the deck. I recognized a few faces, but I didn't know anyone, as we looked for the host to give him the bottle of tequila we brought. Julian mingled with some people he knew and I ventured out back to the deck after I grabbed a margarita.

It was almost summer, and I had a play to begin production on. I was thinking of things I needed to do in the coming weeks. I could see the kitchen from where I was standing. I noticed Carrington standing beside Julian. When he walked away I went back in to meet Julian.

"Carrington just asked me to introduce him to you," Julian said.

"Huh? We've met before."

"Child, good luck!"

"Maybe, he didn't recognize me from the last party because I was wearing that hat," I said. "That's why he didn't speak when we came in. He didn't know who I was."

"Well girl, I told him, 'that's Craig. Introduce yourself.'"

Carrington walked over to me.

"Wait five minutes and meet me downstairs," he whispered.

I didn't know if it was a joke or if he was serious. I went downstairs, but there were so many people that we ended back upstairs in the kitchen. Obviously, Carrington wanted to speak to me privately.

"I'm Carrington."

He was halfway smiling and biting his lip nervously.

"Yea, I know." I smiled. "We met at the Pisces party a couple months ago."

"You were there?"

"Yea, I had on a hat so you may not recognize me."

He was at the fiesta party with his best friend who hosted the Pisces party. Carrington asked if I wanted to follow him to another party when we left.

"I rode with Julian. It's up to him."

He rushed over to ask Julian, and he agreed so we trailed Carrington and his friend to the party. Carrington and I talked on the phone the entire way. There were many things I already knew about him because Julian had told me. I knew he had throngs of guys after him because he was young and accomplished. He had his own dental practice, a home in the suburbs, and was in the process of closing on a condo in Midtown at the Metropolis building. Carrington also had a pattern of attracting men who took advantage of his generosity—including friends.

His best friend drove his car to the next party because Carrington was tipsy. When we arrived at the second party, he walked over to me and kissed me as soon as I got out of Julian's car.

"Carrington, get off that boy!" his friend yelled.

We walked up to the house and somehow ended up kissing in one of the bedrooms while the party continued just outside the bedroom door. We fell on the bed, and his friend came to break us up and escorted us out of the room.

I don't know if the kissed changed the way I saw him, but I was suddenly interested. I told Julian when we left the party he would have to be my witness that Carrington pursued me if Elden ended up feeling some kind of way about it. We weren't about to fall out over a date.

I invited Carrington over for dinner the following week and he introduced me to jazz soul singer Lizz Wright. He played "Open Your Eyes, You Can Fly" from her first album, *Salt.* I loved her voice immediately. It sounded like I imagined warm velvet would feel—smooth and comfortable.

Our conversation had a natural flow to it. We just seemed to click. We had more in common than I thought and we viewed relationships in the same way. We both wanted to find the one that would last.

When he got ready to leave, he leaned in for a kiss, but I back away.

"Nah, maybe on the next date," I said.

"Boy, stop playing and give me a kiss. We've already kissed," he said.

I leaned in and kissed him.

"Ok, I gotta go. It's a school night," he said.

I was anxious to see Carrington again, but didn't want to look too interested too soon because he still had a reputation of leading the boys on and dropping them.

I found out through one of our conversations that he was going to a party at a new spot downtown called Endenu. I called Elden and Julian on three-way.

"We gotta go to this party at Endenu," I said.

"What party?" Elden asked.

"It's Saturday. Call Julian on three-way," I said.

For Elden, it was a no-brainer because he lived across the street from the venue, and I knew Julian would take the drive from Smyrna if we were both going.

"Miss Julian, what you doing?" I said.

"Nothing you bitch. What you want?" he said.

"We going to Endenu Saturday," I said.

"That's what the fuck you called me to say? Child, get off my phone."

We made plans to meet at Elden's before the party.

I saw Carrington drive by as we walked up to the club. He obviously saw me too because he tooted his horn. We were inside by the time Carrington parked and made his way inside. He was with his best friend as always, but he came right over to me.

"What's up man?" he said.

"What's going on?" I said.

"What's up Julian, Elden?" he said.

Julian was also one of Carrington's patients.

"Dr. Woods," Julian said.

"What you drinking?" he asked.

"Rum and Coke, thanks."

Julian and Elden wanted to mingle while I waited for Carrington to return from the bar.

"Girl, we'll be back," Julian said.

I took a seat at one of the tables near the entrance.

Carrington returned with our drinks and sat down beside me.

"How's your weekend going?" I asked.

"It's going good. I worked today. I work one Saturday out of the month. How 'bout yours?" he asked.

"Pretty good. I can't complain," I said.

"I really enjoyed dinner with you the other night. I learned a lot about you," he said.

"Oh yea?" I questioned.

"Mmm hmm," he replied.

"What did you learn about me?" I asked.

"That you have a good heart," he said.

I smiled and looked towards the back of the club.

"I can't wait to do it again. Next time it'll be breakfast," he said with a devilish grin.

"I'm not spending the night with you," I advised.

"Not like that. I'll cook for you. You can come over one morning," he explained.

"Ok, just let me know when," I said.

"What about Monday, since it's Memorial Day? I'm off," he suggested.

"That works," I said.

He went through the motions of planning a menu to make sure he prepared things I liked, and I told him I would call him on Monday for directions to his house.

I got up to look for Julian and Elden. As I passed the dance floor I heard a song I hadn't heard before. The instruments sounded like they were recorded live. It was definitely an R&B track, but it had a different feel. It was a mixture of horns, drums and high hats when the base line dropped. It was "Crazy in Love." Beyonce's first solo cd was about to drop. The crowd was going crazy, so the dj played the track several times that night and we were on the floor each time it played.

On Monday, I called Carrington's home number, but I got his voicemail so I left a message. Normally, I would call the cell first, but I figured since we were having breakfast at his house I would call there. I tried his cell. Again, there was no answer and I left another message.

I never heard back from him. Tuesday, I deleted Carrington's number from my cell. I have a rule, delete the number before you abuse the number. Carrington didn't call Tuesday and I didn't hear from him Wednesday. He called Thursday evening.

I saw his number flashing on my cell phone. Although I deleted the number, I knew it when I saw it even though I hadn't committed it to memory. I was running late for a panel discussion with AIDS Research Consortium of Atlanta (ARCA), but I picked up anyway.

"Hello."

"Hey man," he said casually like he hadn't stood me up three days earlier.

"Who is this?" I asked like I was clueless.

"This is Carrington," he said.

"Oh, you said *'hey'* like I've talked to you," I snapped.

Before he could answer I cut him off.

"I'm on my way to a meeting, so I need to call you back."

"Oh...ok. Call me back."

I really wanted to talk to him and I was nervous that when I called back he may not answer, but I was willing to chance it. He stood me up and he needed to know I wasn't going to be available when he felt like being bothered. I didn't care what his reason was for standing me up.

I called him two hours later. When he answered he made an attempt to have general conversation without addressing the date he missed.

"I have to tell you something before we go any further. This isn't about us not having breakfast because I understand things come up. This is about you not extending the courtesy to me that I would've extended to you. If you weren't able to have breakfast you should've called. There really is no excuse for you not calling because even if something happened to your cell phone you could've reached me because we have mutual friends. I'm telling you this because I don't want to teach you, by not saying anything, that you can pull this with me again," I said.

"You're right. I'm sorry. I had a hangover Monday because we went to the Palace Sunday night. And on Tuesday, I was backed up at work because the office was closed Monday for the holiday, and I work late the first Wednesday of every month, so when I got home that night I had a lot of charts to finish writing up so I called you tonight," he explained.

"The president of the United States had time to run the country, be married to Hillary and have an affair with Monica Lewinsky. If he had time to do all that, you had time to call or text me. You're not that busy," I stated.

"It won't happen again," he said.

We chatted for a bit, but didn't stay on the phone long because it was late when I called him back and his office opened at 7 a.m.

"Alright man. I need to get ready for bed. Hit me up tomorrow," he said.

"Hold on, I need to save your number again."

"You deleted my number?"

"Yea, I did. I didn't plan to use it again."

"Damn."

"Ok, I got it."

I resaved his number, but I refused to initiate future phone calls or plans until he proved he was not playing games. I only called him if I was returning his call. If we were going to spend time together it would be at his suggestion, not mine.

I intentionally missed some of his phone calls so he'd get my voicemail and hopefully begin to step up his efforts. I didn't want to be too available, and when I did pick up I always got off the phone first. I'd make up some reason to get off the line before he could say he needed to go. Hell, I was busy too and if I wasn't, I pretended to be.

Soon, he was calling me a second or third time before I had a chance to return one of his phone calls. I've never been one to play games, but I know how the game is played. When he stood me up, the rules changed for me. I needed to know he was really interested.

We talked on the phone a few times a week and always had great conversations, but he wouldn't suggest getting together and there were days I wanted him to call that he didn't, but I stood my ground. I knew I had his attention when he called from his office in between patients.

Once we were talking and seeing each other every day, I cut off the other guys I was dating casually. I was dating five others, but I was only having sex with one of them. The other four were simply to occupy my time when I wasn't working on funding for the play.

Carrington asked if we could date exclusively a few months after we started dating seriously. Although I wasn't seeing anyone else, I was reluctant to commit because I view relationships as marriage. It's the closest thing we had to marriage and I wanted to take the commitment seriously. I needed to know we would both fight when things became rough and we wouldn't walk away because of simple things. I was also reluctant because I was in quite the precarious financial position at the time with no signs of coming out of it anytime soon.

There were times I completely shut down and closed Carrington out because I was consumed with money matters. Carrington showed up at my place one night unannounced because he couldn't reach me. I had turned the ringers off on my home phone and shut my cell phone off to be alone. I heard a knock on my door in the middle of the night. I got out of bed and looked out the peephole. Carrington was outside my door.

"I couldn't sleep. My stomach kept turning because I couldn't reach you," he said.

He was standing with worry on his face and a black leather duffel bag.

"I have a lot on my mind. I needed some time to think," I explained.

I stepped to the side so he could come into the apartment. I couldn't bring myself to tell him that I was behind on all of my bills and didn't have the rest of the money to stage the show. He climbed in bed with me and we fell asleep.

Very few of the efforts Leslie and I put forth for the play panned out. Media outlets that supported and promoted the show previously weren't interested in covering the play. The only person who knew my financial difficulties in great detail was Elden. His interior design business was bourgeoning and he felt comfortable approaching a few of his clients about running an ad in the playbill for *A Day in the Life.* He even asked Carrington to make a donation.

A few days before the deadline to pay the last installment on the venue Elden gave me a check for $1,500 to cover the outstanding balance.

"Carrington donated a thousand," he said.

I wasn't sure if I was moved most by Elden's thoughtfulness or Carrington's generosity, but I knew I was grateful for both of them.

Later that night, Carrington came over to stay the night. I sat in my living room watching him move around the apartment drying off after a shower. I remembered the chase before we started dating and how close we came to not happening because I deleted his number out of fear of getting caught up. I reflected on the night we had dinner at the Cheesecake Factory in Dunwoody when I finally agreed we could date exclusively. I pled my case one final time that I wasn't in the financial position to date anyone, and his words were simple and direct, "I have enough money for us."

He was drying his ears and singing some song I hadn't heard before.

"What?" he asked.

"Elden told me what you did," I said.

"What'd I do?" he asked with concern on his face.

Carrington was five years older than me, but he always looked like a little boy, especially when he was nervous about something.

"He told me that you gave money for the show. What made you do that?"

"I know it's important to you and I just thought I could help."

"No one's ever done anything like that for me before. I appreciate you doing that."

"You're welcome."

Carrington wouldn't be in town when the show opened because he and his best friend had already planned a trip to Brazil. That trip was the first of many to come that would prevent him from being around when I needed him.

RUNNING ON EMPTY

My third attempt to produce *A Day in the Life* was worse than the second. I was glad Carrington wasn't in town for the show. I was officially depressed. I was angry that I didn't get the same level of support from the local organizations and media outlets that helped with promotion previously, and with myself for not trusting my gut. I knew the timing was off.

I flashed back to my conversation with Tyler and got mad all over again. I was livid he hadn't called back with a change of heart. I blamed him for the show failing a second time and all of the financial setbacks I had. Furthermore, I held Tyler accountable for the rise in the HIV rate for Black women because AIDS wasn't the number one killer of Black women ages 29-34 when I first produced the show. All of which was ridiculous and unjustifiable, but I told myself we could've prevented some of the new HIV cases with *A Day in the Life*—Tyler's demographic was women.

To add insult to injury, one of the cast members sued me, but there was no money to pay him or anyone else. Leslie disappeared when the cast demanded their money, but as he put it, "that's not my responsibility."

I didn't want to tell Carrington how horrible things were, but I did and he was supportive. He never stopped believing that things would turn around for me, but I was beginning to.

Carrington wanted me to move in with him six months after we were together, but I thought it was too soon. I hadn't worked a job in years because I decided I was going to be an artist full time, and that decision made things more difficult for me than they had to be. It was one thing to shuffle and juggle my bills, but I couldn't move into his place and be unreliable from month to month.

"You could just move in with me and focus on writing. You don't have to pay anything. Just have your mom give you enough to buy food for yourself. I'll take care of the rest," he offered.

He knew my mom was financing my monthly expenses because once I trusted him, I told him. It was a truth I was ashamed to admit, but it was the reality. Moving in sounded like a novel idea, but I didn't want to be in a position of being asked to leave if things didn't work out with us, and I didn't want to move in because of circumstances. I wanted to move in because we were ready to graduate to the next level.

"I'll move in once we make it a year together," I said.

That spring, Carrington and I celebrated our one-year anniversary, and I moved into his eighteenth floor condominium at the Metropolis condominiums on Peachtree Street. I wasn't in a position to pay the last month of rent at my 26th Street apartment, so I abandoned it. He and I decided that I would only move in for six months to see how things worked out.

The unit had views of Piedmont Park, downtown, Buckhead and as far East as Stone Mountain. I helped Carrington choose the furniture and paint the walls, but I still felt displaced. Perhaps it was because I parked in a visitor parking space every day because Carrington was only assigned a single space. It wasn't easy coming *home* every day to a place that was completely furnished with things that didn't belong to me, and it didn't help that his custom closet system didn't offer room for the few pieces of clothing I had left that I hadn't sold to pay bills. My things were folded in a corner in *our* bedroom. I also felt displaced because I had things at Cris' and Carrington's. It was a nightmare trying to find things at the condo that I had left at her place and vice versa.

We spent many afternoons having brunch at The Flying Biscuit because it was walking distance from the condo, and by night we were dining out around town and attending plays at the Alliance Theater—Carrington purchased season passes.

We stood in the lobby one night waiting for the house to open and I overheard someone whisper, "that's the guy that wrote the A Day in the Life play." I pretended not to hear him because it was a painful reminder to me that I wasn't doing anything with the show. God had given me a vision, but my hands were tied.

I was stopped at the most inopportune times by people leaving the grocery store or at the gym, and they all wanted to know what was going on with the show. In some instances they came up to me singing the songs from the show. I thought it was God reminding me not to walk away from it, but it seemed more like a carrot being dangled in front of me. I gave a generic answer, "I'm working on funding to tour," but that was just something to say because I didn't want people to think I had given up.

I was drowning with Carrington and he didn't seem to take notice. He was too busy traveling and buying things for himself to cover up the wrong in his life. His business partner was behind in her portion of the bills.

Carrington did his best to help in the way he knew, but that meant dinner and trips. My career was at a standstill. I had a show that had now flopped twice in a row and a stack of greeting card ideas, but no money to print them.

Carrington was standing on a small ladder in the tub repainting the wall around the shower. This was the second color he was trying because he didn't like the first color we used.

"You know what you should do?" he said.

"What?" I asked.

"You should do a greeting card party," he suggested.

"What do you mean?" I asked.

"You know, like a tupperware party except you'll have your cards for sale. Choose the best ones and print a few of each. We can rent the clubhouse downstairs and invite people to come," he explained as dipped the paintbrush back into the bucket.

I was amazed at his generosity, but not surprised because he searched online for a class for me to take that taught me how to write a business plan. It was his idea and he paid for it. Carrington did this at his own will because he thought I would be in a better position to get my business off the ground. I felt foolish for thinking he was unconcerned. His actions were completely selfless and I loved him more because of it.

"How many will we print? I need a budget," I said.

"Ok, let me know how much it'll cost to print ten of ten different cards," he said.

No one had ever loved me in a relationship the way Carrington loved me. At times I didn't know how to receive it because it felt foreign and I didn't recognize myself in that relationship. My emotions were running high because I was in love. I loved Saleem, but I was in love with Carrington. I braced myself for the day it would end—the day things would start to fall apart.

I managed to set up a meeting in Dallas, TX, with Tyler Perry's promoter. Several months before, I was invited to see a play based on one of E. Lynn Harris' books at the Atlanta Civic Center. I met Al Wash in the lobby during intermission chatting with someone I knew. I overheard him giving his cell number, so I memorized it and locked it in my phone. After a few months of relentless calling and leaving messages, he agreed to meet with me. He was supposed to fly to Atlanta for a wedding, but the flu prevented him from flying so I flew to Dallas.

I was so broke that I flew one morning on skymiles and returned the same night. I had just enough money to rent a car and get lunch when I touched down.

Al and I sat in a conference room adorned with posters from all of Tyler's shows and the Tom Joyner cruises. I told him about the success I had with my show and told him how much more could be done with his resources.

"I don't know how to promote a gay play."

"You promote it the same way you promote any other play, but we also need to promote on the ground level. We can tie in the gay pride organizations around the country. Every major city has a pride. If we pay them something they'll help us promote in their market."

"How can you be sure?"

"I have contact with the president of the Black gay pride planning committee. All of the prides are under this one umbrella."

"Ok, if you can get him to agree to help me, I'll do it."

A week after my meeting with Al we had a conference call with the pride federation president who agreed to assist us with promoting *A Day in the Life* nationally. One week from the conference call, Al and I were supposed to have a phone meeting to discuss the tour budget, but it never happened. I called for an entire year, but he never returned my calls.

My suspicions told me Tyler had something to do with it. I was still looking to blame him. I convinced myself that Al contacted Tyler to confirm that Tyler did in fact see my show, but I couldn't be sure. I knew something prevented Al from moving forward with *A Day in the Life.*

With hopes of a national tour down the drain I was forced to take a job at a phone and internet company. I resented having to take a job especially at a call center for little money. I resisted every step of the way. I thought the job was beneath me. After all, my name had been in lights. *What did I look like answering phones?*

I sank to a new level of depression.

The first trip Carrington and I took together was to New York. Carrington had a class to attend for his certification the weekend after Thanksgiving. He sent me an evite invitation asking if I would go with him. When I opened the email I was expecting an invitation for a movie date because he had sent those in the past.

He called those invitations "Date Night". In the "To" field he typed "My Baby" and it listed the movie, show time and the option for me to suggest an alternate time. This evite was different.

I was in the bedroom on the computer when I opened the invitation and he was sitting in the living room at the other computer. When I stepped out of the room to look down the hall he pretended not to notice me. I went back into the bedroom to send my reply.

"Yes, I will attend."

In the comments field I typed, "I would love to."

I walked into the living room and sat beside him on the couch and kissed his lips.

"I love you," I said.

"I love you more."

He often said he loved me more, but I didn't know if love could be quantified. I just knew it felt good hearing him say it.

Carrington and I invited six friends to our first Thanksgiving dinner together. He was excited that we shared the responsibility of cooking everything ourselves. His mom came over to eat with us before our friends came later that evening. Carrington's father died years before, and his mother's only request of her three children after he passed was to be together every major holiday.

After dinner with our friends we told everyone to take a to-go plate, but there was still a ton of food left that we needed to get rid of because we were leaving for New York.

"I guess we'll have to throw it away since we're leaving," Carrington said.

"Let's pack it up and take it to that homeless shelter," I suggested.

"What shelter?" he asked.

"It's right there at Peachtree and Pine. I take clothes there from time to time," I said.

We packed seven plates from the leftovers and took them to the shelter. When we pulled up to the men's shelter the car was surrounded by men who lived in the shelter. They knew we were there with a delivery. The swarm didn't alarm me because I had experienced it dropping off clothes. Carrington looked nervous.

"Pull over right here. I'll get out," I said.

I gave the plates to one of the employees who surfaced among the crowd of men. I jumped back in the car and we pulled off.

"That was really nice of you to think to do that," he said with a smile.

The next morning we were in New York staying in Times Square for the weekend.

Carrington never stopped showing me he valued me, and what we had together, but it was difficult for me to receive it because my career seemed to be going off track. His practice was flourishing and I was feeling stagnant professionally. I had eighteen overdraft fees in one month. I was tired of being in need. It was a place of dependency and I couldn't see my way out of such desperate times, so I couldn't thoroughly enjoy what Carrington and I had. I was miserable and I think subconsciously I was trying to make him feel my misery. I wanted someone's sympathy. My mother witnessed my mood swings.

"Are you sure you're not just a little jealous that things are going well for him and you're having a hard time right now?" she asked. "He can't stop living his life because yours isn't going the way you want it to."

But, I wasn't jealous. I was young and self-involved. I didn't think he understood what I was going through. I had flown to Dallas, to meet a promoter, with no money and Carrington never asked if I needed anything. Pride prevented me from asking him for anything, but I thought he should've asked if I had money. He systematically left town for vacations with friends without asking if I needed anything before he left, and I was often torn between decisions of getting a haircut or gas for the car.

Everything that could go wrong in my life was going wrong. My bank account was overdrawn $600, my grandmother was getting ill, and my car was totaled. My insurance company provided me with a rental car for thirty days, and as the last day to have the rental got closer I was in a rush to find something, anything.

After the deductible, I was left with $4,000 to buy another car. I was still consumed by image and led by ego. *"What kind of car was I going to buy for $4,000?"* God was stripping me of everything I *thought* I needed. This was the *process* Tyler spoke of years before, but I still hadn't gotten the lesson.

I saw a car online for sale by a private owner for $3,800, but I hadn't received the check from the insurance company. Carrington offered to loan me the money until I received the check. We picked up the car just before the rental was due back.

*****

My grandmother had always been strong and faithful even when there was no evidence she should be. A few months before she passed, I called her in tears. I told her I was unhappy with the direction my life had taken. I was pinned in by debt and I couldn't figure out how to get this writing thing to work.

"Keep praying. Only God can change it," she whispered

softly.

I sobbed and hung up the phone because I felt foolish whining about *things* when she had suffered more and still believed. She had recently undergone an operation that left her with one leg.

Mama and I spoke regularly when I was away at school. She often asked if I was still praying on my knees every night. I told her I was praying, but I didn't kneel down on my knees because the floors in my dorm were dirty. She lectured me on the importance of praying *on my knees*. She said it was a sign of respect to God for his grace and mercy. From that day forward I knelt down on my slippers since the floor was filthy. I was still saying my prayers, but didn't think God gave me credit for it. My life was spiraling out of control.

I thought about my grandmother's strength when my mother called to tell her I was gay. Mama didn't need time to adjust to the news. Her response to my mom was, "he's still your son. You can't worry about what people think. I'm still gonna love him."

When my grandmother passed I didn't have money to buy a plane ticket for the funeral, so my mother gave me the airfare to attend the funeral.

Carrington left town again with his friends in a moments notice, and I was looking for a reason to let go. The stress of the relationship was too much. I decided I would leave the relationship. It was clear that he was used to doing what he wanted when he wanted.

This time he and his friends took an impromptu trip to Miami. I was bothered that he consistently made plans to go out of town with his single friends. I never believed he was cheating, but I thought it was inconsiderate of him to make decisions that affected us without having a conversation with me. That's relationship 101. It would have been no different if I removed $5,000 from a joint account and told him after I spent the money. I mentally checked out of our relationship the same weekend he left for Miami.

That Saturday, I walked into Banana Republic at Lenox Mall and met someone else. I ran into two friends in the mall on my way into the store. The three of us walked in as he approached the front of the store. He was gorgeous. I made every attempt not to stare, but he was striking. I had been in this Banana Republic a thousand times to see Brent and had never seen him before. *He must be new.*

He looked like one of the few Black preppy male models in an Abercrombie and Fitch catalog. He was cocoa brown with silky fine hair that was cropped in a neat shadow fade. He was an inch taller than me but thinner. When I smiled he smiled back with a boyish grin. I knew he had to be in his mid to late twenties also. He was dressed in a navy blazer, a collared shirt and heather grey slacks.

"Hey, how you doing? Can I help you find something?" he asked.

218

"Can I see these in a ten," I said holding up a pair of sneakers.

"He is fine," I said when he turned to walk to the back of the store to retrieve the shoes.

"Remember, you're married," my friend reminded.

"I know. I can look."

The sales clerk returned with the sneakers and set them down on the bench for me to try on. I didn't need to buy anything, but I had to splurge this time.

"Where are you from?" I asked.

"Virginia," he said.

"Really? What part of Virginia? I went to Hampton," I said with a bright smile.

"Norfolk," he said smiling.

"What brought you to Atlanta?"

"I'm a theater major at Morehouse."

"I wrote and produced a play," I said.

"Really? What's the name of it?" he asked.

"A Day in the Life."

He squinted his eyes.

"I think I heard of it," he said.

"Yea, I moved here to write music and started writing greeting cards and plays," I said.

"I write music too," he said with laughter.

I still hadn't worked up the courage to ask him for his number. I was nervous because I knew I wouldn't be asking for his number to network. I left the store without asking for his number, but I did buy the sneakers.

My friends and I headed to the food court for lunch at California Pizza Kitchen. The restaurant is situated next to the escalators overlooking the food court below. After placing our orders, we sat talking when I noticed out of the corner of my eye a parade of people marching onto the escalator headed down to the food court. My eyes latched on to a single person amongst the crowd, bobbing and weaving through in a hurry. It was the sales clerk from Banana Republic. He was speed walking. He appeared to be looking for someone. He was looking up and down at the different levels of the mall, and over to the food court.

"He's looking for me!" I said.

"What? That boy ain't looking for you. He's probably on his fifteen minute break," my friend said.

"I'm telling you. He's looking for me. I'm going back to the store," I said.

After we ate I headed back upstairs to Banana Republic.

"Y'all wait here," I said before they could follow me inside the store.

He was standing in the front of the store looking out into the mall. He smiled when he saw me coming in.

"A little birdie told me you were looking for me," I said.

"Huh?"

"A little birdie told me you were looking for me."

"That sounds kinda cocky," he said.

"No, no, no. I wasn't trying to be cocky. My mom used to say that to me when I was a kid. Whenever I asked her how she knew something I knew I hadn't told her, she would say that," I explained.

"Oh ok."

"But were you looking for me? I saw you going down the escalator."

His smile told it all.

"Maybe."

"What's your name?"

"Frankie, but my friends call me Scooter."

"I like Frankie."

We exchanged numbers and I left the store with new kicks and a bit of guilt.

I called him that night on my way to a house party. I pondered how and when I would tell him about Carrington, but I didn't on the first call.

Carrington returned from Miami that Monday. He made every attempt to mend things between us, but I was unforgiving. I stayed a few night's at Cris' place to avoid him.

I invited Frankie to Wind Down Wednesdays, an outdoor concert, at Centennial Olympic Park and happened to run into DJ. Coincidentally, DJ and Frankie knew each other from Morehouse. I was petrified that DJ would blow my cover by mentioning Carrington in front of Frankie, or worse, casually mentioning to Carrington that I was at the show with someone else, but I played it cool.

My cell rang and it was Carrington calling.

"Hey, you wanna go to see Kindred at Centennial Park?"

"I'm already at the show with some friends," I said coldly.

He knew I was still pissed that he went out of town again.

"Oh, ok then," he said stunned.

I didn't show any mercy, although he tried to make amends. Whenever there was discord in our relationship, Carrington was the one to try to keep us on track. This time I wanted him to feel what I felt when he left me for Miami—alone.

I was also acting out behavior I adopted from my parents. Whenever my parents argued, my mom shut down and could go days without speaking to my father when she was upset with him, and my father had a tendency to be abrasive and short with her when he was upset with her.

I started sneaking around with Frankie while Carrington was at work, and got bold enough to do it at times he wasn't. I used Carrington's car for one of my visits to Frankie's. Frankie asked immediately whose car I was driving. He knew it wasn't mine because he had already seen my car.

Carrington was out of town the one and only time I spent a night with Frankie, so I didn't have to conjure a lie. I couldn't bring myself to have sex with Frankie because I was in love with Carrington.

Since Frankie was a songwriter too, I used it as justification to see him, but it became obvious that Frankie wasn't over someone he dated before we met. Many of the songs Frankie wrote were about his ex, and his name consistently came up in our conversations. It was exhausting for me and difficult to see him hurting over a man that didn't want him.

I was attracted to Frankie, but I liked him as a person. I wanted to maintain a friendship with him, so I didn't drag him into my confusion. Besides, he had been through enough with his ex. When I told Frankie about Carrington, he said he suspected I had a boyfriend. My confession gradually changed things for us. We became friends, and it wasn't sexual. Instead, we collaborated on music solely.

I confessed to Carrington that I cheated, even though Frankie and I never had intercourse. Nevertheless, it was a level of deception. Frankie and I had layed and played, and I knew cheating qualified as anything I wouldn't do in front of the person I'm in a relationship with.

Carrington was near tears. It was the only time he showed any emotion in our relationship. He wanted to know who I messed around with, but I didn't want to tell him since Frankie and I were still writing music together, but I did.

"Was it the guy who we met to get that shirt from?"

Carrington saw Frankie because he came with me to get a shirt I bought from Banana Republic using Frankie's store discount.

"Yea, that was him."

"How could you do that to me? Why would you take me with you? He knew who I was the whole time and I didn't know who he was!"

It felt like Appleton Street all over again with my father.

"We didn't have sex."

"It feels like you had an affair on me."

I didn't have the words to try to explain. Nothing I said could mitigate the pain he felt. The truth broke his heart and it fractured our relationship.

After living with Carrington for six months, I began making plans to move into my own place again. With all that happened with Frankie I felt it was best. I didn't tell Carrington right away because I knew he would try to persuade me to stay. And, I was unsure if I'd be able to pull it off financially because I moved from my last place without paying the last month of rent. I wasn't sure if there was an eviction on my credit that would prevent me from securing a place.

I knew it was time to move out after Carrington and I got into a physical fight. I went to a house party with Elden and Julian. I sent Carrington a text message to tell him we were going to Traxx after the party and he replied that it would be best if I found someplace else to sleep that night because he didn't want to be bothered. I ignored the text and went home instead of going to the club.

When I got to the condo, Carrington was in the walk-in closet organizing.

"If you didn't want me to come home you should've told me earlier and I could have made arrangements to go somewhere else tonight. I'll find somewhere to stay tomorrow."

"You stay at Cris' any other time. Why didn't you go there?"

"I'm not going to someone's house at two in the morning. Like I said, if you didn't want me here you should've thought of that earlier."

"You come in here whenever you feel like it! What's the difference?"

I ignored him and began undressing for bed. My grandmother always told me, "a person can't argue by themselves. If you close your mouth, eventually they'll close theirs too." In this case it didn't work.

"You can sleep on the couch. You're not sleeping in here," he grumbled.

"I'm not sleeping on no couch. You sleep on the couch," I barked.

"I told you not to come here!" he yelled.

"You heard what I said!"

This wasn't the first time Carrington flexed his power in his house. He refused to give me access to the voicemail code to check messages on the home phone. It didn't present a problem until I got a callback for a job and he neglected to give me the message because he forgot. Still, he was adamant about not giving me the code, and that was before things became tempestuous.

225

Before I got in bed he sprawled across the width of the bed when I went into the bathroom to remove my contacts. I came back to the bedroom and knelt down beside the bed to say my prayers. I stood up and asked him to move over, but he ignored me.

"Carrington, I'm asking you to move over nicely."

"I'm not moving over," he said with his eyes closed.

The bedroom light was still on.

"I'm gonna ask you one more time to move over—"

"This is my bed. Go sleep on the couch."

Carrington's true feelings surfaced. He was saying what he always felt. Everything belonged to him and he treated it as such. I was just a guest in his house. My attitudes were never about the trips he took, but the position in his life he relegated me to. It was beginning to make sense to me. I was just a character in his show, hence the reason he never gave me the voicemail code or made room for my things in the closet.

Carrington was used to being the most interesting one in his relationships so he could run things. He got away with these things in his past relationships, but I wouldn't allow it. He wanted control.

"Move over or I'm gonna move you."

He exhaled doubt. I was frustrated, sleepy and tired of feeling like I was in his way because it was his place. This was his idea for me to move in. He asked me to live with him.

I picked him up and threw him out of the bed. He crashed

against the floor to ceiling glass wall shattering the metal mini blinds in the process.

"What are you doing? I could've fell out the window!"

"I asked you to move! I told you I don't feel like playing with you!"

He jumped back in bed holding onto the mattress and headboard.

Again, I grabbed him and pushed him out of the bed—this time towards the hallway. He swung to punch me and his fingernail scraped my gum. I could taste the blood. I lunged at him and grabbed him by his throat. His arms flailed knocking fixtures and picture frames from the wall. Glass crashed to the floor, and we were both barefoot.

"Stop! Get off me," he yelled.

"I asked you to stop! I didn't want to fight you."

I let him go and walked to the bathroom to rinse my mouth. It wasn't bleeding, but there was a scratch on my gum.

"I can't do this. I want you out of my life. This ain't right!" he sobbed.

"I'm done and don't come back begging when I leave this time," I said.

Carrington's lip was bleeding. It was strange fighting someone I loved. Carrington threw on some clothes and left the condo. He returned a half hour later. He got in bed and we went to sleep.

I found a place in Vinings that my friend Jamelle told me

about. Jamelle owned a furniture store that Elden freelanced in before he started his interior design company. She and I got close after she agreed to carry my greeting cards in her store.

Once I secured the apartment, Jamelle told me she would allow me to buy all of the furniture I needed at cost. It was a generous offer that made it possible for me to furnish the entire apartment when I moved in. Working for the internet provider wasn't so bad after all. I had money to do some of the things I wanted.

I told Carrington I was moving after I put the deposit on the apartment.

"Why didn't you tell me you were looking for a place? It's like you were sneaking."

"We only agreed that I was staying for six months."

"But, I just figured you would stay. It feels like it's over," he said.

I knew what he meant. It did seem backwards. He was hoping, just as I, that things would be perfect enough for us to continue living together, but they weren't even close.

JUST A KEY

I moved to my new apartment in the beginning of fall. It was nestled right outside the city limits in Vinings again near the first apartment I leased when I moved to Atlanta. Carrington stopped by to help me paint before the furniture was delivered. My flat was a two-minute walk to his dental office, and a fifteen-minute drive to his condo.

It was awkward being in a place of my own again, and he looked out of place standing in my living room. He didn't say much. He just looked around the apartment searching for words to keep the silence out.

Carrington may have stayed one night with me in the apartment. I thought he would have taken advantage of the close proximity to his office, but he didn't. Things were further complicated by the fact we hadn't had sex in months. We satisfied each other sexually, but there was no intercourse.

Our only saving grace for the relationship was a cruise to the Bahamas that was approaching in the New Year. We planned it before things began unraveling. The cruise began as something to do for our moms, but it became a means for us to re-evaluate the relationship and determine if we could repair the damage done.

I had a horrible habit of breaking up with Carrington each

229

time we argued—big or small—because I lacked experience, and it was a defense mechanism. The last time I broke it off was a couple weeks before we set sail for the Bahamas.

Kepri happened to be in town on business from New York, so I was too busy to return Carrington's calls because she and I were running the streets having spa treatments and going to dinner on her corporate credit card. I figured I could get back to him once she left town. I never stopped to consider his feelings or the impact that breaking up and making up would have on the stability of our relationship. Once I returned his call he told me it felt like a real break up that time because he didn't hear back from me. He suggested we just be friends, but I didn't believe he was serious. Plus, we still had the cruise to go on. I figured he was talking out of anger because when I mentioned canceling the trip he didn't want to do so.

My mom flew from Baltimore to Miami to meet Carrington, his mom and me for our cruise. I suggested to my mom that she and I share a cabin because Carrington and I were barely speaking. Of course, I told my mother the idea was in case she and his mom didn't get along since it was their first time meeting.

"I'm not sharing that tiny room with you. When I come out the shower I don't wanna be rushing to cover up. You can stay right with Carrington. You'll survive."

Our mothers hit it off. They laughed and giggled like childhood friends. The four of us did things together, but they left us on a number of occasions to do things without us—forcing us to talk.

Carrington couldn't get the thought of Frankie and me out of his mind, whether we slept together or not. He wanted to know where he was when I was with him. I wanted to move past all of our flaws—the mistakes we both made—to find the place at which we got off track to rectify things. I never really wanted things to end. I was emotionally immature, and lacked the tools necessary for a healthy relationship.

On the flight back to Atlanta, Carrington and I toyed with the idea of taking a trip to Vegas for the Cirque du Soleil show. I told him I would take care all of the details and pay for us to go.

I decided to drop by the condo unannounced one night to surprise him. In my mind, it was a gesture to say I was willing to make it work. We weren't together, technically, but I still had a key to his condo because he insisted I keep it. He told me he wasn't seeing anyone, so it didn't matter if I used it.

In my heart of hearts, I felt he wanted me to keep the key because he wasn't quite ready to let go of me, us, the relationship. For me, the key symbolized the possibility of salvaging the relationship if I held on to it or its finality should I return it.

When I entered the condo, I could see light flashing from the flat screen television mounted on the living room wall. He was asleep on the couch. The sound of the door opening startled him and he sat up.

"Huh? Who is that?" he said looking around.

"It's me. Who else would it be?"

"Why didn't you call first?" he said lying back down.

I could only see the lower half of his body on the couch. He wasn't alone. Someone was seated beside him. I could see a second pair of legs resting on the leather cube that I helped pick out.

"Why do I need to call? I have a key."

My adrenaline rushed with each step I took. I couldn't reach the end of the hallway quick enough. I wanted to see the person's face. *Was it someone I knew? Had he been dealing with him while we were together? Why is he here?* It was after eleven o'clock at night.

"Who is this?"

"Travis," he said.

I noticed *Travis'* luggage parked in the dining room, indicating he was staying longer than a night. To my surprise, the man whose secrets I sheltered and protected from the world had deceived me. In that moment, I considered all the horrible things only he and I knew that could've damaged him professionally and embarrassed him personally. Moreover, I couldn't understand how we had arrived at this. I failed to remember my fling with Frankie, but at least I fessed up. Had I not popped over he would've never told me about Travis. I didn't think my actions were as bad, but there are no lesser of two evils. Still, this was the kind of thing that happened to people in *other* relationships. This couldn't be happening to me, to us.

"What are you doing here?" he asked still lying with his eyes closed.

"I need to see you in the other room," I said as I turned to walk to the bedroom.

I could hear Carrington shuffling behind me.

I looked at him puzzled. I didn't truly know this person. He wasn't the person I respected. This was an impostor. This wasn't how this story, our story, was to play out. We had just discussed on the cruise how to get back to us. Obviously, I missed something or was in denial again.

"Why is he here?" I asked.

"Why didn't you call before you came?" he said.

"Because I have a key! Why do I need to call if I have a key? I don't need permission to come here if I have a key! I asked you if you wanted your key back and you said no!"

"Craig, go home. We'll talk about it tomorrow."

"I'm not leaving. You need to tell him he needs to leave."

"No, I can't do that. He didn't drive here."

"I don't care how he got here. He needs to leave."

Carrington refused to ask him to leave, and I could feel tears welling up in my eyes, so I grabbed my overnight bag and left before they fell.

I called my friend Robbi who lived nearby. I didn't want to go home and be alone. I climbed into bed with her and told her everything that happened. I cried and talked us to sleep.

The next morning, I got ready for work despite the restless and sleepless night I suffered through. I promised myself many years before I would never allow any relationship to get in the way of my livelihood, so I was going to work. I may not get much accomplished while there, but I would be present and accounted for to get paid.

I got an email from Carrington at work explaining it wasn't his intention to hurt me. He said he wasn't expecting me to come over, and that he didn't understand why I was upset because I had ended the relationship. He reiterated that every time I walked out I took a piece of him with me, and it made it hard for him to piece back the feelings he had.

Since I couldn't concentrate long enough to work, I logged into Carrington's Delta Skymiles account. I found out Travis' luggage wasn't just for a weekend at the condo. There were two flights booked to Las Vegas. Carrington was taking him to see the Cirque du Soleil show that he and I discussed seeing on our flight from the Bahamas.

My first instinct was to cancel the flights, but I decided against it. *I'm better than that.* And, I couldn't allow him to make me something or someone I'm not. I sat at my desk with tears in my eyes—some streaming down my face. I placed a few customers on hold because I could barely talk to them about their internet service.

My mind drifted back to when we met. He was the first person, man or woman I fell in love with because we shared so many firsts. Carrington was the first person I lived and traveled with. He was the first guy I dated that believed in my work. I never would have predicted we would end the way we did.

I needed Carrington to know that I knew about his impending Vegas trip. I drafted Robbi to accompany me to Carrington's after work.

"What are you gonna say when we get there?" she asked.

"I don't know. I'll figure it out when I get there."

"Well how are you gonna get in? You don't have a key. He's not gonna just let you in if he is there."

I forgot I had given Carrington my key before I left the night before.

Robbi was my voice of reason, and at first glance, the girl next door. Her slender frame, and black baby doll hair were part of the reason she made it to the final casting call for America's Next Top Model. Robbi grew up in Milwaukee, but spent summers in Chicago, so she had some *hood* in her. She tried to talk me out of going, but my mind was made and she was my ride or die. I had to go.

"He never locks the front door when he's there, so the door is probably unlocked. But, he doesn't know what you look like so if it's locked you can knock and I'll pop up when he opens the door," I explained.

"Ok."

The biggest dilemma was how we would get to the eighteenth floor if he changed the elevator code because each floor had its own code.

I punched in the elevator code and it worked. My heart pounded as we stepped off the elevator making two quick turns to Carrington's front door. I could hear music playing softly through the door.

"He's home," I said.

Robbi stood behind me giggling nervously and covering her mouth.

I grabbed the lever and turned it slowly. The music made it easier for us to make our way down the corridor to the living room without being heard. Carrington looked up in shock. Travis was frozen in the same spot he was in the night before.

"Did he tell you who I was?" I said to Travis.

"Yes," he said.

"He told you we were together?"

Travis looked puzzled. I could hear Carrington behind me saying hello to Robbi as if he was expecting us. He was trying to play it cool.

"Hello. How are you?" Carrington said.

"Good. Hi Carrington. How are you? I'm Robbi."

"Oh hey! Nice to meet you," he said.

"You know I could embarrass you right now. I could really put you out there, but I won't," I said to Carrington.

He stood looking at me with a blank expression on his face. The room was completely still.

"Craig, let's go," Robbi said softly.

We left, and the heartache followed.

A friend told me, *"for every one thing you learn about someone else, there are three things you can learn about yourself"* and it was true. I had learned more about myself, but that relationship taught me so much about people, life, love, emotions, companionship, pain and myself.

Every relationship after, I chose people who would love me more because I never wanted to feel that loss again should it end. I wanted to be strong enough to walk away. I didn't want to be the one who couldn't let go.

TESTING THE WATERS

O ne of the best parts of life is when you can admit the truth to yourself about yourself. Thus, I've come to understand my experience with anonymous sex with strangers I met on the internet resulted from a bout with depression.

With respect to gay people, some use the internet as an entryway to gay life. Others use it as a mechanism for dating because of the many barriers with meeting someone publicly, and there are those who use it for sexual anonymity because they live secret lives.

Cyberspace is a world where one can become something he isn't, but everything he dares to be. One can find whatever he cares to imagine because the biggest part of the illusion is what's created in the mind of the person logging on—it's the story we create about a total stranger that allows us to be enraptured in conversation for countless hours until we're bold enough to meet.

Many of the characters online are there for sex and demand in their profiles that you're naturally masculine, but the sites allow those who are naturally feminine to sound masculine through messages like *sup*.

Some even specify that you be of a particular race, height, weight or physique before you consider messaging them. But, those specifications don't prevent some from being duplicitous by using fake or altered photos.

The internet can serve as a magnet for those of us rebounding from a break up or a resource for the resilient that believe love can be found online and foolish enough to believe the odds are in his favor to find it on a sex site.

Sex sites are the unofficial antidote for loneliness. It's a device for the depressed as well as a sounding board for homophobic men, and those frustrated with being jaded, heartbroken and disappointed.

Because I struggled with the break up with Carrington, I used the internet to pacify the emotional pain I wasn't ready to face head on. I knew it wouldn't be long before Carrington would be with someone new because he is the guy who can't be alone. He has to be with someone because he's a serial monogamist and that bothered me.

My depression moved quickly and deliberately before I realized it was occupying a section of my life. It wasn't just the residual effects of the break up, but career lulls and financial setbacks too. The depression I experienced was rooted in sex, but it wasn't just about the depression. It was years of suppression and denial erupting. My suppression was a conscious suppression. I was clear that I had been holding back feelings of being with men. It was like a disease that lay dormant that suddenly surfaced. I was like a church girl who had been sheltered from the world by her minister father only to break loose and run wild the first time she left home. I went from rigid to over the top. Previously, I wouldn't sit with my legs crossed in the way President Obama and so many other men do—because I thought it was feminine—to wearing cut out t-shirts with safety pins in it.

All of the classic symptoms of depression were present. I couldn't concentrate on anything except what Carrington was doing. There were days I didn't shower or brush my teeth until late in the day, if at all. For the first time, I didn't care what I was wearing or what I looked like.

I knew Carrington's schedule, so my mind danced through his daily routine and to make matters worse I still lived behind his office. Each day that I left my apartment I looked to see if his car was there. I started playing a game with myself. I challenged myself to pass without looking, but couldn't do it.

I broke down driving to work one morning. I called my mother in tears. I couldn't hold back the flood that begged to be released. The moment she answered, I rattled everything I felt.

"I can't stop thinking about it. This isn't what I wanted to happen," I cried.

"What? What are you saying? I can't understand you. Where are you?" she said in a panic.

I sobbed and attempted to repeat myself.

"I'm on my way to work."

"Pull over! You need to pull over before you have an accident."

But, I wasn't far from home. In fact, I was still in the parking lot. I pulled over at the entrance to the complex.

"I've never felt like this before. I can't stop thinking about him. I can't shake it. I don't want to feel like this."

My mom knew we were no longer together, but we hadn't talked about the impact it had on me.

"You have to focus on what you're doing. You have to put your energy in the play, those greeting cards and everything you're trying to do. You just have to take it one day at a time. It'll get easier. The person for you could be someone you'll meet along the way in your field."

"I don't know how you did this. You've been divorced twice. We didn't spend half as much time together building a life, buying a home like you and my father. I can't keep going through this. I don't want a lifetime of going in and out of relationships every two years. I'm tired of starting over. It takes so much out of you to pick up and move on."

The harsh reality that there are no guarantees in lasting love was becoming real despite all the promises he and I made when things were euphoric. Carrington never believed in gay marriage until I said I wanted to be married to someone one day.

I was taking the split personally. A break up has the kind of power to challenge the strongest armor of self-esteem. I was convinced that I wasn't as great as I *thought* I was. I began second-guessing myself. I could now understand how my cousin

Lisa felt after Kendal, and why my friend Justice couldn't just walk away from her boyfriend in college.

I needed validation, so I started having sex with a guy named Bryce that I knew from the gym. He stopped me at the gym many years before because I was wearing a Hampton University t-shirt to tell me that he wanted to attend Hampton when he was applying to colleges.

"I tried to introduce myself before, but you didn't really seem interested," he said.

I didn't recall ever seeing him before, but I was with Carrington during the time he was referring to, so I may have been blinded by love.

"I don't remember that," I said.

Once the ice was broken, we exchanged numbers and made plans to see a movie.

Bryce usually wore shorts and cut off shirts to the gym. He had the body of a grown man, but he was only in his mid 20s. His thighs were thick and muscular like an athlete's, and the way I like them.

He met me at my place before the movie, but he didn't come inside. After the movie, he came up to my apartment. I knew we were about to fuck around when he followed me up to my apartment instead of getting in his car to leave. He was acting shy at first, so I fixed him a cocktail. He loosened up after a few sips of cranberry and vodka.

I was standing in the kitchen when he passed me to put his glass in the sink. I grabbed the waistband of his pants and pulled him close to me. I kissed his full pink lips.

"I knew you were gonna do that," he said smiling.

"You wanted me to."

I kissed him again. I sucked on his bottom lip and started unbuttoning his khaki pants.

"Craig, we can't do this yet."

I reached in his underwear and cupped his nuts. His dick was growing. I moved my hand behind his nuts to play inside his ass. He moaned each time I inserted my middle finger in him. I pulled him over to the couch. He kicked off his flip-flops before lying back on the couch. He lifted his legs so I could slide his pants down around his ankles and then off.

His legs were built like a track runner. His hamstrings were flexing. Bryce spread his legs open so I could lie between them. He wrapped them around my waist. I pulled his dick out of his underwear to taste it. With a few strokes, and licks on his nipples he was ejaculating.

We routinely met at my place after the gym. He showered at the gym, so we could get straight to it. Sometimes I opened the door wearing a towel or nothing at all, holding a glass of wine.

After a few hook ups, I started sliding my dick in Bryce to see if he would stop me, but he didn't. He positioned his ass closer to me, so I grabbed a condom from my nightstand and fucked him.

"What are you doing?" he asked.

"You know what I'm doing."

He felt good. It was tight and wet. This was the first time in months I was inside someone because Carrington and I had long stopped having sex. Bryce's ass was firm and smooth, and it didn't have any blemishes or stretch marks. I turned him on his back and lifted his legs straight in the air. When I entered, he moaned.

"Damn, that feels good," he mumbled.

"You like that?"

"Yea nigga. Don't stop. Gimme that dick."

Sweat poured from my head dripping to his stomach. I watched him watching me until he came all over his stomach and my chest.

Our hook ups became too sporadic because of his grad school schedule, so I set up a few online accounts to find sex. I wasn't interested in getting attached to anyone and I knew I wouldn't take anyone I met online seriously.

I had multiple screen names to increase my chances of meeting someone attractive. The majority of the profiles noted HIV negative under *status*, but I knew better from the work I had done in the HIV community. I knew 1 out of 3 Black gay men was positive. At any given time there were thousands of men online, but only a few listed they were positive on their page and others left it blank—an indicator they were HIV positive too.

The messages I found in my inbox validated me in my depression. In some strange way, they reinforced that I was worthy and deserving. I never used naked pictures nor did I use a face picture as my primary photo because my pride wouldn't allow it. There was some level of shame for me to be online. It felt desperate to some degree, and I knew there was a chance I could be recognized from my show or greeting card business. My profile pictures were photos of my chest, arm or leg, and face photos for my private pictures.

Days became weeks then months of me surfing for sex. This erotic surfing was a poor attempt to avoid emotional wounds that wouldn't heal fast enough for me. It prevented me from thinking too much about what was happening in my life personally, financially, and professionally.

Some rebound from break ups at the expense of another person's feelings, while others *sit* patiently in the pain and process through it. I used the internet to cope. My days consisted of waking up and logging on to see how many messages had accrued overnight. Some days I sat at the computer all day. I'd look up and the day would be over. The only time I stepped away from the computer was to eat or go to the gym.

I was out on short-term disability from the internet company. The time off gave me time to foster relationships with local merchants who would potentially carry *Say it in a Card*, but it also left me with endless hours at home to cruise the internet.

My disability case opened after I called in claiming to have had a death in my family. In actuality, I was exhausted from a greeting card party my coworker Liv sponsored. After seven consecutive absences from work my short-term disability case opened automatically. The one stipulation, I was required to attend counseling with a therapist each week. I agreed to the counseling and I received sixty percent of my pay. Liv and two other coworkers were the only people who knew I was pulling a stunt.

Before I went out on leave, I had greeting card samples that I took to work for my coworkers to preview. The samples circulated through the building and by the end of the day I had a number of orders to fill. After Liv saw the samples she questioned why I was working a *regular* job.

Liv started after I was employed there, so she didn't know the disdain I felt when I first started. I had fought, kicked, and screamed at the idea of taking this job, but I was clear my time employed there would be temporary. Once I shared my story with Liv, she never stopped telling me that I was too talented not to be pursuing my craft fulltime. She agreed to help me get the business off the ground.

The universe has a way of giving us exactly what we need before we realize we need it. For me, it was the job at the internet company because the result was the counseling sessions. Initially, I didn't take counseling seriously. I thought I was getting over on the company because I was getting paid without working and earning money from the greeting card sales. *Say it in a Card* was in four stores, and quickly moving into others.

I had a standing appointment every Tuesday with a therapist. I got in character for each of my sessions. I never went groomed. My hair was never brushed, I didn't bother shaving, and I wore mismatched clothes. I spoke just above a whisper creating stories as I went along. I was *playing* depressed, but underneath it all I was depressed. I just hadn't uncovered it yet. Months passed before I got honest with my therapist about what was happening with me, but when I did I was completely open with her.

I was overdramatizing my feelings about Hurricane Katrina and before I knew it I heard myself say, "I've been having sex with people I meet online."

"When did this start?"

"A while ago. I told two of my friends, but they laughed when I told them."

I had shared the truth with Elden and Julian on one of our three-way calls, but they didn't know the severity of it.

"How did that make you feel?"

"Like it wasn't a problem. Like they didn't take me serious-ly."

"Why do you think you're doing this?"

"I don't know. I can't function. I think it's the effects of a breakup. I'm depressed. I go online every day."

My eyes searched the office for more answers. *Random compliments from strangers fed my ego.* I needed to hear the things I found in my inbox. The internet assuaged the pain—temporarily.

This addiction was monopolizing my time and it had spiraled out of control. Phone calls with my friends and family were met with brevity because my attention was occupied by online conversations. No one could compete for my attention. I was locked in a trance reading the messages and scrolling through the naked pictures on the other profiles.

I left social gatherings early to return home to surf online. There was a science to my madness. I kept the site up while I was gone, so I could accumulate messages while I was away from the computer. I sometimes returned to double-digit messages flashing *for me*.

For my own peace of mind, I made small talk with the guys I met in person, so they weren't total strangers to me when we had sex. It was my way of mitigating the shame I felt of having sex with someone I didn't know. I even rationalized the sex by reminding myself that I was fucking them—they weren't fucking me. But I still couldn't get used to the emptiness.

I invited a guy over, but put him out less than five minutes after entering my apartment. After I saw him, I couldn't remember chatting with him, and it was because he had used a picture of someone else to entice me.

"That's not you in the picture," I said.

"Ok—" he said casually.

I was standing in nothing but a towel. He was a couple feet from me using his right foot to remove his left sneaker without bending down to untie it.

"I'm not feeling it," I said.

"Ok," he said.

He slipped his sneaker back on and left as casually as he had waltzed into my place. It was as if he thought I was desperate enough to overlook his deception.

Rarely would I drive to someone's place for a hook up. Even still, if I wasn't interested I didn't have a problem saying so. On one of my trips, I got to the guy's apartment and when he opened the door I told him I wasn't feeling him and walked back down the stairs.

Casual sex felt empty, and it was making me cold and callous. I didn't care about their feelings. With each counseling session, my epiphanies were coming more consistently. I gained clarity through hearing myself speak my truth out loud.

I lowered my standards a few times. I slept with a few that I would've never considered had I not been sinking in depression. I stopped in the middle of sex a few times because I wasn't completely aroused. I knew my behavior was strange from the looks I got when I asked whomever it was to leave.

It was embarrassing running into guys I met on the internet at parties or social events only to pretend we didn't know each other because neither of us wanted to fess up to meeting in such a desperate way. It's a sick secret so many share.

I wondered whom I chatted with online, and revealed my face pictures to that may have told friends of theirs that they saw me online even if we never hooked up.

I couldn't recognize myself. I had morphed into someone I didn't know. I was doing what Leslie and his friends had except I was using the internet as opposed to the chat line. I had judged them, possibly because they contracted HIV in the process, and yet I was doing the same thing. The only difference, I hadn't contracted HIV. In some ways I was still searching for what was comfortable for me as a gay man, my niche in this new world.

Monica saw a difference in me, and she didn't know half of what was really going on. Her question was simple, *"What happened to the person you were?"* She was referring to the man I was when I moved to Atlanta, the man who didn't allow curiosity or hormones to decide for me. I was rushing into relationships with guys because they were interested in me. Not because I was really into them.

Once I dug up the root of it all, I closed my internet accounts. It didn't happen overnight; it was gradual. But after two years of casual sex, I found the person I was before I came into *the life*. I found the person who exercised sexual restraint, and set boundaries. I rediscovered the man that didn't abuse sexual opportunities because he could. I was finally realizing, again, my worth. No longer did I allow myself the excuse *everyone else is doing it.*

It being the internet or any other vice so many get tangled in, sometimes indefinitely. It's a web of confusion, uncertainty, hopelessness, emptiness and despair because we, as a community, don't know our worth; thus, we subject ourselves to the most scurrilous predicaments.

After six months of playing charades, the HR department began pressuring me to return to work. Things were going too well with the greeting cards to drop everything to go back to answer DSL internet phone calls. When I refused to return to work I was terminated, which was perfect because I was able to collect unemployment for six months and continue building *Say it in a Card.*

Liv and I stayed in touch after I was terminated. She often called or texted me on her pay periods to give me money, and it was always perfect timing. Even when I told her I was managing, she insisted on giving me money to help me out.

My friend Karyn—who was fired from IBM with me—took a job working for Evander Holyfield and was in a position to help pay my utility bill. She, like Liz, always encouraged me to call if I needed them, but pride wouldn't allow it even if it meant going without.

Initially, I resented taking the job at the internet service provider, but meeting Liv was one of the best things to come out of my time there—her support kept me afloat.

DREAMING WHILE AWAKE

I met Brandy Norwood at Nseya Salon and Spa while restocking the greeting cards, and she was getting her hair done. She was seated next to Cris' station getting her hair pressed when I walked in. Brandy was with Keisha Knight-Pulliam and a girl named Lori.

"Oh, come here Craig. I wanna introduce you to my girlfriend Lori," Cris said as I was passing by.

Cris was part of the reason the salon owners took a chance on *Say it in a Card*.

"Craig, this is Lori. The girl I was telling you about that's getting married. I wanted you to meet her and maybe you can write a card for her fiancé."

"Hey, how are you?" I said.

The entire time I cogitated how to ask Brandy if I could submit some songs for her next album. Marcel, my former songwriting partner, had dreamed for years of writing for her and here she was sitting a foot away from me. I did everything in my power not to stare at her, but she was looking at me while I was talking to Lori.

"Hi, nice to meet you. Cris told me you write these cards and I wanna give my fiancé his last gift as his girlfriend, you know?"

"Yes, I get it. We can do that. We just need to set up a time to meet so I can get a feel for the relationship and what you wanna say."

"Ok, you have a card?"

"Sure," I said handing her a business card and I took the liberty of giving one to Keisha and Brandy too.

Brandy looked at the card immediately, "break up cards! You actually write break up cards? People actually send break up cards?"

"Yea, and they do well."

"Oh wow."

"Craig I'll call you to set up something with Lori so y'all can meet or whatever," Cris interjected.

"Ok, that's cool. Just let me know."

It wasn't the time to pitch Brandy on any song ideas. The environment was too relaxed and it didn't feel like the time, nor did I have any demos with me anyway. Besides, music was that relationship I knew I had to walk away from because I wasn't getting out of it what I was putting in, but I kept going back hoping for different results.

I walked away from music after *American Idol's* first season contestant Tamyra Gray made it to the finale. Elden called to tell me Tamyra was on this new show that I had never heard of at the time. He came with me to the studio when Marcel and I recorded with Tamyra, and Elden remembered her.

Tamyra demoed two songs for Marcel and me before making it to the show. We hoped to record more songs with her, and she and her manager wanted us to write for her debut album, but we were no longer able to contact her after she made it to the finale.

Several weeks passed and Cris couldn't manage to set up a meeting for Lori and me to construct a personalized card for her NBA player fiancé. Instead, Cris decided to reach out to Lori's fiancé, Michael Carter. Since their engagement party was approaching Cris figured Michael could hire me to do a card for that occasion. Before I met with him, Cris made it clear that I was to charge him far more than the $25 fee I was charging for personalized cards at the time.

Cris came along with me to the consultation that lasted about forty-five minutes. I suggested a scroll made from parchment paper with dried flowers embedded within the paper then tied with a decorative ribbon. Michael invited me to the engagement dinner where he would present it to his fiancé in front of his and her family.

On the way home Cris asked how much I was going to charge for the work.

"One seventy."

"Mmm hmm, that's good. You probably could've got more, but that's good. He'll pay you."

Cris and I arrived at Prime Steakhouse before the couple or their families. The engagement dinner was held in a private dining room at the restaurant. We could see Lori and her fiancé through the window when they arrived in a forest green Flying Spur Bentley coupe he bought for her 26th birthday.

When Lori walked in, she greeted Cris and me with a hug, but looked a little shocked to see me since she and I never met to create a personalized card together for Michael.

"I'm sorry I never called you. I've been so busy trying to plan the wedding."

"It's ok. I understand. Don't worry about it."

After several courses and glasses of wine, Michael gave Lori the scroll. She stood up and unrolled it to read it. Midway through the script she started crying, along with a few of the people in the room. Lori's fiancé walked around to her side of the table to hold her.

"Oh my God. I love this," she said with her head on his chest. "When did y'all have time to do this?" she said in her Mississippi accent. "I want to do something like this for the wedding. What if we did something like this for my brides-maids? What do we have to do?"

"We just have to meet. I was trying to meet with you before," I said smiling.

"I know, I know!"

"Once we meet, I'll ask you about the relationship you have with each of them and I'll draft it up for you."

"I love this. You are so talented. And you have to come to my wedding. Here, I have an invitation in my purse."

There were six bridesmaids in the wedding party and Brandy Norwood was one of them. *Perhaps I would get the chance to talk to Brandy about writing music for her after all.*

Coincidentally, Cris and I sat on the same pew as Brandy at the wedding. We sat close to the aisle and she sat on the opposite end nearest the wall. Apparently, Brandy decided at the last minute she wasn't going to be a bridesmaid, which explained why she wasn't in attendance of the rehearsal dinner or the bridal shower at the Ritz Carlton Buckhead. Each bridesmaid received the personalized cards and David Yurman bracelets from the bride-to-be.

Every once in a while, I snuck a peek at Brandy during the ceremony. *I wonder if she'll remember me from the salon?* There was no time after the ceremony to reintroduce myself because everyone left the church immediately for the reception at the Four Seasons Hotel. Brandy was surprisingly social with everyone at the reception. At the time she was engaged to Quentin Richardson, who was a groomsman, so I expected her to be close to him the entire time.

"You look familiar," she said as I was passing her and Keisha Knight-Pulliam.

"Where do you know him from," Keisha asked.

"I wanna say he's friends with—"

"No, now you reaching," Keisha said.

"Well, I wasn't too sure, but I know his face," Brandy said.

"Yea, we met at the salon that day. I write the break up cards."

"Yes, see I knew I knew him!"

"I write greeting cards, but I moved here to write music. How can I get some songs to you for your next album?"

"I'm actually going in the studio soon. Get my number from Lori."

"Ok, I'm serious. Don't act like you don't know who I am when I call you."

"No, I'm serious too. Let's work."

"Ok, I'm gonna call you."

A part of me was thinking she was just talking because she could have given me her number herself while we were standing there, but I didn't press the issue.

After Lori and Michael returned from their honeymoon I texted her to get Brandy's number. She replied instantly with the number.

*****

Brent and I thought it was time for the Hettabrinks to take our first trip together. We shared the idea with the rest of the group and everyone went on the trip except DJ. We paired up in rooms by twos. I roomed with Elden for the getaway to the Dominican Republic.

The all-inclusive trip to Punta Cana was amazing. We spent time on the resort property as well as in the city with the residents. We lay on the beach whenever we weren't on an excursion. We signed up for a few day trips, some of which included snorkeling and some water sports.

The trip to the D.R. changed our friendships in many ways. I found myself mediating an argument between Elden and our little brother Jude who came along on the trip. Jude and Devon were the only two who spoke fluent Spanish, and here we were in the middle of a Spanish speaking country and they took issue with translating for the rest of us. Jude told Elden it wasn't their responsibility to translate. The two of them erupted into a screaming match late one night in downtown Puerto Plata just after we stepped out of a cab. I was embarrassed and paranoid we might be hauled off to jail so I grabbed Elden and Julian pulled Jude in the other direction. I hailed another taxi to return to the resort. It was ugly, and the taxicab ride back was worse. Elden and Jude didn't speak for the four remaining days of the vacation. Tension was palpable whenever both of them were present.

To add insult to injury, Jude invited a stranger he met lurking around the property to his and Twiggy's room. Twiggy was pissed the next morning when he woke up to see the stranger in the bed across from him cuddling with Jude.

The biggest shock on the trip was Brent disclosing to Devon and me that he was involved with a girl from his full-time job. He said he really liked her and that he always knew the day would come that he would *go back* to women. Essentially, he was tired of being single. Brent hadn't been in a relationship with a guy since he had his heart broken by a guy he dated before we all met. He said he would still be friends with us, but he wouldn't hang out at the gay clubs or parties anymore.

By the time we reached our connecting flight at Miami International airport the friendships were divided, and Jude realized his iPod was missing. He was the only one unable to believe his vagabond friend stole it while he and Twiggy were asleep.

I walked over to baggage claim to retrieve my bag and decided to give Brandy a call. Her voicemail came on and while I was leaving a message she clicked in on my other line.

"Hello," I said.

"Hi, did someone just call this number?"

"Yea, hey Brandy it's Craig. We met at Lori's wedding."

"Oh, hey. How are you?"

"I'm good. Just wanted to give you a call. I'm still interested in working with you."

"Ok, do you have something I can hear that you've done?"

"Yea, definitely. I can send some songs I demoed. Just let me know where to send it."

"Well, I'm actually gonna be back in Atlanta for the Bronner Brothers show. I'm doing some work with a wig line."

"Ok, cool. I can meet you when you come to give it to you."

Brandy gave me the dates she would be in Atlanta and I made a note in my Blackberry to call her when she got to Atlanta, but little did I know we would begin speaking on the phone daily.

I was afraid to call Brandy too much at first because I didn't want to come off as a worrisome fan, but she called and texted me before I could call her. She opened up to me about her relationship with 'Q'. She said they were no longer together, but it hadn't been released in the press yet. We talked about music, but mostly about her break up. I could relate because I was still mourning my break up with Carrington.

Brandy wanted me to call Q's phone a few times to see if he would answer my call because she thought he was avoiding her calls. I called, but he didn't answer. I pitied her because I pitied my own loss.

"You have to let go," I said.

"I know, but it's hard."

"Each day you'll get stronger, but each time you call or text you reopen the wound. I know from experience. You only feel worse when you don't get the results you hoped for," I said.

"I really appreciate you. I'll never forget how you helped me through this," she said.

When Brandy came back to Atlanta, Elden and I met her at the Ritz Carlton downtown to give her a cd of songs I had written. One of the songs on the cd was a song Tamyra Gray demoed for Marcel and me.

"I listened to the songs. I can tell from the words that you're really passionate about what you do. I definitely want you to come to see what you can do with the other writers."

It was still up in the air if she and Rodney "Darkchild" Jerkins would reunite for the album.

"Is he gonna be cool with me coming to Jersey to work? Do you need to tell him I'm coming?"

"Yea, it's cool. I just need to see if we'll be in Jersey or LA, but I'll let you know."

"Ok Brandy, you can't wait 'til the day before to tell me. My money ain't like that to buy a plane ticket for the next day."

"Ok, I got you. We'll work it out. We'll get you there somehow. Jet Blue, something."

A couple weeks later she called me on a Thursday afternoon. I was having lunch with Elden and another friend when Brandy's number popped up on my cell phone.

"Hey, what's going on?" I answered.

"Hey, what you doing?"

"Having lunch with two of my friends."

"Oh, ok. I want you to come to LA Tuesday."

"This Tuesday?"

"Yea."

"Ok, and return when?"

"I don't know yet. Just get a one-way ticket. I'll take care of everything else."

"Ok, I'll let you know when I get it."

"Ok, bye."

"What she say?" Elden asked

"She wants me to come to LA!"

"Alright now!"

"Yea, but how much is that plane ticket gonna cost?" I panicked.

"Who knows, but you're going if we all gotta chip in to buy it," he said.

It turned out that Brandy decided not to work with Rodney Jerkins on the album. She opted to record with two producers from Denmark who went by the name Maximum Risks.

My father spent years trying to redeem himself for allowing a woman—whom he divorced—to change the dynamic of our relationship. Just before I flew to LA he deposited $1,000 in my account, and my mom gave me the money for the flight. I booked a 7 a.m. flight for the following Tuesday and texted Brandy the details.

I was seated on the plane when I realized I had a slew of voice messages I had yet to listen to. Three of the messages were from Brandy's mother who works as her manager.

"Hi Craig, this is Sonya Norwood. I'm calling to get your itinerary. If you would, give me a call back at 818..."

I hung up to place the call because one of the flight attendants was closing the door of the plane as another made the announcement to turn off all electronic devices. It was imperative that I leave a message with my flight details before the flight took off. The phone rang twice before Sonya Norwood picked up.

"Hello," she mumbled.

"Oh, I'm sorry. I thought I was calling an office number."

"No, it's ok. I always forward the office phone whenever Brandy or Ray is traveling."

"Oh ok. This is Craig Stewart. I just got your message. My flight gets in at 12:25."

"What are your arrangements?"

"I'm not sure what you mean."

"Where will you be staying?"

"I don't know. Brandy just told me to book a one way flight and she would take care of the rest."

"Well, I didn't know anything about this. We have a budget for this kind of thing. We have producers here from out of the country and we have to pay for their accommodations. The hotel where everyone else is staying is already booked."

"Brandy didn't tell you I was coming?"

"Yea, but I thought you were just coming to hang out."

"No, I don't just hang out, but I have to get off the phone because the flight is about to take off."

"Ok, well call the office when you land and my assistant will tell you what to do."

As the flight taxied to the runway I thought about the conversation I had with Brandy's mom. The excitement I had was beginning to wane. My first trip to LA was supposed to be exciting. I was going to write for Brandy, a multiplatinum selling recording artist, and the air was just let out of my balloon.

When I landed at LAX, I contacted Sonya's office and spoke to her assistant. She told me there was a car waiting to take me to a hotel in Glendale that was five minutes from the studio. She also asked who would be footing the bill for the hotel. When I told her *they* were she stammered, but said she would get back to me.

I checked into the hotel without putting a credit card on file. I got settled into my room and climbed into the bed for a nap. No sooner than I got in bed I heard the phone ringing

"Hi, this is Sonya Norwood."

"Hi."

She had already tested my nerves and I knew she was suiting up for round two.

"So, I need to talk to Brandy about all this because I didn't know anything. All of this stuff should go through the manager."

"I understand what you're saying, but it sounds like you're taking this out on me. Brandy should have articulated to you that I was coming. I assumed she worked all this out before I got here."

"Well, you're right. I need to talk to Brandy. You do understand that you aren't going to be paid, right?"

"Yes, I understand how the music industry works. I'm not paid unless my song appears on the album."

"Ok, well get ready because Kenisha will be there to pick you up to go to the studio."

Kenisha had written many of Brandy's hits on the *Full Moon* album, so I was familiar with her work because I typically read the cd jackets.

Kenisha called my cell phone about fifteen minutes after I hung up with Sonya to say she was on her way to pick me up.

On the way to the Glendale studio, Kenisha told me how much she enjoyed working with Brandy. She said Brandy was the quickest artist she had ever worked with in the studio outside of Michael Jackson. Kenisha worked with Rodney Jerkins on Michael's *Invincible* album.

Once we arrived at the studio, Kenisha introduced me to Maximum Risks, two unassuming white guys with incredible ears for what was musically fresh. An hour or so later, Brandy appeared at the studio. She stuck her head into the sitting room that all the songwriters were in.

"Hey y'all."

"Hey," we all said in unison.

"Craig is in the building!" she said with an enormous smile.

"What's up?" I said unable to contain my smile.

"I want you guys to hear what we have so far to get an idea of the direction," she said beckoning us to the studio next door.

Brandy asked the producers to play a few of the tracks for us. The first song they played was "Sweet Nothings." The song was airy, futuristic, and European. It was a hit. Brandy looked at me and whispered, "you like it?" I shook my head and whispered back, "yea, it's hot."

Brandy asked all of the songwriters to begin writing to some of the other tracks that were submitted to her. I came back in the studio when I heard her recording. I had to *see* her in the booth to say I was there when she recorded a song. She sat on a stool in the vocal booth and layed her vocals and ad libs with ease. Her voice stacked effortlessly over the track. It was like her voice had become a part of the music. It blended so well.

I didn't see Brandy outside of the scheduled recording sessions. She was busy taping *The Tyra Show,* and going about her normal routine. I mistakenly thought because we had bonded that she would show me a bit of LA since I didn't know anyone in California.

Fortunately, I spent time with two of the other songwriters I met. They were convinced I was guaranteed to get a song on Brandy's album because we were friends. I never believed that. I knew their chances were as great or slim as mine.

My communication with Brandy was becoming sparse, and it became clear why. She and her mom were still having discussions about the expenses they were incurring with me being in LA. There was the car service from the airport to the hotel, the hotel, the car service back to the airport and the flight back to Atlanta.

The night before I left LA, Brandy and I got into a heated argument, but this wasn't our first. My guess this time was that her frustration was misdirected at me after her mom chewed into her for not giving her notice that they were picking up the tab.

But in reality, her mom was right. Brandy should have informed her that I was coming to LA to work, not hang out.

"I brought you out here to give you a shot. I didn't have to do that!" she shouted.

"You're right, you didn't. But, you ain't doing me no favors either. The problem is you never told your mother I was coming and she's pissed with me!" I yelled.

"I don't have to deal with this! I'm a star. I'm rich," she said.

"I don't give a fuck how many albums you've sold or what you have cause that shit ain't benefitting me, and even if this means I don't get a song on your album so be it 'cause what God has for me is for me!"

"When do you want to go back to Atlanta?" she asked.

"Tomorrow!"

"Alright, I'll call you right back."

After she called back with my flight itinerary I called Cris.

"I can't do this shit no more Cris. I give up," I said.

"What happened? Why are you crying?" she asked.

"Me and Brandy just got into it."

I told Cris what happened from the beginning and couldn't help but cry in the process.

"You know what, fuck that bitch. I told you she was crazy. Don't you let her kill your dreams Craig. You can't stop writing just because of this. This is what you do. Stop crying. It'll be ok."

Cris was right, but I had slammed into this wall one too many times. Perhaps, I was on the wrong course in life.

I was on the first flight back to Atlanta in the morning.

I knew without a doubt that from the beginning Brandy and I regarded the *friendship* differently. This experience was my first dose of celebrity reality. She was only dependent on our interactions until she healed her broken heart. I never had a problem reaching Brandy by phone. She answered every call I made and text message I sent. I had even skipped some of my counseling sessions because she *needed* someone to talk to. It was a hard pill to swallow.

*****

It was already Christmas again, and as usual my friends and I were planning to pull names for secret Santa. Brent kept his word two months after we returned from the Dominican Republic. He truly had cut in half the time he spent with us. We kept up with what was going on with him through Devon who was still his roommate. Once Devon got a full-time job, they moved from Brent's one bedroom apartment to a two-bedroom they shared.

Devon was first to sound the alarm that Brent and his new girlfriend were expecting a child. Our concern was had he told his girlfriend about his past, and was his past truly the past or was this a phase he was going through because anyone can abstain from sex—the feelings are always there.

DJ, the eternal skeptic was sure Brent wasn't done with men, so he made constant jokes about it.

"I guess we gotta find Brent a straight Christmas gift. Bitch, what are we supposed to buy him, tools?" he chuckled.

"Shut up fool," I chuckled.

We laughed, but it was a clear indication that it was the end of the friendship as we knew it, and no one was laughing about that. Shortly thereafter, Devon also became estranged from the group and moved back to New York.

Brandy and I spoke a few times after I returned to Atlanta from my trip to LA. We managed to patch things up enough to remain cordial, but we stopped communicating. Weeks later, I saw a report that Brandy was involved in an automobile accident that killed a woman. I sent a text message to her offering my prayers, but I never heard back.

SURRENDERING ALL

Things weren't coming together for me professionally. I was so close to my dreams at times I could taste it, but still I felt so far away. Everything I had attempted failed to come to fruition—the play, music and my greeting card company. I felt like I was in possession of three winning Lotto tickets, but couldn't cash them for whatever reason.

I sat in church countless Sundays praying for movement in my career. Praying every night on my knees like my grandmother told me, but none of it helped. I was stuck and at my wits end. I was waiting on a sign from God telling me which way to turn.

The only time I heard the voice of God I was seated at New Beginning Full Gospel Baptist Church in Decatur, GA with Twiggy and DJ. Vanessa Bell Armstrong was the musical guest and she was preparing to sing "Peace Be Still." Before she began the song she was preaching and her words touched home.

"Somebody in here needs a turnaround. You've been working on an idea for some time now and it just doesn't seem to be working out. He told me to tell you it's gonna be all right, if you can just hold on a little longer. But before things get better, they're gonna get a little worse. He told me to tell you PEACE!"

The choir echoed, *"Peace! Whenever the Lord says Peace, be still..."*

I heard a voice clearly underneath Vanessa Bell and the choir, *"I know you've been working hard. Your work hasn't gone unnoticed. If you trust me, I got you."* I looked around because I thought someone in the church was talking to me.

I had seen people burst into tears in church, but it had never happened to me until now. I never felt the need to cry in church before. I thought it was embarrassing to get that emotional in public, especially in church, but I couldn't hold back. I could see DJ nudging Twiggy through my tears. Twiggy put his arm around me and rubbed my back. He knew some of my struggles as an artist. I had borrowed money from him on a few occasions to pay my bills, and he never questioned me. If he had it, I had it.

When I left church, I felt free enough to cut off contact with a guy I was dealing with just to have someone around. Transitioning from casual sex to dating was cumbersome. I only dated people that I knew would fall harder for me than I would for them. It was a defense mechanism I developed after Saleem and Carrington. There were men I cared about, but not anyone that could ever capture my heart, so if the time came for us to go our separate ways I'd be strong enough to do so.

That service was my first glimpse of clarity.

Elden was having trouble finding reliable staff to accommodate the business opportunities that were pouring in, thus, he contracted Wendell to assist him with the labor on some of the jobs. One of his newest clients was a widow named Camille who lost her husband in an unfortunate accident while playing professional football five years before. Elden was excited to work with Camille because she was carefree with spending money, and his most open-minded client who allowed his creative autonomy to shine through.

Camille hired Elden to assist her with her move from a large Buckhead home to a modest one in Morningside, and from those interactions a friendship bloomed.

"I gotta introduce you to Camille. I really think you two would get along. She's a Taurus too. Y'all remind me a lot of each other," he said on a few occasions.

Elden's chance to introduce us came when Camille hired him to stage a benefit at her new home for her non-profit organization that adopted underprivileged schools, supplying them with accoutrement to run the schools properly. The foundation also provided supplies to the students. The catered dinner was $250 a person, and Elden contracted *Say it in a Card* to design and print the invitations.

Elden and I gave Camille several cardstock options to choose from for the invitations. I also brought samples of the greeting cards to show her some of the work I had done previously. She was impressed with the variety of greeting card offerings that included the Break up cards that grabbed Brandy's attention when we first met, and the Troubled Relationship, and Troubled Friendship cards.

"Did you write all of these yourself," she asked.

"Yea, I did. Most of them I wrote to myself, secretly wishing someone had given a card to me that said those things," I said.

The bulk of the *Encouragement* and *Wisdom* cards I wrote while I was depressed.

I could see why Elden felt at ease with Camille. She was very likeable. She wasn't what one thinks of when considering she had inherited millions. Camille was very unassuming. She wasn't boastful. I knew she was rich because I saw the way she lived. Not because she ever said it. As she put it, "real money never speaks money."

Camille and I scheduled a few meetings outside of the ones we had with Elden, which allowed us to bond. She really took an interest in *Say it in a Card*. Six weeks after we met she gave me $6,000 to market the line.

The following week, she flew me with her to Miami for the Final Four games. We stayed in a posh 2-bedroom suite at the Setai Hotel on Collins Drive with Elden, her childhood friend Kimani, and one of her girlfriends.

*****

Kencil invited me to a 4th of July barbeque at her friend Orlando's house. Kencil and I met at the gym during my fling with Bryce. Although she and I had known each other for a while, I had never met Orlando. Kencil mentioned he was in real estate and made millions when the market was booming.

I decided to tag along with her because I didn't have any other holiday plans. I figured I would run into some people I knew because Orlando was gay and the circle is pretty small. Almost immediately I saw a guy I knew from the gym who was an aspiring actor.

"What's up, I didn't know you knew Orlando," he said.

"I don't. I came with my friend Kencil."

"Oh ok. You know Tyler is having auditions for his new movie," he said.

He knew I had written a play, but he definitely didn't know our story.

"He's not one of my favorite people," I said.

Apparently, Orlando overheard me because he looked my way.

"We have history," I said.

I could tell from Orlando's facial expression that he thought that I was insinuating that Tyler and I dated because of my reply. He looked at me inquisitively.

"Not like that. I wrote a play and he came to the show," I said to Orlando who was now eavesdropping on our conversation.

"Oh, what happened?" he inquired.

"I don't really want to get into that here."

Orlando beckoned me to the staircase so we could speak privately.

"What happened?" he asked.

"Basically, he said he would help me get in touch with a promoter, but he didn't."

"Did he say why he wouldn't help?" he asked casually.

"It was too controversial," I replied.

I was close to checking out of the conversation because I vowed I wouldn't produce *A Day in the Life* again because I endured enough pain and stress as a result, so any conversation about it was pointless. And I didn't want to draw any attention from his other guests. I only continued talking to him because it was his home and I didn't want to be rude and close the conversation abruptly.

"What was the name of the show?" he prodded.

"A Day in the Life," I said.

"A Day in the Life?" he mumbled.

His eyes wandered around the room as if it sounded familiar.

"A Day in the Life! Kenji called me about that show asking me to invest in it," he said.

He and Kenji dated years before and remained friends. Kenji was a friend and former sex buddy of Leslie's who came to the play.

"Really?" I said in shock.

I was impressed that Kenji thought so highly of the show to ask someone for funding.

"Yea, and Tyler called me three days after Kenji raving about it," he injected.

I couldn't believe my ears. After almost four years and countless financial and personal struggles I found out Tyler was *raving* about a show that he refused to help me produce.

"Have you reached out to him since?" he asked.

"No, he's not gonna help," I said.

"Well, he may have had his reasons then," he said.

"Yea, because the show is gay and he's afraid to touch it. Tyler could have been a silent investor. No one had to know he was involved. He could have produced it and profited from it too. It wasn't about competition because my show could've toured on one coast while his was on another," I explained.

"Tyler's actually one of my closest friends and I'm not a fan of his stuff and he knows this. He was staying with me when he was writing one of them shows," Orlando said.

"My focus is my greeting card business, *Say it in a Card,* because it's providing me an income. I don't have any desires to do the show again," I said.

"Well, if he told you it was brilliant and I'm telling you he called me talking about it then you should use that as your inspiration to make it happen," he said.

"I can't make it happen without the money," I exclaimed.

"Find it," he said.

"I've tried to. No one cares about gay people or HIV. I'm done with it."

On the way back to Kencil's house, she told me she knew Tyler when he was a struggling writer with a big imagination and dreams. As hard as I tried I couldn't imagine him in the same desperate financial and emotional position I was in because his life had done a complete one eighty.

"It's gonna happen for you Craig. It may not come through Tyler, but it's gonna happen. I've seen it happen for several of the people around me and I see it in you," she said.

I had no idea that Kencil knew Tyler. She had never mentioned him.

A month after my conversation with Orlando, Camille asked how much it would cost to stage the show.

"Could you do your show for 50g's?"

"Hell yea I could."

"If you can do it for 50g's, I'll give you the money."

I knew if she said she was giving me the money she would, but my concern was whether or not I could muster the strength and energy to ramp the show again and face another possible flop.

That October, my friend Lane and I flew to New York for Kepri's 30th birthday dinner party. Lane was a beautiful dark skinned country boy from Slocomb, AL, with much style. He was the darkest-skinned person I had ever seen in person, and gorgeous. Camille and I used to tell him he missed his calling to be a model. His skin was creamy and his hair boasted roots from his grandmother's Native American heritage.

Lane and I flew into Laguardia airport and stayed at Camille's Ritz Carlton Battery Park apartment that overlooked New York harbor. I still hadn't given Camille a definitive answer about producing my show again, but Lane, Monica and I attended an Off-Broadway play called *Platanos and Collard Greens* that inspired me.

The show was in a small theater, but it was sold out. The writer's brother came out at the end to thank the audience on behalf of his brother who wasn't in attendance. He said the show would be moving to a larger venue in Tribecca because word of mouth created more demand.

I was anxious to get back to Atlanta to tell Camille face-to-face that I was ready to do the show. I got to Camille's and she asked me to ride with her to pick up her son from school. We were driving down Monroe Drive in her black Range Rover when I told her about the Off-Broadway show.

"Camille, their show was simple. They barely had a set and it was sold out. They probably didn't have $50,000 to do that show!"

"Ahh, hello! That's what I know."

"I wanna do the show!"

"Ok, well look, put together an outline of how you're gonna spend the money, so I can see it. Just put it in a WORD document. It ain't gotta be all fancy—show me how much you need for each month leading up to the play and when you need it by. And whenever possible you can put whatever you can on that good AMEX card so that way you can hold on to your cash just in case I'm out of town and you can't catch up with me."

"Right. Ok, I'll email you the budget this week."

Camille gave me the first portion of money in December 2006 just before I flew home to Maryland for Christmas.

I put a deposit on the Balzer Theater in January to reserve the venue from March 15th through March 25th. I wanted to do thirteen shows over the ten days.

When I left the theater, I headed down Edgewood Avenue for my barbershop appointment. It was a windy day. The kind of wind you can feel and hear gusting from inside the car. I noticed a guy walking down the right side of the street. He was wearing a beige button down shirt, beige slacks, but he wasn't wearing a coat. His hands were shoved in his pants pockets. The wind was pushing him along slightly. As I got closer I recognized his walk. It was Saleem. I pulled alongside him and pressed the horn. He looked and flashed a smile when he saw me.

"Hey," he said leaning down to the car.

"Where's your coat?"

"I just ran across the street to get lunch," he said like he owed me an explanation.

He didn't look like himself. He was thinner, and the sparkle I was used to seeing in his eyes was missing. Saleem looked defeated. I was searching for the man I loved and lost to HIV, but he wasn't there. Saleem didn't look well. He didn't look sick, but I knew he wasn't at his best. His skin was ashy gray and he appeared a little frail. He was always smiling, but there was a haze over it this time.

"Where you going?" he asked.

"I'm going to the barbershop, but I just came from putting a deposit down on a theater. I'm doing the show again in March,"

I beamed.

His smile was as grand as mine. Saleem knew he was part of my inspiration for writing the play.

"Let me know when the tickets go on sale. I'll be there opening night," he said.

"Ok, I'll let you know."

"I'll call you later. I love you," he said.

"I love you too."

I knew he wouldn't really call. That was his way of saying goodbye when he didn't know what else to say. Every so often, Saleem and I ran into each other at a club or on a rare occasion, a party. After he was diagnosed with HIV he wasn't very social. He told me he didn't want to meet anyone because it would lead to dating, and dating leads to sex, and sex would mean disclosing his status.

Saleem was suffering silently because of fear. On occasion he met guys, but stopped returning their calls when he felt them trying to get too close. When he knew they were starting to really like him or vice versa he pulled away.

I continued down Edgewood to the barbershop.

I got busy with plans to stage *A Day in the Life* for the first time solo. There was a bit of trepidation for other reasons too. The show flopped the last two times it was produced, so promotion was key to me. I was in search for a publicist, but Lane told me he knew a local promoter.

"Baby, before you meet with anybody you need to meet with

Don. He promotes all this shit that comes through here except Tyler's shit. I'm telling you, he works with everybody and them shows *be* giving sold out bitch! If you want your show to sell out, that's the motherfucker you want. At least meet with him Craig."

"Ok, what's the number? I'll call him," I said.

Lane gave me some of the best advice throughout our friendship. He was wise beyond his 33 years. We spent many late nights eating at various Waffle House restaurants around town after leaving a club. Although money was usually tight for me, I bought food for some of the homeless men that wandered into the restaurants we found ourselves in. Lane thought it was such an admirable thing to do, but I was only paying it forward because I learned compassion from needing it from others.

"Craig baby, right now you're just praying to be able to pay your bills, but your prayers change. What are you gonna be praying for when your play is *giving* sold out on Broadway for eight months straight bitch?"

"I don't know Lane. Something else I guess. I don't know what that will be."

"Baby, it can happen like that," he said snapping his fingers. "God could pull your number tomorrow bitch! He could be like *'ok, it's his turn!'*" he said stretching his eyes wide.

After a series of meetings and other referrals I determined Don was capable of promoting the show. I wrote him a check for $18,000 to buy radio spots on V103, the number one radio station in Atlanta. The commercials would begin airing thirty days before the show opened. Don also secured a street promotion team to canvas the city two weeks before opening night, and a publicist responsible for the press release and bookings for me on radio and print interviews.

After I held auditions and the show was casted, I flew to Dallas to relax and have a good time because I knew the next six weeks would be nonstop work. Meanwhile, Camille, Julian and I were strategizing to do an intervention for Elden once I returned because his drinking had spiraled out of control.

Collectively, we couldn't pinpoint the impetus of his binge drinking. I was uncertain if Elden was burned out from running his business alone or his broken relationship. He and his ex reunited for a third attempt at the relationship. We simply knew he was driving around town, sometimes en route to a client's home, with empty Grey Goose bottles rolling on the floor of his Mercedes SUV, and McDonald's cups full of vodka disguised as soft drinks.

I got a call from a guy Elden dated while I was in Dallas. He told me he ran into Elden the night before at Phase I, a nightclub in Decatur. He said Elden seemed out of character. According to him, Elden was being loud and cursing people out. I was stunned when he asked if Elden was on drugs. He said he didn't *look* healthy.

I knew it wasn't just a random call because Julian and I had experienced similar outbursts in public with Elden. Elden's behavior had become pretty erratic and uncharacteristic of the person we knew. After that call, I texted Elden to say I wanted to have a heart-to-heart with him when I got back to Atlanta, and I called Julian to devise a plan.

I took the first flight from Dallas and went straight to rehearsal. When I got home that night I was exhausted. I got a call from Elden. He asked about my trip and the first day of rehearsal. Just before the call ended he asked what I wanted to talk to him about.

"Camille, Julian and I wanted to talk to you together," I said.

"About what?"

"We've noticed you drinking a lot more and it seems to be a little out of control."

"Why are y'all having conversations about me behind my back?"

"We weren't talking about you in a negative way. We were speaking out of concern. That's what friends do."

"Well I don't have a problem. I don't drink any more than anyone else."

"Well, that's not true. Elden, there are times that we're together and I may not even have a drink. Can you say that?"

"Oh, Craig don't do me! You are really trying it!"

"Trying what? I'm asking you. Can you honestly say that you've turned down a drink ever?"

"I am not an alcoholic!"

"No one said you are, but this is how alcoholism begins. It has to start somewhere."

It was obvious that he wasn't ready to have a discussion about it because he was defensive. I called Julian and Camille, and we decided against the intervention.

Because I was the one to uncork the subject, Elden kept any and all future details about his life from me. It was difficult at times being isolated, but it was a price I was willing to pay. I would rather speak up about his drinking problem than stand by and say nothing only to see him have a fatal car crash killing himself or someone else. Elden had already experienced a handful of blackouts. He called me on two separate occasions trying to retrace his steps from the night before because he couldn't remember.

THE WRITING ON THE WALL

I met Raylon at a birthday party at Georgia Tech in December after Camille gave me the first deposit for the show. He was standing with DJ and Twiggy when we caught eyes. When Raylon turned away I asked about him. Twiggy said Raylon was a friend of DJ's visiting from Nashville, Tennessee, but he and Raylon were sort of talking.

"He's married child," he said.

"Married? Well, what's he doing at a punk party then?"

"Right!"

"And why are you fooling with him?"

"Child..."

Yet another confused, late bloomer turned me off. Raylon continued making eye contact until I walked away. If he was interested in Twiggy, he certainly didn't act like it.

In February, DJ called to tell me Raylon was in town for the weekend, and was asking about me. I was running errands before going to the gym to meet Kencil when my cell phone rang.

"Hey, what you doing?"

"Nothing, what's going on?"

"Raylon's in town."

"Raylon? Who's that?"

"Raylon, from Nashville child!"

"Oh, the married one."

"Girl, he's divorced. He's been asking about you since that party. I kept telling him you weren't tryna date nobody 'cause you were getting ready to do the show, but I got tired of him asking about you."

"Mmm hmm. Twiggy said they were talking. Wasn't Raylon staying with him when he visited?"

"That's 'cause I was staying there too. She likes him. Child, Raylon don't like her. Hold on, somebody wants to talk to you."

Before I knew it, Raylon was on the phone. I had no clue he was in the car with him, but DJ was known for calling me up on a three-way call without telling me someone else was on the call with us until after I ran my mouth too much. I should've known better.

"Hello."

"Hello?"

"This is Raylon Jermaine Lewis."

I thought it was a little corny for him to say his full name, and his thick Tennessee accent didn't help.

"Hi," I said.

"I wanted to know if you would come with me to see Alvin and Ailey tonight."

Alvin and Ailey? It's Alvin Ailey. He is country.

"I have been saying I wanted to see the show," I said.

I looked at the clock. It was almost 6 o'clock and the show was starting at 8 p.m.

"Yea, I'll go. You need me to pick you up?" I asked.

Raylon was staying at his friend's apartment near the Georgia Dome.

"Yea, that's fine."

"I'll call you when I'm on my way."

By the time I got home, showered, and dressed it was almost showtime. I called Raylon to tell him I was en route and he admitted that he hadn't bought the tickets for the show.

"What? How you inviting me to the show and you don't have tickets?"

"I was gonna get them at the door."

"Suppose the show is sold out?"

"Well, we can get tickets from a scalper."

"A scalper? We're already late. We still gotta find parking, and you're counting on tickets from a scalper? We're not going."

"Well, let's go somewhere to eat."

I should've left his ass where he was, but I picked him up from an apartment complex directly across from the Vine City train station off Northside Drive. He was in the parking lot walking over to a rental car when I pulled up. He was getting a puffy ski coat from the car.

We drove to Buckhead for dinner at Café Dupri, Jermaine Dupri's restaurant. Raylon was trying to be refined, but I could see through it when he ordered.

"Would you happen to have some Thousand Island salad dressing?" he asked.

Strike one. Not that this restaurant was upscale, but it certainly wasn't McDonald's either.

"Where you from again?" I asked.

"Memphis originally, but I've been in Nashville for the last twelve years," he said.

Raylon was employed at a university and living with a friend of his as a result of his divorce. From the conversation, I knew he was carrying more baggage than I was willing to help carry.

Raylon was extremely judgmental of his friend that was giving him a place to sleep, and of his ex-wife. He claimed his friend's place wasn't clean because he had cats and his ex-wife got everything in the divorce because she lied maliciously. Let him tell it, he was the victim.

"I just let her have everything. It's not worth it to me. God will give it all back. That's what He promised me. If my name means *anything* to Him, He'll do it for me just as sure as my name is Raylon Jermaine Lewis."

After dinner, Raylon and I went to Caribou Coffee on 10th St. because he wasn't ready to end the night. He told me he was struggling with his sexuality because he was raised in the church, and he was taught, like most of us, that homosexuality isn't of God. I was grateful that I wasn't still living for other people.

The irony of it all, he was involved with a married minister when he was 19 years old. I hit him with a barrage of questions, and tried not to judge him.

"How are you still confused?"

"You've been dipping since you were a teenager?"

"How did you reconcile having sex with a married man and be sooo religious?"

The cogs in my head were turning. *He's like the rest of the hypocrites in church.*

He looked at me a moment before he answered.

"I never really went to gay clubs though. Whenever I went I felt like the place was gonna go up in flames."

"But you thought you were safe dealing with a married man who happened to be the pastor of a church?" I asked.

"Yea," he answered nonchalantly.

"So, how has praying it away worked for you?" I asked.

"My wife and I had counseling with our minister and it worked for a while. But, whenever I got the desire to be with a man I would tell her, and we would have sex so the urge would go away," he said.

"So, she knew you were gay before you got married?"

"Yea, we were friends for years."

"Did you ever cheat on her with a man?"

"Not when we were married?"

"But, when you were dating?"

"Yea."

"What about when you were engaged?"

"Well, we didn't live together until we got married."

"So what does that mean?"

"I had a boyfriend. She never stayed the night at my apartment—"

"Did he spend nights?"

"Yea."

"Oh my God. That's a mess."

Raylon's entire circle of friends in Nashville were living double lives, and suffering through the opinions of their fellow church members.

Raylon left his wife because he grew tired of going to counseling sessions with their pastor, and praying with his wife that the feelings would fade away. His wife was under the belief that she was enough to quell his desire for men. She was wrong hence our dinner and coffee date. Sadly, everyone at his church found out why he and his wife split.

Raylon tried to shift the conversation to another topic as I yawned and was beginning to lose interest with this all too familiar story.

"You ready to go?" I asked.

I still had to take him back to his friend's place in Vine City.

"I don't wanna go back yet," he said.

Raylon had a smirk on his face that I recognized from other undercover freaks I had met in the past.

"Where you wanna go," I asked.

"I wanna go to Vinings," he said.

He knew I lived in Vinings from our earlier conversation when we were planning to see Alvin Ailey.

"You wanna go to Vinings? What you wanna go to Vinings for?" I asked.

He smiled, so I knew what he wanted. Rehearsals for *A Day in the Life* were underway, so I wasn't concentrating on dating anyone seriously. I purposely hadn't had sex with anyone in several months to stay focused on the show. I was in the middle of a dry spell, and I didn't need any unnecessary distractions.

"Let's go," I said.

Raylon didn't drink, so I wondered what ploy he would come up with to have sex. We sat in my living room watching television. He made himself comfortable. He took off his shoes and the button down shirt he was wearing, which left him wearing a white tank and jeans. He sprawled out on the couch with half of his body on the couch and the other half on the floor. He was pretending to be asleep. I reached over and unbuttoned his pants and started removing them. Raylon *woke up* and pulled them down the rest of the way.

We kissed and I pulled him off the couch and led him to my bedroom. He scooted onto the bed. He slid himself backwards to the middle of the bed and opened his legs. I climbed between his legs and continued kissing his lips and licking on his ears.

He was an avid runner, so he had nice thighs and a high booty. I had seen it in his jeans, but I wanted to see it naked, so I turned him over on his stomach and spread his legs. I kissed and licked his back and his shoulders before I pressed all of my weight on him. I grabbed his right leg and opened his leg wider and began sliding inside him.

"Craig, what are you doing?" he said laughing.

"You know what I'm doing. Open your legs," I whispered.

Raylon opened his legs wider, and as I penetrated deeper inside him he closed his eyes slowly. I watched his eyes roll back in his head as he moaned.

The next day, DJ called after Raylon was gone.

"Raylon told me he stayed the night last night. Bitch, he said the sex was everything!" he laughed.

I was disappointed in myself for sexing him without a condom because I knew better.

For the next several months Raylon made trips to Atlanta to visit me. On the first few trips he stayed with the friends he already had in Atlanta. I wasn't dating anyone, but I was certain I wasn't interested in him other than for sex from time to time. I started noticing how manipulative and strategic he could be, even in the beginning. I had a busy weekend approaching with rehearsals and interviews for the show, but Raylon insisted on visiting that same weekend until I caved.

Raylon sent emails and text messages all day from his work email while I was in rehearsal, so most times I couldn't reply, but he continued messaging as if I had. His persistence was flattering on some level, but annoying too. He knew DJ had been casted in the show, so he asked him for the address to the rehearsal location to send flowers. On the surface, his gestures were thoughtful, but it was his control issues shining through.

Eventually, I allowed Raylon to stay at my place on his visits to Atlanta. I was decidedly single, but it felt good to have someone to spend time with in my down time. I know that I like being in a relationship. I prefer the person I am with companionship, but the decision to continue seeing Raylon was a poor decision that I made out of loneliness. He wasn't the kind of guy I normally got involved with, but he managed to weasel his way in my life because he was consistent and persistent while I was distracted with *A Day in the Life*.

I knew Raylon was troubled by his religious upbringing. He married because he thought it would cure his craving to be with men. I had thought the same thing at one point, so I could certainly relate.

I felt sorry for Raylon. He had confusion written all over his face. He was conflicted with whom to be in public, at work, and in church. At 33 years old, he didn't know who he was because he was too busy people pleasing.

Raylon wanted to be liked and he went out of his way to be accepted. He paid for most of the things we did together, and when my friends came along he paid for them too. I told him it wasn't necessary for him to take on that responsibility, but he insisted it was just money.

It came out during conversation that he didn't have a car. He was renting cars every week to visit me, and I didn't notice because he stayed with friends on his first few visits. I urged him to focus on stabilizing, not a relationship. His response was always tied to the Bible or God. Raylon quoted Bible verses every three sentences, but was far from practicing what he preached.

I did my best to affirm him. I challenged everything he [we] had been taught by family, religion and society as it relates to sexuality. He decided he wanted to be with me, but I wasn't into him. I had a pattern of trying to save people from themselves then slipping into relationships with them though I didn't want it. Once I helped Raylon erase some of his concerns about being gay, I worried that if I walked away he would be convinced all gay men were the same, so I hung around.

*****

I contracted Frankie to co-write some of the music for the show because we make great music together. It was clear during one of our writing sessions that there was still an attraction between us. The session ended with us naked on my couch kissing. It was sweet, not sexual, but it couldn't happen again because we had work to do that couldn't take the backseat.

I got a call from Frankie one evening I was home planning the rehearsal schedule for the week. He sounded different— something was on his mind.

"What was the guy's name that you dated who had the funny name?" Frankie asked.

"Who Saleem?" I asked.

"Yea, I think he died," Frankie said.

"What?! Where did you hear that?" I yelled.

"Well, you remember he and my old roommate were friends? He said they rushed him to the hospital because he was having trouble breathing."

"When did this happen?"

"Like Monday."

It was Wednesday.

"Let me call you back."

I frantically dialed Saleem's home number. I wasn't crying or sad because it didn't *feel* like death. The day didn't feel off. The kind of day with moments when the telephone rings and before you answer you know its bad news. This day didn't feel that way.

Saleem had moved his mom, niece, and nephew from Philadelphia to help his mom raise them because their parents were estranged. It was my mother's story with my nephews all over again. I had met his mom a few times before she moved to Atlanta, but I didn't think she'd remember me. And, if it was true, she definitely wouldn't know to call to tell me, let alone invite me to the funeral.

A woman answered the phone, but it wasn't his mother. Before I could hone in on the voice, I heard gospel music blaring in the background, traditional gospel. This song wasn't anything I recognized. It was layered with heavy organs.

"Hello."

"Hi, may I speak to Saleem?"

There was a brief pause.

"Hold on."

If she's putting me on hold she's going to get him. This was a false alarm.

"Hello," she said again.

"Yes," I said.

"Munchie's gone. He passed," her voice quivered.

"Oh no. I'm so sorry. When is the service?" I asked.

She rattled off the details.

"You wanna speak to his mother?" she asked.

"Yes, is she able to come to the phone?" I asked.

"Hold on," she said.

I had just seen him a month ago on that cold day in December.

I flashed back to the year before. I called Saleem a few days in a row leaving messages for him, but he never returned my call. On the third attempt to reach him he answered.

"I've been meaning to call you back. I saw you called," he said.

"Where you been?" I asked.

He explained he had a boil he was nursing and had been back and forth to the doctor for treatment.

"Awe, you were worried," he teased.

"Yea crazy. I hadn't heard back from you," I said.

"I'm still here. I ain't going nowhere," he replied.

But this time he was really gone. His aunt came back to the phone and said his mother couldn't talk. She gave me the information for the funeral service again. It was in two days.

Saleem's funeral was on a cold, dreary, rainy Thursday evening in Tucker, GA. I debated all day if I was going to the funeral.

He had progressed with his treatment. He was a person that refused medication, but became someone that stuck to his regiment. Saleem became undetectable, but I've learned through my experience is attitude plays the biggest part in whether a person lives or dies from AIDS.

Saleem's spirit was crushed once he learned he was HIV positive. The stress kills the majority of people living with HIV. No matter how hard he tried to appear to be happy, I knew he carried that burden. It was visible each time we saw each other. He told me once that I was a reminder that he was positive whenever he saw me.

There was always a moment that we were excited when we first saw each other out, but it was always interrupted by an awkward silence when we had nothing else to say. In that silence, we were remembering his status—our story. We could be standing in a room full of people, and were the only ones in the room that knew his reality. His secret was our secret.

I decided against attending the service because I wanted my last mental picture of him to be from that crisp day on Edgewood Avenue. Saleem's death reminded me why I was committed to *A*

Day in the Life and why I couldn't walk away from the show. I didn't want anyone else to live to tell this story.

The cast and crew were on stage preparing for the last run through of the show before we opened Tuesday, March 15, 2007, while I paced nervously outside the theater. I said a few more prayers and answered more calls. My phone was ringing off the hook. Friends and family were calling and texting their best wishes for the show.

My mom was in town to assist me with selling the greeting cards in the lobby during intermission. I commissioned a couple of the HIV organizations to set up information booths in the lobby as well. I walked back inside the theater to check on things and the telephone for the theater was ringing incessantly. The box office manager was behind the desk on a phone call. She stopped me before I went into the house.

"Congratulations Mr. Stewart. You just sold out your first show."

"Really? Thank you!"

I sent Camille a text. *The show is sold out!*

A Day in the Life had another successful run and no one was more relieved than I. It was time for a mini getaway to celebrate. Lane and I took a road trip to Nashville because Raylon had asked me on several occasions, but I always refused. After the show closed, I had no excuse.

Soon after Lane and I arrived, Raylon and I got into an argument. Raylon was different in Tennessee. He was snappy and all of his comments to me were flippant because I was now in *his* city, so he assumed he could get away with it.

His arrogance in front of his friends was an attempt to look less interested in me than he was because they all had ill thoughts about gay relationships too. Their cynicism provoked a few of Raylon's friends to marry women because it was said to be easier than dealing with gay drama.

Lane and I were excited to be in Nashville and ready to see the city. Our eagerness caused us to be indecisive about what we wanted to do. Lane wanted to go to some shops and I wanted to eat, but didn't know what I wanted to eat. Frankly, Raylon was rude and snapped.

"Look, what the fuck y'all wanna do? Y'all getting on my goddamn nerves now!"

I had never heard him curse before. He prided himself on never cursing or drinking. I was baffled by his aggravation. I had never seen this side of Raylon.

"Who are you talking to like that?" I yelled.

"I'm talking to your ass! Lane wanna go here, you wanna get something to eat! Y'all need to make up y'all mind."

"You ain't talking to me like that, and so what!"

"Raylon, you need to pull over while we do this 'cause this is my truck we driving," Lane interjected.

"Lane, I'm not gonna crash your car."

"You can take us back to the house. We going back to Atlanta," I said.

"That's fine Craig. You are not hurting my feelings."

We got back to Raylon's friend's house and grabbed our weekend bags to get back on the highway to Atlanta. We hadn't been in Nashville two hours. Raylon ran in the bedroom when he saw I was serious. He closed the door so his friends couldn't hear him apologizing and begging us to stay.

"Craig, I'm sorry. I don't know what came over me. Lane, tell him to stay please. Don't you wanna stay?"

"Well, it's up to Craig."

"I'm sorry Craig. It won't happen again. Give me another chance."

Raylon went to the living room to gain more support from his friends. The moment he left the room Lane whispered, "Bitch if you wanna go we can hit it 'cause you know I don't even give a fuck!"

"I'm ready to go," I said.

"What is his motherfucking problem, bitch? He is doing full fledge stunts and shows! Is he tryna show his ass for his country ass friends?"

"I don't know what's wrong with him, but we're leaving."

"Bitch, I thought he was gonna put his hands on you."

"That motherfucker ain't crazy."

"Bitch, I don't know, but we would've fucked him all the way up, hear? And, I'm not saying I'm the baddest bitch 'cause you just *might* be able to kick my ass, but you gonna know I was on yours! See Craig, I don't do all that arguing and shit 'cause that sends your blood pressure up all high. I'd rather just fight and get the shit over with."

Lane and I emerged from the room with our bags. Raylon's friend who was hosting us asked if we would stay because it was too dark to leave. He said it would be better to leave in the morning, so we stayed.

Camille called the next night at almost midnight to say Elden collapsed at her house. I had never heard her distressed before.

"Oh my God, Craig! I'm sorry to be calling you this late 'cause I know you're out of town, but Elden was at my house and he just fell out and hit his head. Blood was everywhere. I called 911 and they just took him to the hospital."

Camille said she called DJ and Julian to go up to the hospital because she was home alone with her nine-year old son.

"Was he drunk?"

"I don't know 'cause he didn't have nothing to drink here. I mean he took like a couple sips and he got up to go in the house to use the bathroom. We were sitting on the porch like we always do, and when he stood up he fell in between the couch and the table. He opened his eyes, looked up and said he was really sleepy, but that wasn't no sleep Craig. So, he made it in the house. Next thing I heard was BOOM. I ran in the house and he was just still. He didn't want to go to the hospital, but I was like he gotta go. I was scared."

"We need to call his mother," I said.

I thought it was important for us to have each other's parents' phone numbers in case of an emergency, and this was an emergency.

"You know he's gonna be mad if we call," she said.

"He'll just have to be mad. Hold on."

I put Camille on hold and called Elden's sister in Houston on three-way to tell her what happened. Subsequently his mom and sister flew to Atlanta the next morning and rushed to Piedmont Hospital. Doctors stitched Elden's head and told his family he had a *ridiculous* amount of alcohol in his system.

As expected, Elden was upset with Camille and me for calling his sister, but we thought it was the best thing to do, especially if his condition worsened in the hospital. Quite frankly, I was exhausted from babysitting and I felt someone in his family needed to know. His drinking was taxing me.

We all kept a watchful eye on Elden when we went out to make sure he wasn't close to fighting someone because his demeanor became belligerent at times, and someone was responsible for getting him home. It didn't help that he wanted to stay until the club closed.

Elden became secretive about his drinking. He thought he was doing a good job of hiding his drinking. In front of us he had one or two drinks instead of multiple like in the past, but we knew he was drinking at home because he reeked of alcohol when he showed up.

It seemed the more he drank, the louder his cologne became to mask the smell of vodka on his breath and seeping through his pores. It amazed me that he wouldn't admit to me that he had a problem, considering I reached out to him and Julian two years before when I was struggling with an internet sex addiction. The only difference, I was ready to be open and honest about it.

YOU'RE GONNA LOVE ME

Raylon was intent on changing my mind about being in a relationship with him, so he began making plans to move to Atlanta two months after we met. His random flare-ups were more than enough reason for me to discourage the move.

"Don't move to Atlanta for me because that's not gonna change how I feel."

"Eighty percent is for you Craig, and twenty percent is for school. I'm going to AIU."

"I just don't want you moving here thinking we're getting together. I really don't want a relationship."

"I think things will be different once I'm there. I'm gonna make you happy. Just give me a chance."

It's no accident that Raylon believed he could change my mind about being in a relationship because we were already functioning as such, and that was my mistake for leading him on. We were seeing each other regularly and having sex. I had a habit of *not* giving things a title for fear they wouldn't work out, and in the event they didn't I could reassure myself with, *"we were just hanging out."*

With all that was compounding in Raylon's life, I got a second chance to see the monster reappear, but still I continued playing along.

Raylon told his mom he was gay and she was curious to meet the man special enough to keep her son from dating women, and he was equally ardent to show me off as he did whenever we traveled back to Nashville with hopes the news would travel back to his ex-wife.

When Raylon moved to Georgia, he lived in Smyrna with a friend of his from Memphis, but after a few months his friend moved to Baton Rouge, LA, for a job leaving Raylon with no place to live. Living with me was not an option, but I allowed him to use my second bedroom for storage once he moved in with a coworker that gave him the ok to sleep on her couch.

Raylon and I packed for a weekend in Memphis to visit his mom, and for a roller skating competition. Everything was coordinated perfectly except the time we actually got on the road. We drove in silence for five-hours because Raylon was angry that we got on the road later than he wanted. The only sound was gospel music blaring from the car stereo.

The plan was to drop off his car for service at a mechanic in Memphis because his mother was paying for the work, and for him to get a haircut while the car was being serviced.

I was aggravated because I could have stayed home, especially since he was in a foul mood.

"Can you turn the music down some?"

"No, I cannot. I need this to stay awake while I drive."

If looks could kill he would've died that day. *I don't know why I didn't stay home.*

We didn't speak again until we arrived in Memphis.

"Are you gonna pout all weekend or are you gonna act like you have some sense 'cause I came to have fun," he barked.

"You're the one acting crazy. This is the second time you've done this. Why do you wait to get out of Atlanta to act a fool?"

"You need to decide what you gonna do 'cause you can get on the bus and go back to Atlanta. Now, are you gonna act like you got some sense or what?"

I ignored him like the stranger he was.

"I'm going to get my haircut."

When he walked into the barbershop, I called Delta and booked the first flight back to Atlanta. I headed across the parking lot to the grocery store to ask how far the airport was from the shopping center.

I happened upon a little white woman with mixed silver and black hair pulled back in a bun. Her reading glasses were propped on her head.

"Excuse me," I said.

Her hands were full, but she was squatting down looking at some knick-knacks on sale.

"Yes," she said standing to her feet.

"Do you know how far the airport is from here?"

"I would say about twenty five minutes or so."

I was processing the steps I would have to take. My luggage was still in Raylon's car, which was at the mechanic and that was ten minutes from the grocery store. I had to move fast because my flight was leaving in two hours. The woman looked around the store then back at me with a quick once over.

"Did you need to get to the airport?"

"Yes, I do. I'm gonna take a cab."

"Well, I can take you if you don't mind waiting for me to check out real fast."

This truly had to be God working on my behalf. I would've never predicted this little white woman would offer me, a strange Black man, a ride to the airport.

"I would really appreciate that."

"Ok, let me just check out," she said scurrying to her cart.

We walked out to a little pick up truck and loaded her things in the cab of the truck. Just before I climbed in I noticed the seats were marred with dog hair, but this was one day I didn't care. I was getting in.

I couldn't remember the name of the street where the mechanic was located, but after circling the area a few times we stumbled upon it. I jumped out and grabbed my bag from the car and we headed to the airport.

Come to find out, this little lady was married to a Black man and this wasn't her first time being a Good Samaritan. He had told her many times before not to pick up strangers, but I was glad she ignored his advice this time.

Just as we pulled up to the airport Raylon texted, *"I don't know where you at, but I'm ready to go."* I ignored his text and offered the woman $20, but she refused to take it. Once I stepped out of the car I tossed the bill back into the truck and thanked her again.

By the time I arrived in Atlanta I had fifteen text messages and ten voice messages. The messages ranged from, *"I'm about to leave you!"* to *"Baby, I'm scared. Just let me know you're alright."* I deleted them all without responding and he called all weekend to no avail.

I was able to piece together things I couldn't when Raylon was living in Nashville. His whole life was a lie. He was leaning on friends and family financially. He told his mom he moved to Atlanta for graduate school and she co-signed for a car to help him—the exact same model and color car I was driving.

The truth was he didn't want his mom to know he left his job at Tennessee State University and was now unemployed in another city because he wanted to be with a man, so he lied. This was the same person I had seen screaming, shouting, and running up the aisles in church.

Raylon turned over stones looking for me once he returned to Atlanta, but I was done. I couldn't pretend anymore. He popped up at my part-time job smiling, but he couldn't redeem himself. I was done with the late night screaming matches and calls to 911 because he wouldn't leave my place.

It was the middle of January, when the east coast is coldest, when Raylon retaliated. He entered my apartment while I was at a meeting and stole all of my winter clothes. He even picked up clothes that I had at the dry cleaners. Some of the clothes he stole were things my booster got me to wear for the show, so I couldn't really be upset about those because I hadn't gotten those things legally, but it was the principle.

Raylon's story became undone when his mom called asking me for money to make his car payment. Apparently, Raylon told her that he gave me money to deposit into her bank account to cover his car payment.

"I don't know anything about money for his car payment. He hasn't given me anything," I said.

"Why would he tell me that? I need that money to put in my account because the bank is drafting my account," she said.

"I don't know, but he stole from me. He came into my place and took my clothes, so if you talk to him tell him I'm filing a police report."

Raylon's mother worked for the bank that was sifting from her overdrawn account, but he didn't care.

"I called him about the money, but he was whispering. He said he couldn't talk because he was in class," she explained.

"Class? What class? Raylon's not in school," I said.

"I don't understand what's happening. Why would he do this?"

"He's a thief!"

I didn't have time to make sense of things for his mother, especially after she confessed that this was the second car she co-signed for with a similar outcome. I wondered what else he was lying about. I had fucked him without a condom.

I called Raylon's cell phone, but he wouldn't answer. I kept getting the voicemail, so I sent text messages to let him know that I knew what he had stolen from me.

He replied, *"I have a whole lot more LOL."*

I wanted revenge. I couldn't have him think that he had gotten over on me so easily. I replied, *"I'm gonna get you when you least expect it..."*

I changed my locks the same day and filed a police report with Cobb County police. They wouldn't issue a warrant for his arrest because he had a key and there was no forced entry. Furthermore, his fingerprints were gonna be present because he was my *boyfriend.* I was pissed, but was left with no choice but to let it go for now.

Seemed like everyone who knew the story ran into Raylon somewhere around Atlanta except me. I got constant phone calls with reports. The calls became too much, so I refused to entertain them any longer. The one call that bothered me most was from Elden. He called the day after he saw Raylon at a gathering. Elden said when Raylon entered he walked past him without speaking, but he stopped Raylon to ask why he didn't speak. Raylon told him, *"I thought your loyalty would be to Craig."*

Elden went on to say that he asked Raylon for a hug and they exchanged phone numbers to hang out another time. It was clear that Elden no longer respected our friendship. I've never been one to expect my friends to cut ties with people I've dated because we broke up, but this motherfucker had stolen from me. I shouldn't have had to explain that to Elden. That's friendship 101. And, he claimed he didn't like Raylon when were seeing each other so what was different now?

I thought back to a secret Elden kept from Wendell. Elden found out shortly after our trip to the Dominican Republic that Wendell's boyfriend slept with another friend of ours that was living with Wendell and his boyfriend. Apparently, they hooked up while we were away, but Elden never told Wendell. I could now understand the betrayal Wendell felt once he found out Elden knew, but never told him.

I believed my friends and I were cut from a different cloth because we didn't sleep together nor did we sleep with or date each other's boyfriends, past or present.

Elden was someone I could count on. He was one I cared about tremendously, and I still do. He loaned me $16,000 to pay off my American Express card without questioning if I'd be able to repay him in two days as I promised. Our parting of the ways was as traumatic as my split with Carrington. We went from inseparable to no communication at all.

We vowed, in our 20s, not to be the old gay men in the club trying to fit in with the young boys by dressing too young for our age. I was transitioning from the clubs and Elden was going out more than he ever had and understandably because the club lends itself to drinking and drugs. We said we would be different, but I began to see us becoming everything we said we wouldn't. We were the same.

Initially, I thought we were drifting apart because our schedules had changed or because we were involved in relationships, but our lifestyles had changed. There were secrets built on lies, deception, and an array of untruths. I felt the toxicity in our friendship. I knew there was no other option but to pull away when I could no longer be honest about the things happening between us, and if I couldn't be honest, we couldn't be friends.

Slowly but surely I re-categorized Elden's placement in my life. I spoke when I saw him, but the days of being in close contact were over. I resolved that it was time to move on to make room for healthy friendships in my life. Elden's interaction with Raylon was a problem greater than his drinking for me.

I tried moving past being robbed because it wasn't worth the energy I was expending. Plus, I didn't know where Raylon was living to get him back. Two months passed, and I had come to terms with what happened despite the fact I was still discovering things that were missing.

I noticed my car door was unlocked one afternoon before I activated the keyless entry. I couldn't remember if I had locked the car door the night before after returning from the grocery store toting bags. *Maybe I was remiss in not locking the doors.*

When I got in the car I noticed my cds were missing and the bag of loose change that I kept in the car for tolls and parking meters was gone. My first instinct was to file a police report with Cobb County police because there had been random car burglaries in my apartment community, so I did.

In the days that followed, the battery in my keyless remote was dying. I searched for the spare remote control in my nightstand and it was gone. I knew Raylon was the culprit for what I thought had been a car break in. I went after him with two of my friends, Kimani and Xavier.

I dressed in a pair of old Timberland boots and sweats. We hunted him down that night with a car jack in hand. Our first stop was Cascade Skating rink. I didn't see his car in the parking lot, so we stopped at Utopia next. I knew the guy working the door there, so we didn't pay to do a walk through.

Our last stop was at Django's on Peachtree Street. Xavier and I searched upstairs and Kimani took the basement level. I knew he was there. I could feel it. Kimani spotted him, and called my cell. We waited for him outside the club in my car. Raylon stayed until the club closed.

We watched him exit from the rear of the club crossing Courtland Street. I pulled slowly behind him with my headlights switched to the off position. When he turned and saw us creep-ing behind him, he picked up his pace. I drove on the sidewalk and sped up. He was wearing one of my shirts. I jumped out of the car with the car jack in my hand.

"Oh, but you don't know what clothes I'm talking about? Where did you get that shirt?" I yelled.

He ran and I chased him into a tavern on Piedmont Avenue. Raylon ran to the backside of the tavern near the bar begging the bartender to call the police. The bartender saw the car jack in my hand.

"Get out of here! I'm calling the police!" she screamed.

"Call the police! He stole from me and I'm gonna fuck him up!"

"Miss please! Please call the police! I can't go back out there. It's three of them." Raylon begged.

"You better not come out here 'cause I'm gonna fuck you up," I said walking back outside.

I was in the middle of a domestic dispute in downtown Atlanta with someone I didn't want or love. I was giving him control. This was what he wanted—a reaction. It was the reason he kept baiting me.

The police arrived and threatened to arrest me because I was disturbing the peace. I told them they wouldn't arrive in time the next time he and I crossed paths. One of the cops pulled me to the side and told me he had gone through a similar situation with a guy he dated that stole his identity and bought a new car on his credit. He urged me to put it in God's hands.

"I'm telling you I'm gonna fuck him up, so when something happens to him just know I'm responsible," I said.

Raylon was smirking and laughing while the officer's back was to him.

"Keep laughing. You won't be laughing when I catch you!" I yelled.

Kimani and Xavier settled me down enough to leave, but for two consecutive weeks I woke up in cold sweats. In my dreams I caught Raylon and bludgeoned him to death. I was allowing him to win by my reaction. He wanted this because he craved my attention. I was allowing him to make me someone I'm not. I was considering violence.

I started praying for peace of mind. I asked God to remove the disdain I had towards him because it was no longer about the things he stole. I was trying to get back at him so he wouldn't think he had gotten over on me. The things he stole weren't worth going to jail for. I also asked God to keep me from seeing him.

Since the police weren't any help in prosecuting Raylon, I moved. I couldn't risk him knowing where I lived and being defenseless. I broke my lease and moved into Kencil's until I was ready to move into my own place again.

Staying with Kencil allowed me time to reflect. I had overlooked many of the signs that pointed to Raylon's instability, mostly because I was too busy to slow down to see what was there all along. Raylon used religion as a cover. Religion was the centerpiece for his manipulation and conniving spirit. It was an expensive lesson I paid, but worth every bit of wisdom I pulled from it.

PATTERNS

One of the biggest epiphanies for me, after Raylon, was the realization that I had developed a pattern of dating men whom I thought needed me to help them with whatever they were struggling to cope with. I settled for men that lacked a sense of self to some degree, and I thought it was my responsibility to save them from their demons because I could relate to the struggle. I had my role confused with the responsibility of *A Day in the Life*.

I thought if they came to me damaged and in need of repair, I could fix them. Some were uncomfortable in their sexuality while others suffered from abandonment issues. I thought if I *invested* in them by walking with them through their stuff—like a good partner—I would get a return, and that return on my investment would be monogamy, loyalty, consistency and longevity. I discovered those things weren't guaranteed because there are no guarantees that we'll get back what we put into people.

My friend Liv, from the DSL company, made it simple for me, "stop allowing people to choose you, and start choosing who you want to be with." Every man I dated had chosen me.

I began taking inventory of the extremes I went to prove myself. Even as the players involved changed, I was the one constant. I was the common denominator in each scenario and I was allowing them to choose me. I lowered the bar because I thought it was too high for most to reach and I grew tired of waiting to be with someone worthy and deserving.

In many ways, I was subconsciously substituting. I was replacing my dreams with finding a partner. My career suffered whenever I got into relationships because I couldn't strike a balance between the two. My sexuality was consuming me and practically monopolizing the other parts of my life. I spent more time investing in relationships than I was in becoming a writer. Every other year from the time I was 22 and dating men, I was in a relationship with only a year or so in between each.

We're taught that a relationship requires us to help our partner become whole, when in fact he or she should be whole when they come to us. I exerted time and effort pouring into men that should've been preparing for the relationship before we met. I ended up playing counselor in a few of my relationships instead of being a partner. It's one thing to work with a person because they're impatient, stubborn, unorganized or procrastinates, but it's another when we try to teach him or her fundamental core values.

I managed to break my relationship patterns when I took time to be single.

After living with Kencil, I moved into an apartment at Atlantic Station. Brent and I weren't in contact frequently, but I still considered him a friend. He was a leasing agent at the property I moved to. He helped me shift some numbers around to qualify for a beautiful one-bedroom apartment under the tax credit program. The market rate for the apartment was $1,200 a month, but with our creativity I got the apartment for $778 a month.

It was time to be tested for HIV. For the first time in my life, I was paranoid about getting tested because I didn't really know Raylon after all. Before the counselor administered the test, he asked if I had put myself at risk. I used to think that question referred to people who had unprotected sex with strangers. It took on a whole new meaning that day.

"Yes, I have."

"Ok, do you have reason to believe you're positive?"

"No, but…"

"How do you think you'll respond to a positive test result?"

"I have no idea."

"We have resources for you should your test come back positive. The test takes twenty-minutes, so I'll have you wait in the waiting area and I'll come and get you."

"Ok."

I thought about Saleem and everyone I knew who was positive. I thought about the promise I made to myself to remain negative after I told my mother I was gay.

The counselor called me back into the room.

"Your test was negative."

I felt like I was starting over.

All of the drama with Raylon and Elden was over, and no one knew where I lived. It was freeing and lonely at the same time, but something *shifted* inside me in my thirties. I became less anxious and worried about things I couldn't control, including the things I heard about myself after I was no longer in touch with Elden. I was a bit more patient, understanding, and less judgmental.

The things I needed in my twenties were less important or no longer necessary at all. My needs changed because I was evolving. I was no longer reaching and grabbing for things outside myself in an effort to make success happen faster than God intended.

I've always believed great things would happen for me, but I thought I could manipulate it. I was under the impression that I could connect the dots faster if I took bigger risks; however, I realized I made things more difficult than they had to be because of poor choices I made. I thought I had to choose between being an artist and working a nine to five.

With solitude came many epiphanal moments. The debut show sold out and I got lost in the hype. I got caught up in the shine. I forgot I had been chosen by God to tell a story to spread a message of hope and awareness that He could've chosen anyone to tell. I forgot His instructions, so He took it all away and I struggled financially because of it.

It became clear to me why the show hadn't gone on tour, and it wasn't because Tyler didn't help. Yes, I met with a national promoter who agreed to take the show on the road, but without warning he disappeared because God had more lessons for me to learn. I believe everything happens for a reason in the spiritual realm and in the physical realm.

In the physical realm, the show didn't tour because the promoter didn't follow through with his promise because he was afraid to touch a gay play. But, in the spiritual realm, God knew I wasn't ready for the success; thus, He set things in motion that would prevent the promoter from following through with a tour. Everything that I went through was a part of the process Tyler spoke of—I finally got it.

Everything that happened to me had happened for my greatest good even when I was unable to see how at first. All the things that I feared manifested in my life, including dating men who were living with HIV. I was afraid I would fall behind in my car payment, so I did. I was scared I would be late paying the rent and I was. I *never* feared becoming HIV positive, thus, I've remained negative. So, it was clear that my thoughts were creating my destiny.

*****

I walked into the parking deck of my apartment building with plans of going to the gym. I knew I was behind in my car payment, but I was sure they weren't looking for my candy apple red Acura 3.2 CL coupe in Atlanta because I had it registered in Maryland.

I looked around the parking deck trying to remember where I parked because I had parked on the wrong floor before. My first inclination was that the car was stolen, but I decided to call the finance company and, much to my chagrin, the car had been picked up from my gated community.

This was the first time since I was seventeen that I was without a car. My mom was retired and made it clear she would not be cosigning for a car for anyone. Fortunately, I was living in the heart of midtown at Atlantic Station, so I was in walking distance to the gym and grocery store. If I needed a ride some place, I could get a ride from a friend because I was centrally located. Still, this was humiliating. *What will I say when people ask what happened to my car?* I had judged people in the past for being a *certain age* without a car.

My friend Zoe relocated to Boston for a job with Bristol Myers, but prior to moving she was having an incredibly difficult time financially in Atlanta. She was staying with a friend rent-free as I had with Kencil, so I could relate. Every so often we ran into each other at the gym and I recognized depression in her face. She tried masking it with a smile and her piercing brownish-green eyes, but depression and I had an on again and off again relationship. I knew it when I saw it no matter how it was dressed.

Zoe and I went to HU together, but she and I only spoke in passing. I was friends with her older sister. Zoe and I ran into each other years later at Crunch fitness after recognizing one another. We exchanged numbers after crossing paths multiple times, and subsequently, she came to the show.

She and I never really got a chance to hang out when she lived in Atlanta, but I invited her out a few times just to get her out of the house. Soon after, she called with news that she was moving for an incredible salary.

I texted Zoe two days after my car was repossessed just to catch up and see how she was adjusting to life in Boston. I usually avoided reaching out to people I didn't speak to on a regular basis because the question that always seemed to come up was, "what's going on with the play?" and since I didn't have an answer, I wanted to dodge those conversations if possible.

I told her my car was repossessed and that I was looking for a job because I was two months behind in my rent.

"Oh man, well, I can help with one of those problems. I have a company car that I use and my car is just sitting. If you don't mind coming to Boston and driving it back to Atlanta, it's yours for as long as you need it."

"Are you serious? Hell yea, I'll drive it back!"

Zoe was still paying the car note on her Honda Accord. It was only three years old and fully loaded with satellite radio and less than 50,000 miles.

"Ok, I'll even buy your plane ticket to Boston. When do you want to come?"

Before my car was repossessed I was praying for financial relief, but I didn't expect for the car to be taken though it was a blessing in disguise. God freed me from that worry, and supplied another car.

I flew to Boston a week and a half later with a guy I was dating who worked for the same airline, so he was able to fly for free. He helped me with the drive back.

I suggested that Zoe and I draft an agreement to spell out the terms of the car loan. I agreed to take care of the scheduled oil changes and pay any tickets for parking or moving violations. Zoe continued making the monthly car payment and paid for all major work the car needed like tune-ups and brakes. She also noted in the contract that I was to be the only driver once we got the car back to Atlanta.

When we arrived in Boston, she picked us up from the airport. We drove to Zoe's to sign the agreement and to pick up the car before we checked into our hotel for the night.

The next morning he and I drove to Baltimore to stay at my father's, and spend time with the rest of my family for a few days before we continued to Atlanta.

*****

Two years passed without running into Raylon until I saw his car parked outside a party. I thought because he had been out of sight and out of mind I was over what happened, but I wasn't. I decided not to go inside the party. Instead, I drove home for a few supplies. I grabbed a butcher knife, hammer, tennis racket and a couple cans of paint leftover from a spruce up job I gave my apartment.

I called Neequaye on my way back to the party. He moved back from DC after two years, and his new place was close to the party. I told him what I was about to do, and he had to be there to witness it.

I wanted to total the car. I slashed each tire on Raylon's car. I used the tennis racket to shatter every light on the car and to break both of the automatic side mirrors. When I was done they were dangling from the car. I only stopped when cars passed or to grab more supplies from my car.

I opened the gallon of rust colored paint first. I poured it on his sunroof down to the front windshield so he couldn't see out to drive. Neequaye pulled up as I poured the last drop of baby blue paint from the sunroof down the back window. It was after midnight and frigid, which helped dry the paint almost instantly.

"You damn ghetto Baltimore skeezer. Bitch, you *is* crazy," Neequaye laughed.

"And I can't wait to see his face."

"You gonna wait out here til he comes out?"

"No, we're gonna go to your house and come back when the party is over."

I followed Neequaye to his apartment and we waited until the party was over to drive back. I knew Raylon wouldn't leave the party until the last car left the parking lot. Neequaye and I drove his car because I didn't want Raylon to see me driving Zoe's car. I couldn't afford for anything to happen to it should he retaliate a second time.

We parked across from Raylon's car to have a clear view of him as he approached.

"There he is," I said.

"Where?"

Neequaye had never seen Raylon before, but he knew the entire story.

"Coming up right there with the blazer on. I wonder if he has on some of my shit."

"Oooh, that would be a mess," he chuckled. "That's him?"

"Yea, that's his ass."

Raylon was by himself. He was walking swiftly to his car because it was bitterly cold. I could see his pace slowing the closer he got to the car. Neequaye giggled because he knew, like I knew, that Raylon could see from a few feet away that his car was vandalized. He got closer then walked slowly around it to see it from all angles. His face had shock and disbelief written all over it.

Partygoers passing in their vehicles slowed up to get a view as they left the party. Neequaye and I could hear some of them laughing with us.

Raylon pulled out his cell to make a call. I figured he was calling the police, and possibly someone to come pick him up. It was 2 a.m., so it would be virtually impossible to find a ride at that hour. Neequaye and I laughed hysterically watching him pace back and forth, cold and confused.

"I gotta fuck with him. Watch this," Neequaye said snickering as he pulled closer.

He put his window down.

"Hey man. What happened to your car?"

Raylon couldn't see me because of the tint on Neequaye's windows.

"I don't know. I just came out. I was at the party," Raylon explained.

"Damn, that's fucked up. Yo, you need to call the cops."

"Yea, I just did."

Neequaye rolled up the window and let out another laugh as we pulled away. He was really getting a kick out of this. He turned the car around to pass Raylon twice more.

Finally, Raylon got in the car and started it up to get some heat.

"Honey, I told you you should've got a potato to put in that tail pipe. That ho wouldn't have started at all! He would've sat in that car cold honey," Neequaye giggled.

When the police arrived we left the scene. We laughed all the way back to Neequaye's apartment.

"I told that ass I'd get him when he least expected it. He'll be up all night trying to figure out who did it and I'll be sleeping peacefully."

I sat at Neequaye's until almost 4 a.m. I couldn't resist passing by again to see if Raylon was still there, and he was.

LEAVING ATLANTA

Friendships weren't the only things being recycled in Atlanta. There was a line of gay men at a revolving door waiting their turn to date the same men, but the trend didn't stop there. The same was true of the gyms, nightclubs, and apartment complexes that we flocked to as they sprouted up in the city. We were in search of something or someone. It was like watching a merry go round of people taking turns sleeping with the same people. The usual six degrees of separation was more like two degrees in Atlanta—part of the reason HIV is running rampant.

After years of losing touch with Chance, Neequaye and I reconnected with him via Facebook. He was living in Phoenix running his very own mobile dog grooming business, and with his newfound freedom came wisdom that wasn't given, but earned. Chance disclosed that he was HIV positive and from time to time he struggled with depression, but he sounded happy. He confessed that he contracted the virus from John. Chance was planning a move to DC, but didn't hesitate to give his two cents on Atlanta as he saw it after he moved away.

"Y'all girls in Atlanta aren't as progressive as you *should* be. It took stepping out of that bubble for me to see that all y'all seem to care about is who has on what, who's driving this kind of car and who's fucking who. It's sad. And, I'm so glad I'm not trying to be on the *A list* anymore just to get invited to a party."

Most of what Chance said I was feeling. I questioned whether short-lived relationships were endemic of Atlanta or if it was community-wide wherever gay men were. The easier it became to have sex, the more elusive love became, but I was unhappy living in Atlanta for reasons bigger than the drawbacks of the gay scene. I couldn't create because my mind was clogged with fear of not being able to survive financially day-to-day, thus creativity was blocked without a way to come through. I was too busy worrying to recognize the many *mini* miracles in my life that had pushed me forward. God was placing lily pads before each step I took. They didn't look stable, but they held me up until it was time to leap to the next one. God sustained me through the generosity of the people who appeared in my life.

My time in Atlanta was up, but fear paralyzed me. I was still convinced I needed to remain there to get my *big break*. I knew too many people and had a plethora of contacts there. Atlanta was the city where I had written music, developed a line of greeting cards that was carried in seven retailers, and the place *A Day in the Life* was born. I talked myself into believing there were more reasons to stay than there were to leave.

I was comfortable, yet on edge in Atlanta. I grew accustomed to waiting for the next financial crisis to occur in my life. I wasn't breathing. I was slowly suffocating and the universe was squeezing the life out of me in an effort to force me out of

Atlanta. It was the reason my car was repossessed, and it was difficult to pay the rent month after month. God was pinching me hard enough to make it too uncomfortable in Atlanta for me to want to stay. He was forcing me to leave, and I couldn't continue ignoring the signs.

In December 2010, I felt a tugging in my spirit. It was the first of it's kind. I had never considered leaving Atlanta, but my instincts were telling me to move to Los Angeles. I came close to moving to New York when George Faison called and asked if I'd be interested in working with him on a show. George choreographed the stage version of *The Wiz* and won a Tony for his work. He said there was talk of staging a play based on E. Lynn Harris' first novel, *Invisible Life*. George wanted me to assist with the music that was being produced by Ashford & Simpson, but when the funding failed to come through I canceled plans to move.

I never had a desire to live in LA, but I knew a seed was planted in me this time. I called two friends living in LA who had previously lived in Atlanta. I told them I was thinking about moving, and they encouraged me to put some serious thought behind it to make sure it wasn't a rash decision. I was planning to move because I had the nerve to believe God was telling me to go, not because it was impetuous. I prayed that if it was God's will for me to move to LA that He would make it a seamless process.

I began saving money and flew to LA in March 2011 to put things in motion. My nephew's cousin worked for an airline and the round trip plane ticket only cost me $100. During that trip, I secured a place to stay with a college friend's parents. They told me I could live with them rent-free until I found a job and enough money saved to move into a place of my own.

When I got back to Atlanta, I set my move date for April 28th so I'd be in LA for my birthday on May 4th. I hired a moving company to move my furniture from my apartment to Kencil's unfinished basement to store. Coincidentally, on the day the movers came, there was a yard sale in Kencil's neighborhood. Instead of having the movers take my things to Kencil's, I had it transported to the yard sale. To my surprise, everything sold.

I waited a week before my move to call my nephew's cousin again to book my one-way flight to LA, but he had been terminated. I was afraid to check the price for the flight because I knew it would cost a fortune. I thought I would have to push back the date to get an inexpensive flight. I reluctantly signed onto Delta's website to check the prices. The one-way fare was $127 including tax. I was ecstatic. I couldn't believe the fare was so cheap.

Just before I purchased the ticket, I recalled receiving a $75 travel voucher from Delta after writing a letter to customer service about a previous flight. In total, I paid $69 for my flight. It was meant to be.

Leaving Atlanta

Thoughts of leaving Atlanta made me very emotional. Despite the tough times I had, there were many fond memories, and I met some amazing people who I count as friends. I worried that we would lose touch in the way I lost contact with friends from college, but I knew this move was what I needed. Kencil reassured me we would never lose touch.

I packed my luggage in Kencil's car and we headed to the airport. I was in tears before we hit 85 South. I was leaving the place I called home for 13 years.

"You're just a plane ride away. I'll come there and hell, you can visit Atlanta. It'll still be here. You're young, and you don't have any kids. This is the time to do it. Baby live. This is gonna be good for you Craig. I'm not gonna cry. Unh onh. I'm not 'cause I know I'm gonna see you again. I'll miss you though," she said.

Kencil started out as my workout partner, but she became like a sister, mother, and spirit friend to me. Though she's fifteen years my senior, I could talk to her about anything and she never judged me. We taught each other about personal growth, and much about loving the people in our lives without fear of rejection. We laughed together and cried for each other when love didn't bloom in our lives or when we faced career lulls.

I jumped out of the car when we pulled up to grab my suitcase from the trunk of the car.

"Ok, Craig. You got everything?"

"Yea," I mumbled.

"Ok, give me a hug."

Kencil reached up for a hug and I could feel all of her weight on me. Her 5'6" frame felt like a ton of bricks weighing me down. She was crying.

"I'm gonna miss you so much. I love you so much. You're such a beautiful spirit."

"I love you too,"

"Ok, let me stop. I said I wasn't gonna do this."

I knew she would do it all over when she found the letter I handwrote the night before that I tucked in her lingerie drawer.

"Let me know when you make it," she said.

"I will."

I checked in and headed to the concourse train to my departure gate. When the doors of the train opened I saw Carrington.

"Hey, where you going?" he asked.

"I told you I was moving to LA."

Over the years we stayed in contact, mostly because of his efforts, so we weren't completely out of touch. And, several of my friends were still his dental patients. He used his chair side conversation time with them to ask about me, and the things he didn't ask them he learned from my mother. Carrington continued sending Christmas gifts to my mom every year after we broke up, and she often reciprocated.

"You're leaving today?"

"Yep, today is the day. Where you going?"

"I'm going to Philly for a class."

"Oh, one of those certification classes?"

"Yea."

"Oh ok. How was Hawaii?" I said with a slight grin.

"Damn, how did you know I went to Hawaii?"

Two friends told me Carrington and Wendell were dating secretly. Well, at least they thought they were clandestinely. Apparently, they didn't want anyone to know because neither would
own up to it, but they were spotted having dinner on Valentine's
Day. I knew it was true because the two people who told me
didn't know each other, and I learned from Lane that two people
who don't know each other can't tell the same lie.

What I didn't tell him was that I overheard his boy toy telling
Jamelle—my friend that owned the furniture store. I was on the
phone with her weeks before and she happened to see Wendell in
passing. I overheard Wendell telling her that he was just getting
back from Hawaii with a friend. I put two and two together. I
knew Wendell didn't have money to go to Hawaii unless the trip
was sponsored, and I knew who sponsored it. Besides, Carrington and I had talked of going to Hawaii, but never made it there.

I wasn't bothered because I was over Carrington. It was typical Carrington style to be with someone who needed him financially to make it difficult for them to leave him, and Wendell's
modus operandi has always been to find a man willing to provide
because he didn't like to work nor did he have a clear career path
in all the years I knew him. Wendell spent years bouncing from
one *big* idea to another, so they were perfect for each other.

"You know Atlanta is small," I said.

Carrington realized if I knew he went to Hawaii that I also knew he was dating someone that was a friend of mine. This was my way of letting him know that I knew he was dating Wendell. What he didn't know was that I didn't care.

Before Carrington could probe me for answers the train stopped at the concourse for my flight.

"It was good seeing you. Take care," I said.

"Alright man. You too."

As I settled into my first day in Los Angeles, I got a text from Carrington asking the name of a restaurant my mom and I took him to many years before in Maryland when we were together. I knew it was just a *feeler* text. There was something else he really wanted to know, but he had to work his way up to it.

I kept it simple. I replied with the name of the restaurant and hit send. I didn't bother including any small talk. He responded, *"How did you know I went to Hawaii?"*

I never responded.

The closing doors on the train were symbolic of the final closure on that chapter of my life, and similar subterfuges in Atlanta.

EPILOGUE

This book is for any person who struggled to come to grips with his or her sexuality, and anyone that's ever apologized for simply *being*. It's for young gay people with few or no examples of progressive gay people in their lives to show them ways of entry into *the life* other than internet sex sites or gay clubs. I gift these words to the many parents conflicted with whether to continue loving children they brought into the world after discovering he or she is gay. Lastly, this book is for those who find it difficult to understand *how* a person is born gay.

Despite the number of people we *come out* to, there's still a journey of self-affirmation that has to take place, otherwise we remain in constant search of self-acceptance. It took years before I reached a comfort level in my skin. After many wasted years living in a shell hoping, wishing, and praying to be something other than what God made me, I was finally able to breathe when I concluded God made some of us gay, straight, bisexual, Black, Asian, White and Latino. The more I knew, the taller I stood.

Coming to terms with one's sexuality is a lifelong journey. The journey doesn't end the moment we come out or act on the feelings we suppressed. Conversely, the point at which we come out marks the beginning of the journey to be free. I was twenty-two years old when I tested the waters, so I imagine it will take another twenty-two years or more to undo *untruths* that I learned about my sexuality.

We've been conditioned to believe gay is wrong because it's what we've always been told, but repetition doesn't equate to truth. Many gay relationships end before they begin because one or both people involved battle with themselves at one point or another. Being gay isn't a sin. Improper use of sex is the sin, and that's true for gays and heterosexuals.

The battle with HIV is prolonged because we spend more time pointing blame and less time having honest conversations about sex and sexuality in our community. The Black church blames gay men for AIDS, and women hold bisexual men responsible. In reality, we exist in a community where young girls and women have children with many different men—at times with no knowledge of who the father is. The same holds true of our young boys and men with multiple *babies' mamas* living in the same city or neighborhood. We all have culpability. This disease will continue to devastate our community until we stop resisting truth and end the finger pointing. The church avoids dialogue about HIV because the conversation would lend itself to talks about premarital sex—although we know it happens.

It wasn't until I moved to Los Angeles, and began the process of writing this book when a friend helped me realize I hadn't forgiven my father. I was still the hurt little boy my father reprioritized during his marriage. Consequently, I cut him out of the significant details of my life. I never invited my father to any of the productions of the play, the greeting card launch parties, and most importantly I didn't tell him I was gay until I was near finished with this book. Though we've never lost touch, my father hadn't been to Atlanta since I moved there after college. I had to forgive my dad for the same reasons I had to forgive Tyler—to move past it.

I pray this book gives voice to the lesbian, gay, bisexual, transgender, questioning (LGBTQ) people who have been muzzled and ignored. The LGBTQ community is comprised of God's most gifted and talented people. Give yourself permission to be who you are and live confidently. This book is for you.

Stay Connected

Contact: bookthewriter@gmail.com

Craig Stewart itsok2write@gmail.com

Twitter: @wordsneverspokn or @therealcstewart

Facebook: facebook.com/wordsneverspokenbyCraigStewart

For media inquiries, interviews, book club discussions, and review requests please contact: bookthewriter@gmail.com.

Made in United States
Orlando, FL
12 January 2025

57113120R00214